OVERCOMING BODY DYSMORPHIC DISORDER

2nd Edition

A self-help guide using cognitive behavioural techniques

OVERCOMING

DAVID VEALE, ROB WILLSON
AND ALEX CLARKE

ROBINSON

ROBINSON

First published in Great Britain in 2025 by Robinson

Copyright © David Veale, Rob Willson and Alex Clarke, 2025

1 3 5 7 9 10 8 6 4 2

The moral right of the authors has been asserted.

Important Note
This book is not intended as a substitute for medical advice or treatment.
Any person with a condition requiring medical attention should consult
a qualified medical practitioner or suitable therapist.

All rights reserved.
No part of this publication may be reproduced, stored in a retrieval system, or
transmitted, in any form, or by any means, without the prior permission in writing
of the publisher, nor be otherwise circulated in any form of binding or cover other
than that in which it is published and without a similar condition including this
condition being imposed on the subsequent purchaser.

A CIP catalogue record for this book
is available from the British Library.

ISBN: 978-1-47214-847-6

Typeset in Bembo by Initial Typesetting Services, Edinburgh
Printed and bound in Great Britain by Clays Ltd, Elcograf S.p.A.

Papers used by Robinson are from well-managed forests and
other responsible sources.

Robinson
An imprint of
Little, Brown Book Group
Carmelite House
50 Victoria Embankment
London EC4Y 0DZ

The authorised representative
in the EEA is
Hachette Ireland
8 Castlecourt Centre
Dublin 15, D15 XTP3, Ireland
(email: info@hbgi.ie)

An Hachette UK Company
www.hachette.co.uk

www.littlebrown.co.uk

Professor David Veale is a consultant psychiatrist in cognitive behavioural therapy. He leads a national service for people with body dysmorphic disorder (BDD) at the South London and Maudsley NHS Trust and in private practice. He is a visiting professor at the Institute of Psychiatry, Psychology and Neuroscience, King's College London. He was a member of the group that wrote the NICE guidelines for treating OCD and BDD in 2006. He is an honorary fellow of the British Association of Behavioural and Cognitive Psychotherapies (BABCP), and a fellow of both the British Psychological Society and the Royal College of Psychiatrists. He is an ex-trustee and now patron of the charity, the BDD Foundation. His website is www.veale.co.uk.

Dr Rob Willson PhD is a cognitive behavioural therapist in private practice, an author and researcher. He has been involved in treating individuals with body dysmorphic disorder (BDD) for more than twenty-five years. Rob regularly teaches on the psychological treatment of BDD, and supervises numerous therapists who specialise in treating the condition. He is a trustee and chair of the charity the Body Dysmorphic Disorder Foundation. His website is www.robwillson.com.

David Veale and Rob Willson are the authors of *Overcoming Obsessive Compulsive Disorder*, *Overcoming Health Anxiety* and *Managing Your Mood*, also published by Robinson.

Dr Alex Clarke DPsych is a consultant clinical psychologist, specialising in the psychological aspects of altered body image and plastic and reconstructive surgery. Formerly in clinical practice at the Royal Free Hospital, London, she is now a visiting professor at the Centre for Appearance Research (CAR) at the University of the West of England, where she concentrates on research. Together with colleagues at CAR, she is the author of *CBT for Appearance Anxiety*, published by Wiley.

The aim of the Overcoming series is to enable people with a range of common problems and disorders to take control of their own recovery programme.

Each title, with its specially tailored programme, is devised by a practising clinician using the latest techniques of cognitive behavioural therapy – techniques that have been shown to be highly effective in changing the way patients think about themselves and their problems.

Many books in the Overcoming series are recommended under the Reading Well scheme.

Titles in the series include:

OVERCOMING ALCOHOL MISUSE, 2ND EDITION
OVERCOMING ANGER AND IRRITABILITY, 2ND EDITION
OVERCOMING ANOREXIA NERVOSA, 2ND EDITION
OVERCOMING ANXIETY, 2ND EDITION
OVERCOMING CHILDHOOD TRAUMA, 2ND EDITION
OVERCOMING CHRONIC FATIGUE, 2ND EDITION
OVERCOMING DEPERSONALISATION AND FEELINGS OF UNREALITY, 2ND EDITION
OVERCOMING CHRONIC PAIN, 2ND EDITION
OVERCOMING DEPRESSION, 3RD EDITION
OVERCOMING DISTRESSING VOICES, 2ND EDITION
OVERCOMING GAMBLING ADDICTION, 2ND EDITION
OVERCOMING GRIEF, 2ND EDITION
OVERCOMING HEALTH ANXIETY, 2ND EDITION
OVERCOMING HOARDING
OVERCOMING INSOMNIA, 2ND EDITION
OVERCOMING LOW SELF-ESTEEM, 2ND EDITION
OVERCOMING MILD TRAUMATIC BRAIN INJURY AND POST-CONCUSSION SYMPTOMS
OVERCOMING MOOD SWINGS, 2ND EDITION
OVERCOMING OBSESSIVE COMPULSIVE DISORDER, 2ND EDITION
OVERCOMING PANIC, 2ND EDITION
OVERCOMING PARANOID AND SUSPICIOUS THOUGHTS, 2ND EDITION
OVERCOMING PERFECTIONISM, 2ND EDITION
OVERCOMING RELATIONSHIP PROBLEMS, 2ND EDITION
OVERCOMING SEXUAL PROBLEMS, 2ND EDITION
OVERCOMING SOCIAL ANXIETY AND SHYNESS, 2ND EDITION
OVERCOMING STRESS
OVERCOMING TRAUMATIC STRESS, 2ND EDITION
OVERCOMING WEIGHT PROBLEMS, 2ND EDITION
OVERCOMING WORRY AND GENERALISED ANXIETY DISORDER, 2ND EDITION
OVERCOMING YOUR CHILD'S SHYNESS AND SOCIAL ANXIETY
STOP SMOKING NOW, 2ND EDITION
THE OVERCOMING LOW SELF-ESTEEM HANDBOOK

Contents

	Acknowledgements	vii
1	Why does appearance matter?	1
2	Do you have body dysmorphic disorder?	23
3	How BDD develops	52
4	Setting yourself on the right course	73
5	What keeps your BDD going? Building your 'vicious flower'	87
6	Thinking about thinking	135
7	Taking action	183
8	Tackling depression and reclaiming your life	229
9	Helping someone with BDD	254
10	Compulsive skin-picking, hair-pulling and other habits	271
11	Special problems of disfiguring conditions	299
12	Psychological aspects of cosmetic procedures	334

13	A guide to medication for BDD	365
14	Finding help	396
	Appendix 1 Useful contacts and information	409
	Appendix 2 Further reading	413
	Appendix 3 Assessment forms and progress charts	417
	Index	449

Acknowledgements

We would like to acknowledge the host of individuals who have inspired or taught us, and who have done most of the research into body image. We have not included full references in this book, but most of the research findings are taken from the publications of Ulrike Buhlmann, Tom Cash, Jamie Fuesner, Asmita Jassi, Georgina Krebs, David Mataix-Cols, Anne Möllmann, Benedetta Monzani, Sandra Mulkens, Fugen Neziroglu, Lauren Peile, Katharine Phillips, Nichola Rumsey, Roz Shafran, Oliver Suendermann, Sabine Wilhelm and many other researchers too numerous to mention. Lastly, we thank all our patients, from whom we have learned so much. We recognise the struggle they face every day, and hope that this book will be helpful to them and others.

1

Why does appearance matter?

First impressions

Appearance is important. First impressions depend partly on what we look like and partly on how we behave, so our appearance is a major source of information in social encounters. Faces have several functions. Our faces allow us to express ourselves and communicate. Our emotions – such as happiness and sadness, disgust and anger – are all conveyed through our facial expressions. When we communicate with someone, we are constantly noting (whether consciously or not) what their eyes, mouth and stance are telling us, as well as what we are hearing in their words and tone. Is the other person interested in what we are saying? Or are they bored? Faces and the way we use our hands to gesture communicate vital information as we find our way through a conversation, showing that we are listening, indicating questions or taking turns to speak. Our physical appearance also indicates age and attractiveness, ethnicity, gender, and familial or racial characteristics. There are many reasons why our appearance, and our faces in particular, are important in human behaviour. Therefore, it can be particularly difficult if something about your own appearance worries or disturbs you.

Similarly, we all pay attention to 'body language'. By this we mean the way we behave to convey additional information to other people. If you are excessively concerned or anxious about your appearance, changing the way you look may seem the obvious or only way of changing how you feel. But you can also manage your concern about your appearance by thinking and behaving differently. The goal is therefore to become less preoccupied with your appearance rather than to radically change it. It also means being able to get on with what is important in life, despite what your mind is telling you. This will be explored in later chapters. First, we will discuss appearance and body image in more detail. What is a normal appearance? And what is normal in terms of how much we think about it and try to change it?

What is body image?

Psychologists use the term 'body image' to describe our internalised sense of what we look like. They refer to it as being 'multifaceted', in other words having both a subjective and objective component, an evaluative component (whether it is viewed in a positive or negative light) and a salient component, i.e. the level of importance body image has in an individual's sense of self-worth.

Body image can be thought of as a mental representation or map of our body, against which we judge our external appearance. The idea of body image was first developed by neurologists who were investigating how the brain interprets information that it receives from different parts of the body. For example, after people lose a limb, they often experience phantom pain or sensation – as if the limb were still there. For this to occur, the brain must have an internalised representation of the limb. This mental image takes time to adjust once the external appearance has been altered. The body image of people with eating disorders has also been studied, and their perception of their body size may differ greatly from their actual size. People with anorexia may feel normal or fat, even though in reality they are very thin. Once again, their internal body image is providing inaccurate information about what they look like.

For most of us, there is a relatively good match between what we think we look like (subjective appearance) and how we appear to other people (objective appearance), although it is interesting how often people dislike photographs of themselves. To some extent, our body image is idealised (based on how we would like to look). It is also based on a mirror image of our actual appearance. Other people see animated or moving images, whereas we view our own image mainly through photographs or mirrors where expression is still. Body image also changes slowly as we get older. We recognise our image as 'our self' when we are children and as we grow into adults. However, when our appearance changes suddenly, perhaps after an accident or because of disease, it can be very disconcerting, and it can take quite a long time before we 'see ourselves' once more when looking in the mirror. Even a dramatically different haircut can be quite shocking when we catch sight of an unexpected reflection, for example in a shop window.

Body image can also be studied in terms of what we look like in the eyes of an observer. What other people see and what we think they can see – the outside and inside view of body image – are like two sides of a coin, as they both contribute to how we feel about our looks. For example, we might receive positive or negative feedback about our appearance that might influence the way we think and feel. Equally, the way we act and feel about our appearance will have an impact on others. For example, if you keep your head down, don't make eye contact and say very little then others will think you are not interested in them. They could be critical and reject you, not because of your appearance but because of your actions.

Body image can therefore be positive or negative and can vary over time. It is just one aspect of the way you feel about yourself. For instance, you might have a negative body image and a high sense of worth about other aspects of yourself, or vice versa. Ideas about body image overlap with feelings of high or low self-esteem. If low self-esteem is generally a problem, then it may take longer to overcome your body image problems, and we will discuss this in Chapter 2.

Body image across the lifespan

Attractiveness is difficult to define, but there are several common factors across different cultures. For instance, someone with a very symmetrical, balanced face is usually rated attractive. More symmetrical features may be a sign of good health and fertility, as an infection at a young age can interfere with facial symmetry. One theory is that the human brain has a built-in mechanism for detecting symmetry because it demonstrates to others that the person has good genes and does not have any serious illness. Even babies are born with a tendency to pay attention to attractive faces. Studies have found that a baby's attention is held for slightly longer by images of faces that that have been rated as very attractive compared to images of faces rated unattractive. Older children also play for slightly longer with attractive dolls.

Very young children show little awareness of their own appearance, and they don't make value judgements about other people based on the way they look. However, from the age of about seven, children become more aware of their own appearance, and may begin to discriminate between 'good' and 'bad' appearance and ascribe characteristics to other people based on what they look like. Children's literature reinforces this development by linking the ideas of beauty and goodness. Fairy tales such as 'Cinderella' and 'Beauty and the Beast' (variations of which can be found in all cultures) reinforce the idea that beauty is rewarded and is therefore to be prized, while ugliness is associated with evil. This assumption appears even in films for adults, where the hero is generally strong and good-looking and the villain characterised with a scar or disfigurement. One of the few 'plain' heroines in literature is Jane Eyre, but she is not married to Mr Rochester until he has been blinded in a fire and has acquired additional disabilities! Images from social media increasingly link physical attractiveness with exceptional success and celebrity, although in reality the celebrities featured often seem to find that their fame brings them problems rather than happiness.

Adolescence is the period when people's appearance changes most noticeably, and over a very short period, as they reach puberty. Before puberty, male and female children have very similar body shapes. After puberty, girls develop breasts and curvier hips. For boys, the trunk slims, the shoulders broaden, facial features become more masculine, and facial hair starts to grow. Although breast development is characteristic of girls, some boys also experience breast changes. 'Man boobs', as they are sometimes called, can be very worrying for teenage boys and may lead to teasing, but they usually disappear as puberty continues.

Most importantly, appearance becomes linked with sexuality during puberty. The way people look affects their attractiveness in the eyes of other people. It also influences the way they see themselves. While girls are usually thought to worry most about their physical appearance, young men are also very concerned with how they look. However, while girls aspire to an ideal weight and shape, boys focus more on fitness and well-defined muscles.

The hormonal surge that occurs at puberty not only triggers the physical changes mentioned earlier; it can also impact on other very visible aspects of appearance, such as people's skin. For example, acne (caused by excessive production of sebum in the skin) can cause very visible and painful pimples across the face and shoulders. Although associated with adolescence, acne can continue throughout someone's life and often causes considerable unhappiness and anxiety about appearance. Fortunately, this condition can usually be well controlled with a combination of medications, which reduce the production of sebum and combat infection. Acne is a good example of a condition that is common but often misunderstood. Although it is usually seen as a minor issue or a 'normal' part of growing up, the level of distress experienced by some acne sufferers may be highly significant. While it may be assumed that someone with severe facial burns will experience more distress than someone with acne, this is not necessarily true. Any form of altered appearance may cause distress if the individual feels that it makes them different from their peer group and puts them at a disadvantage compared with other people.

The self-consciousness associated with these rapid changes in appearance is perfectly normal. Adolescence is a time when people can become acutely aware of body changes, particularly if they are either the first or last in their peer group to, for example, develop breasts. While some people enjoy the sense of being different or exceptional, it is far more common to want to 'fit in' or be 'unremarkable'. Therefore, comments about appearance can make people feel acutely uncomfortable. Unfortunately, adolescence is also a time when bullying is most common. And, since appearance is the most immediately obvious thing about people, bullying remarks will often concern their appearance. Thus weight, shape, hair or skin colour, height, obvious scars or birthmarks, and skin conditions such as acne, can all become the focus of bullying.

However, it is important that the problem here is recognised as the bullies' behaviour rather than the young person's appearance. Bullies pick on the things about which people feel vulnerable, and schools should therefore take measures to prevent bullying about appearance in the same way as they try to prevent the expression of racism and sexism. Bullying is not a good reason for seeking to make changes in your appearance, particularly during adolescence, but it is a good reason to develop some strategies for managing intrusive or bullying behaviour from other people. Furthermore, 'ghosts from the past' can influence us in the present. People who have been bullied or abused when they were younger often feel, in adulthood, that they are still being humiliated by others (when they are not) and may become excessively preoccupied with their appearance.

Body image is often assumed to be less important for older people. Look at the vast and lucrative industry devoted to helping people to slow down or prevent the obvious signs of ageing, however, and a different picture emerges. Many older people are clearly still very interested in their appearance. Likewise, younger people often anticipate that they will be more relaxed about their appearance 'once they reach forty', but people whose sense of self-worth is largely determined by their appearance are unlikely to change as they grow older. In some work settings, particularly those in the media, such as television, personal appearance is perceived to be an important commodity, and an attractive individual may do better when competing for a high-status job. This has led many older employees to worry about the effects of ageism and pursue a more youthful appearance to protect their employment.

Cultural factors and changes in the body image ideal

Changing fashions have promoted different body shapes in different decades – for example, female waist-to-hip ratio has alternated between a more voluptuous and an androgynous body ideal. However, some body image 'ideals' have remained relatively unchanged over the centuries. Well-defined breasts are widely valued, and breast surgery has become one of the commonest forms of cosmetic surgery. Similarly, a smooth and unblemished skin has been prized in women across all the cultures that have been studied throughout history. Thus smallpox, which left the skin very pockmarked in previous centuries, led to women wearing veils and being considered less attractive as potential wives. In modern times women in some developing countries are sometimes attacked with acid to cause facial burns that may result in them being unable to find a husband. Unblemished skin is thought to be prized because it is associated with youth and therefore fertility; ageing is most visible in the skin, compared with other organs. Disease is also very apparent in skin appearance, so smooth, healthy skin is likely to have a strong evolutionary advantage and to be prized in all cultures. Other aspects of appearance may vary with socioeconomic conditions. Weight is a good example. In cultures or at times when food is short, plumpness becomes a sign of wealth and is valued. However, with the advent of cheaper mass-marketed food in the West, obesity is becoming prevalent, and a slimmer, more muscular, 'physically fit' ideal has developed. Tanned skin, associated with wealth in European populations before the advent of cheap travel, is becoming less desirable as it becomes more easily achievable for all, although this may also be a result of the negative link between sun exposure and skin cancer and premature ageing. This change in ideal body image therefore associates appearance with wealth and status.

Social networking and the promotion of unattainable ideals

For those of us growing up before the advent of the internet, the images we compared ourselves with were on TV or in magazines, or those of the people around us who lived locally or went to school with us. Now these everyday comparisons are made on a worldwide and cross-cultural level, and the universal ideals of attractiveness are, for many of us, unachievable. Ideals of appearance are also promoted by commercial marketing, which often exaggerates their benefits with the aim of selling to a wider audience (for example, fairer or whiter skin is prized and promoted by manufacturers of skin-whitening creams in Asia). As a result, body image anxiety is increasing, particularly in young people.

Those who are influential in fashion are now being asked to select models from a wider range of body shapes and sizes, to help reduce the pressure felt by vulnerable young women. However, we are still far from having models who represent the range of body types and sizes. Another, related, problem arises from the increased use of modified photographic images, in which a perceived defect can be airbrushed out. An image can be created from a variety of sources. For the average person, it is impossible to tell a real image from a fabricated one, and this is an additional concern for those working in the field of body image research where images are still idealised and sought after by some people even when what they show is impossible to achieve.

Comparing ourselves with others is not necessarily harmful. However, when we are concerned about an aspect of appearance, we tend to make upward comparisons. This means we seek out examples of people with a 'better' or 'ideal' feature, thus increasing our level of concern and self-consciousness about our own. The healthier approach is to stop making comparisons. Unfortunately, social media encourages us to make the upward comparisons that drive appearance dissatisfaction.

The wide use of social media to communicate at work and with friends brings not only the positive benefits of facilitating social interaction but the negative effects of social comparison as described above. 'Selfies' (posed pictures taken by and of the individual) – carefully selected and modified with the use of filters to present an idealised version of the self – are circulated, with comments invited.

The number of 'likes' and responses are then monitored, with the aim of boosting self-esteem. Since sensitivity to negative evaluation by others is a major contributor to body image anxiety, this is a high-risk strategy, both for the person initiating it (no amount of positive approval is ever going to be enough and this simply perpetuates an unhelpful preoccupation with appearance) and because, in inviting upward comparison from others, it promotes body image problems more widely.

Social networking sites are not the only online issue. During the long periods of lockdown associated with the worldwide management of Covid-19, work teams used online meeting platforms to continue work activities. Recent reports suggest that the day-to-day exposure to one's own image in team meetings has led to an increase in facial rejuvenation strategies, suggesting that overexposure to appearance has focused attention in an unhelpful way.

'Normal' body image

How can we define a normal body image, if it is clear from research and from the vast amounts spent on clothes and make-up that most of us attempt to modify or change our appearance to some extent on a regular basis? Even without knowing the cultural history of body image, most of us recognise that there is a certain pressure on women, and increasingly on men, to look good. Media that promote celebrity status and unachievable body images also carry critical articles that mock popular figures for their appearance, weight and choice of clothing. While this does help to show that no one looks like a magazine photo all the time, it is very similar to the bullying experienced at school or in the workplace by those whose appearance is unusual. Most people respond to this pressure by, for example, dressing in an appropriate way for work.

In the Western world, most of us shower or bathe regularly. We have more than one set of clothing, and while most of us have a certain 'style' that we adhere to, there is a tendency to take more time and trouble over our appearance in situations where we are meeting people for the first time. This is perhaps because we know that, while some judgements about us will be made based on our appearance in an initial meeting, subsequent meetings will focus much more on our behaviour, personality and competence (in a work setting). Appearance therefore becomes less important in longer-established relationships.

Use of make-up, removal of some body hair, colouring of hair, body piercing and tattooing are all regarded as normal in modern Western society. Using surgery to enhance our appearance is much more accepted than it used to be, although someone who undergoes multiple or repeated procedures may be excessively concerned with their appearance.

The factors that distinguish someone with a normal body image from someone who has a body image problem are linked with the way they think and act. Different kinds of body image problems will be described more fully in Chapter 2. However, it is important to realise that you don't have a body image problem simply because you dislike certain parts of your body, think that you would like to lose a few pounds, regularly wear make-up or love clothes. Nor do you have a body image problem if you have a significant disfigurement or an unusual appearance. Many people whose appearance falls outside the 'norm' live perfectly happy lives and celebrate the things that make them exceptional. Body image disorders are much more to do with thinking about your appearance to the exclusion of other activities, and avoiding social situations, workplaces or relationships because of the way you look. Believing that you can only feel confident or be happy if you change the way you look, or that your appearance is preventing you from participating in certain activities, is also typical of body image disorders. Excessive worry, repeatedly checking your appearance, consistent use of very heavy make-up or refusal to leave the house without make-up are all extremes of normal behaviour, though they tend to reinforce the idea that your appearance is abnormal, thus increasing body image anxiety.

Why does being attractive matter?

There was a prevailing belief in the latter part of the twentieth century that 'what is beautiful is also good'. Being attractive might have a 'halo effect' – in other words, others might believe that someone who was attractive physically had a number of additional positive qualities. More recently, researchers have come to understand that this relationship is more nuanced. Psychologists at the Centre for Appearance Research at the University of the West of England, UK, have proposed the concept of 'beauty myths' that underlie not only beliefs about attractiveness but the marketing of cosmetic interventions to achieve change. Common myths include:

- Occupational success: All things being equal, a very attractive person might have a slight advantage in getting a particular job. However, this premium will not last for long if they lack the skills to do the job effectively.
- Successful relationships: Despite the marketing, relationships are built on far more than looks: there are many couples in which one partner is much less physically attractive than the other. Being very attractive can also have disadvantages such as attracting unwanted attention or inhibiting others who feel that they can't match such a high standard.
- Success in social situations: 'Looks' may open doors to particular social groups, but the social connections made behind these doors may not be rewarding – again, if membership is based on 'looks', many experience insecurity about the likely longevity of these social relationships.
- Happiness: There is no relationship between what someone looks like and their psychological wellbeing. People from all backgrounds, including those with a very visible difference in appearance, live confident and happy lives.

Attractiveness is influential in the first encounter and impacts on the forming of initial impressions; other qualities, such as social skills and self-confidence, are then more important in the long term. However, being attractive is about much more than just your physical appearance. For example, it includes the following factors:

- Your body language and posture. For example, are you playful and do you flirt appropriately? (Or do you keep your head down, make little eye contact and hope that others will go away?)
- Your sense of style. Do you dress well in clothes that suit you? (Or do you wear worn-out, badly fitting clothes?)
- Your manner. Do you act as if you have charisma and enthusiasm? (Or are you someone with little to say and not much interest in others?)

Research has shown that the way someone feels about their appearance has far more influence on their quality of life than how physically attractive they are to others. An individual with a disfiguring condition can have a good quality of life, and an individual who is considered attractive by others may be deeply distressed and have a poor quality of life. The examples of Katherine, Rusha and Sabine below illustrate either end of this spectrum.

Rusha's preoccupation with the shape of her nose

Rusha is preoccupied with the shape of her nose. She believes that it is misshapen, too big and does not suit her face. Overall, she feels that her nose is very noticeable, 'ugly' and abnormal, but others cannot observe anything noticeable or abnormal. When Rusha highlighted her nose to her friend, who viewed it very closely, she could see a small bump where Rusha thought it was misshapen but certainly did not view it as ugly. However, her friend was viewing her as a whole and did not define her by her nose.

Rusha had had a number of cosmetic procedures earlier in her life, most notably work on her chin, which she said she was happy with but that it made her nose look worse by contrast. She had approached a number of cosmetic surgeons who did not consider her a good candidate for further surgery. She spends at least six hours per day preoccupied with her appearance, feels down much of the time and frequently feels anxious about her appearance. She works a few hours from home, having withdrawn from her office, and rarely socialises. She experiences a felt impression of her nose in her mind, which she looks at as an observer. Sometimes this leads to doubts as to how exactly she does look and to frequent checking of her nose in mirrors, which have to have the right lighting. This often leads to further doubts. She avoids bright lights that cast a shadow. She compares herself to old photographs of how she used to look and to the noses of other women of the same age. Her relationship has broken down as her partner was unable to cope with her behaviour.

Sabine's preoccupation with her skin

Sabine is a twenty-four-year-old single woman living with her parents. Her main problem of several years' duration is a preoccupation with her skin. She feels that her cheeks have become saggy and there is fullness of the lower face, causing lines and ageing. Her skin also has acne scarring. She is preoccupied to a lesser extent with wrinkling and sun-damaged skin. She desires intense light therapy or cream for ageing and wrinkling skin, and a skin peel. It is on her mind for at least ten hours a day; she is checking in mirrors or reflective surfaces about twenty times a day. She avoids having photos or videos taken; however, she will take a photo of herself in her camera phone, which she uses to compare with photos of when she was much younger. She is constantly comparing her features to those of people in the media or other people she meets in person. She tries to hide her face with her hair. She has been significantly depressed for some time and does nothing at home apart from watching TV and trying to change her appearance in her mind. She feels constantly tired, often sleeps during the day and wakes early. Her appetite is variable and she has lost a bit of weight. She often believes the future to be hopeless, and has suicidal ideas but no plans. She is extremely self-conscious and fearful of others quietly laughing at her and humiliating her, and avoids social, public situations. She avoids staying over at other people's houses, going to shopping centres, going out with friends or seeing an old boyfriend. She has no enjoyment of anything and does not plan anything. If she does go out, then her mind is elsewhere, comparing herself to others. She may try to convince her mother about how unattractive she is. She may push her cheeks up to where they used to be. She tends to brood on the past and wonder why she was born this way and how she could change her skin. Overall, she feels that her face is extremely noticeable (e.g. to a stranger passing at a distance in the street), but others could not observe anything abnormal. She had some acne problems when she was about eight to ten years younger, when she was teased about having a 'pizza face'.

Katherine's adjustment to visible difference

Katherine's face was severely disfigured from burns in a road traffic accident. Most people would rate her appearance as unusual and would not have come across someone who looks so visibly different in their everyday experience. To start with, after the accident, Katherine was shocked by her appearance, and failed to recognise herself in the mirror. After a period of rehabilitation, she is now familiar with her new looks, accepts that no amount of surgery is going to restore her previous appearance, and has rebuilt her self-esteem by acknowledging all her talents, abilities and skills. She is a good partner and parent, and a full member of the community, functioning well in society. Sometimes the questions and curiosity about her story get her down, but generally she has learned to manage other people's curiosity and is confident and at ease in social situations.

We are not saying that individuals who have a visible difference in appearance do not experience problems or that an attractive person does not have a slight advantage in life. What we are saying that people's quality of life does not depend on their objective appearance. What makes the difference is how you think and act about your appearance. For instance, Katherine knows that she has a disfigured appearance, but she also recognises that this is only one part of how she is perceived by other people – particularly those who know her best. Rusha, however, sees her appearance as the major factor defining who she is and how she relates to others. Rather than changing your appearance, the key to changing quality of life lies in changing the way you think and act. This is the key to understanding and changing all body image problems. We understand this is not easy, as these patterns of thinking and behaving have often built up over many years, but many people have succeeded in overcoming body image problems using this approach.

Making the most of life

Appearance is important. It influences how people view us, particularly when they meet us for the first time. Beauty has always been and remains highly prized, though most of us aim to fit in rather than stand out. This may lead us to modify our appearance to some extent, to fit in with our job, lifestyle and peer group. Feeling happy with our appearance may make us feel positive about ourselves, as well as giving us the sense of others being attracted to us and being positively regarded.

If we don't keep this in proportion, however, we can become excessively preoccupied with appearance in a way that is very unhelpful. Far from working to our advantage, this will increase any beliefs about being abnormal and viewed negatively by others. If we check our features excessively or avoid certain situations, we end up not only limiting our own lives severely, but also affecting those around us, and this in turn influences how attractive we are to others.

In the following chapters we will help you to assess the way you think and act. We will also help you to make changes that will allow you to enjoy taking an interest in your appearance without this limiting your life and opportunities.

> **PIT STOP**
>
> Let's stop and think about what you have just been reading. Can you summarise the key ideas you have taken on board? What is sticking in your mind? Maybe write it down. If you have any questions, jot those down too. You can return to them once you have had a chance to digest the information.
>
> What is sticking in my mind from my reading so far?

OVERCOMING BODY DYSMORPHIC DISORDER

1.

2.

3.

2

Do you have body dysmorphic disorder?

Body dysmorphic disorder (BDD) involves an extreme preoccupation with one or more features which are not that noticeable or abnormal to others. People with BDD usually feel they are ugly, that they are 'not right', and are very self-conscious. They usually have compulsive behaviours such as mirror checking that are difficult to resist. They may resort to needless cosmetic and dermatological procedures with which they are either dissatisfied or that have little impact on their preoccupation and distress. People with BDD also tend to be very secretive and reluctant to seek help because they are afraid that others will think them vain or narcissistic. (Of course they are not vain at all, as their goal is to fit in rather than to stand out and they usually hate their appearance.)

The older term for BDD, 'dysmorphophobia', is sometimes still used. The media sometimes refer to BDD as 'imagined ugliness syndrome'. This isn't particularly helpful, as the ugliness is very real to the individual concerned.

Some people with BDD acknowledge that they may be blowing things up out of proportion. At the other extreme, others are firmly convinced of the reality of their supposed abnormality. Whatever the person's degree of insight into their own condition, someone with BDD usually knows that others believe their appearance to be 'normal' and will have been told so many times.

The degree of disability caused by BDD varies from slight to very severe. Many people with BDD are either single or divorced, which suggests that they find it difficult to form relationships. It can make regular employment and family life impossible. Those who are in regular employment or who have family responsibilities would almost certainly find life more productive and satisfying if they did not have the symptoms of BDD. Their partners may also become involved and suffer greatly.

The questionnaire below highlights the key characteristics of BDD and your answers should indicate whether or not you have the condition.

QUESTIONNAIRE: HAVE I GOT BDD?

Please answer the following for how you have felt about your appearance over the past week.

1. How often do you **deliberately** check your feature(s) (not accidentally catch sight of it/them)? Please include looking at your feature(s) in a mirror or other reflective surfaces like a shop window, or looking at it directly or feeling it with your fingers.

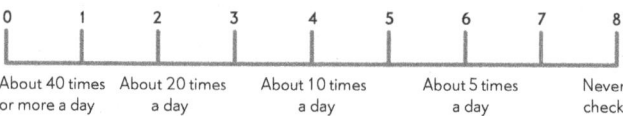

DO YOU HAVE BODY DYSMORPHIC DISORDER?

2. To what extent do you feel your feature(s) are **currently** ugly, unattractive or 'not right'?

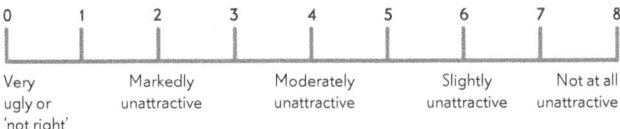

0	1	2	3	4	5	6	7	8
Very ugly or 'not right'		Markedly unattractive		Moderately unattractive		Slightly unattractive		Not at all unattractive

3. To what extent does your feature(s) **currently** cause you a lot of distress?

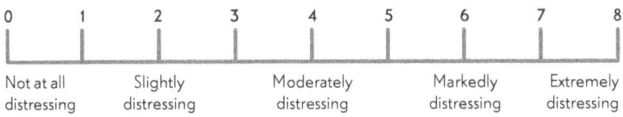

0	1	2	3	4	5	6	7	8
Not at all distressing		Slightly distressing		Moderately distressing		Markedly distressing		Extremely distressing

4. How often does your feature(s) **currently** lead you to avoid situations or activities?

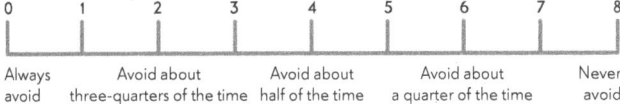

0	1	2	3	4	5	6	7	8
Always avoid		Avoid about three-quarters of the time		Avoid about half of the time		Avoid about a quarter of the time		Never avoid

5. To what extent does your feature(s) **currently** preoccupy you? That is, you think about it a lot and it is hard to stop thinking about it.

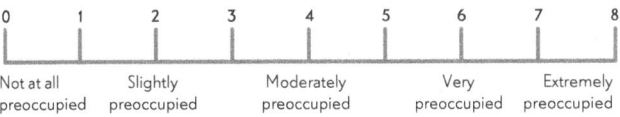

0	1	2	3	4	5	6	7	8
Not at all preoccupied		Slightly preoccupied		Moderately preoccupied		Very preoccupied		Extremely preoccupied

6. If you have a partner, to what extent does your feature(s) **currently** have an effect on your relationship with them (e.g. affectionate feelings, number of arguments, enjoying activities together)? If you do not have a partner, to what extent does your feature(s) **currently** have an effect on dating or developing a relationship?

| 0 | 1 | 2 | 3 | 4 | 5 | 6 | 7 | 8 |
| Not at all | | Slightly | | Moderately | | Markedly | | Extremely |

7. To what extent does your feature(s) **currently** interfere with your ability to work or study, or your role as a homemaker? (Please rate this even if you are not working or studying: we are interested in your ability to work or study.)

| 0 | 1 | 2 | 3 | 4 | 5 | 6 | 7 | 8 |
| Not at all | | Slightly | | Moderately | | Markedly | | Very severely, I can't work |

8. To what extent does your feature(s) **currently** interfere with your social life (with other people, e.g. parties, pubs, clubs, outings, visits, entertaining at home)?

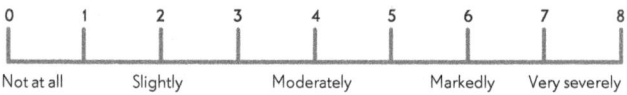

| 0 | 1 | 2 | 3 | 4 | 5 | 6 | 7 | 8 |
| Not at all | | Slightly | | Moderately | | Markedly | | Very severely |

9. To what extent do you feel your appearance is the most important aspect of who you are?

| 0 | 1 | 2 | 3 | 4 | 5 | 6 | 7 | 8 |
| Not at all | | Slightly | | Moderately | | Mostly | | Totally |

Source: Based on Veale et al. (2012).

DO YOU HAVE BODY DYSMORPHIC DISORDER?

The questionnaire assumes that you do NOT have a defect that is easily noticeable, or one that appears only slight to others. The judgement on how noticeable your feature(s) is/are is made by a health professional. Items are scored from 0 (least impaired) to 8 (most impaired). The score is achieved by summing all the items. Items 1, 2 and 4 are reversed (for example, if you circled 8 then you score 0). Possible total scores range from 0 to 72. Higher scores reflect greater interference in your life and the likelihood of a diagnosis of BDD. Individuals who score 40 or more are more likely to have BDD.

If you score between 30 and 40, then you may still have BDD and might benefit from further assessment. If you score under 30 then you are unlikely to have BDD. You might be unhappy or dissatisfied with your appearance, but you are unlikely to have BDD.

Remember to repeat the questionnaire before and after any new treatment to see if there is any change in severity of your symptoms. A blank copy of the questionnaire can be found in Appendix 3, or can be downloaded from https://overcoming.co.uk/715/resources-to-download.

How common is BDD?

We now know that around 2 per cent of the world's population may have BDD, and it may be more frequent in some cultures where cosmetic surgery is more common. It is recognised to be a hidden disorder, as many people with BDD are too ashamed to reveal their problem.

Both sexes are equally affected by BDD. People with BDD are most commonly concerned with their skin, followed by concerns about their nose, hair, eyes, chin, lips or overall body build. People with BDD may complain of a lack of symmetry or feel that something is too big or too small, or out of proportion to the rest of the body. Any part of the body may be involved in BDD, including the breasts or genitals. Although women are more likely to have hair concerns (e.g. that hair is the wrong colour, or it lacks body, or there is excessive body hair), men are significantly more concerned with hair thinning or baldness.

The sex differences also occur with body size and shape. Women are more likely to be preoccupied by their breasts, hips, weight and legs, usually believing that they are too large or fat. In contrast, men tend to be preoccupied with their body build, which has also been described as muscle dysmorphia (described below). Another significant sex difference is that men are more likely to report preoccupation with their genitals (usually a concern that their penis is too small), or be concerned about breast development, which they see as too feminine. Women may also feel that their genitalia or labia are too large and seek cosmetic surgery to reduce their size.

Muscle dysmorphia is a variation of BDD in which a man is worried about being too small or too skinny or not muscular enough. Despite such concerns, many such men are unusually muscular and large. Many of them spend hours lifting weights and pay great attention to nutrition. Others may abuse steroids. In our experience, such individuals are less likely to seek help than other people with BDD and may be less disabled by the condition.

BDD usually begins in adolescence, a time when people are generally most sensitive about their appearance.

However, many people wait for years before seeking help. They may repeatedly consult dermatologists or cosmetic surgeons but often get little satisfaction from these treatments. When they do finally seek help from mental health professionals, they often ask about other symptoms, such as depression, social anxiety or obsessive-compulsive disorder (OCD), and do not reveal their real concerns. However, people with BDD are often also depressed, with a high rate of attempted suicide.

Treatments for body dysmorphic disorder

In the UK, the organisation responsible for producing treatment guidelines is the National Institute for Health and Care Excellence (NICE), which is highly regarded throughout the world. Experts in BDD, including doctors, therapists and individuals who have experienced BDD, have got together to review the evidence and produce the guidelines, based on published research into BDD. At present, there is still relatively little research into BDD – compared with, say, depression or OCD. Furthermore, the published research is only a snapshot of current evidence, which will be updated as new evidence becomes available. There are now a number of good-quality research trials of cognitive behavioural therapy for BDD.

The treatment guidelines on OCD and BDD can be downloaded from the NICE website (see Appendix 1). The guidelines are based on scientific 'evidence' – that is, studies in which people with BDD are randomly selected to receive one or more different treatments or to remain on a waiting list. One group might be given a placebo (or dummy) treatment so that researchers can see to what extent the attention of a doctor or therapist and the passage of time affects the outcome. At the end of the study the researchers retest participants to see which treatments are more effective.

In all the guidelines, there is particular emphasis on patient choice and on the patient's experience with previous treatment. However, treatment options partly depend on the availability of therapists and local resources. If you are seeing a doctor or therapist, they will advise you as to what is best for you given the resources available. It isn't always obvious which treatment is most effective for a particular person. Sometimes you may have to try two or three different approaches before you find one that works for you. The core message, though, is that there is evidence that BDD is treatable and you can get back to a normal life.

Cognitive behavioural therapy (CBT) for BDD

CBT was initially described by Aaron T. Beck, who revolutionised the psychological treatment of depression in the early 1970s. It has been adapted for BDD and has been shown to be effective for adults. CBT is therefore recommended by NICE for treating BDD. This book is based upon the principles of CBT and is ideally used with the support of a trained CBT therapist. More research is needed to compare CBT with other psychological treatments. At present, there is no evidence that psychodynamic therapy or hypnosis is effective for BDD. This means that people with BDD should first be offered CBT from a competent practitioner, as it has been shown to be effective. Sometimes you may have to get someone to advocate for you to ensure that you get a good trial of cognitive behavioural therapy and that it follows the protocol that has been shown to be effective.

However, change *is* possible with the support of a friend, family member, volunteer or even alone. Many people with body image problems find that they may have to wait many months to see a therapist, so getting started with self-help can be a really good first step.

Medication for BDD

Anti-obsessional medication (a serotonin reuptake inhibitor) is recommended as an option in treating moderate to severe symptoms of BDD in adults or adolescents. This medication is not recommended for mild symptoms of BDD. However, medication may be suggested when symptoms are mild but occur repeatedly. Likewise, if a patient's doctor believes that the BDD symptoms are likely to get worse (or if the symptoms have lasted for a long time) medication may be prescribed. We discuss the use of medication in more detail in Chapter 13.

Combining medication with CBT

In general, we do not recommend using medication alone because there is usually a higher rate of relapse when a person stops taking their medication. Results tend to be better when the medication is combined with CBT (and for relapse prevention purposes most people need to take medication for at least a year, which may be beyond the course of therapy). However, a few people can do fine on medication alone – the difficulty lies in identifying such individuals.

If you are seeking treatment for BDD, you need to think about the function of medication for you. If you have tried more than one course of medication and you are hoping that your doctor will come up with a drug that will get rid of your bad feelings, you are not really helping yourself. As we will show in Chapter 5, trying to escape from a bad feeling actually becomes part of the problem and maintains the problem. The main goal of medication is to stop you feeling distressed, whereas the psychological approaches described in this book are generally geared to helping you do the things you value in life, despite the way you feel. We have no evidence that one approach interferes with the other. People with more severe problems may do better on a combination of medication and CBT.

It's worth being aware, though, that more research is needed on the long-term effects of combining medication and effective psychological therapies. Mental disorder is complex and there are no easy answers. Whatever approach you take, make sure you monitor your progress with the rating scales in this book so you can decide (with your therapist or doctor) what is helping and whether to try something else.

> ## INEQUALITIES IN FUNDING FOR MEDICATION AND PSYCHOLOGICAL TREATMENTS
>
> After you recover from your body image problem, we hope that you will think seriously about campaigning for better access to evidence-based psychological treatments so that there is a real choice for everyone. For this to happen, there needs to be better funding for research into the use of psychological treatments in BDD. One area that needs research is psychedelic-assisted psychotherapy.
>
> Pharmaceutical companies have plenty of money for research, whereas scientists who want to investigate psychological treatments have great difficulty in obtaining grants because the pot of money available is much smaller. This is partly related to the stigma of mental disorder – scientists studying cancer or heart diseases have a relatively easier time raising funds for research.

Skin disorders and body disfigurement

Individuals with disfigurement or a very noticeable defect can have many or all of the body image problems related to preoccupation and shame about appearance described above. They may also have to cope with additional problems such as intense curiosity from others, teasing and bullying (for children), staring, comments and questions (for both children and adults). Disfigurements can be caused by a congenital disorder (people are born with them) or they may be acquired at any stage in life because of injury or disease.

Because severe disfiguring conditions are relatively rare, most people seldom come across someone who looks visibly different. This means that when they meet someone with an unusual appearance they tend to notice, do a 'double take' or even ask the person how their condition was caused. This response to anything out of the ordinary is a natural human reaction; our brains are 'hardwired' to take notice of the unique or unusual. But for someone who is constantly being stared at or asked questions, life can become frustrating and annoying. It can then be easy to slip into a pattern of avoiding social situations, particularly when there are likely to be lots of new people present.

Medical and surgical solutions for disfigurements are not always possible. Therefore, treatment is based on understanding the responses of others, learning to pre-empt any problems by taking the initiative in social situations, and building on the research evidence that people respond to behaviour as much as to appearance in building relationships. Although it might seem inevitable that having a disfigurement will cause psychological problems, this is not the case. Nor does a more severe visible difference necessarily lead to a greater degree of psychological distress. Many people with a significantly unusual appearance live happy, successful and normal lives. These issues are explored more fully in Chapter 11.

As yet, there have not been any controlled trials comparing one psychological treatment with another for people with visible difference or physical anomaly. The main approaches continue to be social skills training (see Chapter 12) or CBT or a combination of the two. Both face-to-face treatments and online programmes are effective in reducing anxiety and increasing social interaction, and there have been several new online interventions and apps developed at the Centre for Appearance Research, both for adults and young people. These are currently in different stages of their assessment for effectiveness.

More recently, researchers have been testing the acceptability of acceptance and commitment therapy in managing visible difference. This variation of CBT is still focused on the relationship between cognitions, emotions and behaviour, but, rather than challenging the content of thoughts, works to help people 'observe' rather than 'buy into' their content.

Visible difference is a relatively new subject for research, and the lack of evidence about which treatment works best is due to the lack of large research studies rather than because psychological treatment methods are not effective. However, it is important to note that CBT methods are much more effective than no treatment at all, and that written self-help programmes – such as this book – are effective in helping with the psychological aspects of visible difference.

This book therefore uses the principles of CBT, which can be applied to body image problems involving disfigurement, and the specific problems of disfigurement are discussed in more detail in Chapter 11.

Body integrity dysphoria

BDD is sometimes confused with 'body integrity dysphoria' (BID). These are conditions in which people want one or more of their fingers, toes or limbs to be amputated. Individuals with BID feel that one or more limbs are not part of their 'self' and that amputation will lead to them becoming more able-bodied. This preoccupation is based not so much on a feeling of being defective as a feeling that they would be so much more comfortable if one or more of their limbs or digits were amputated. Prior to amputation, people with BID may live as if they had a disability and are known as 'pretenders'. For example, they may live with a wheelchair, crutches or leg braces. When surgeons refuse to operate, some individuals even carry out self-amputation.

Although such people are preoccupied with becoming disabled, they do not believe their limbs to be defective or ugly (as in BDD), nor do they wish to alter their limbs cosmetically. BID is therefore more akin to gender incongruence, in which an individual feels they are trapped in a body of the wrong gender. BID is an unusual condition, but people who have it are suffering a great deal, and there are clinical reports that suggest they may benefit from amputation. Fortunately, this condition is rare, and it should not be confused with BDD.

Body modification or self-mutilation

There is a group of individuals, sometimes mistakenly thought to have body image problems, who modify or mutilate their bodies as a form of art. Alternatively, some of them may transform their body so that it resembles a particular animal. Self-mutilation commonly occurs in young women – for instance, they may cut themselves on the forearms with razors or other sharp implements. Several studies have linked childhood abuse with subsequent self-mutilation, especially in people with an emotionally unstable personality. In the 1990s, body piercing and tattooing became increasingly popular. The growth of sadomasochism may also have been a factor in these trends. Decorative implants of various sorts are also popular, including some inserted under the skin. These include lobe stretching, ear scalpelling, tongue piercing and various modifications of the genitalia. For most people, body modification appears to be simply a lifestyle choice. However, a few people who have modified their bodies might have BDD and be using the modification as a way of camouflaging their 'defect' or distracting attention from it.

Lolo Ferrari, who died in 2000 at the age of thirty-seven, became famous for having the largest breasts in the world. She had twenty-two cosmetic operations in five years, especially on her bust, which gradually increased from 37 to 71 inches. She had difficulty breathing and was unable to sleep on her front or back. She was a colourful but sad figure who made her name as a presenter on late-night television shows in Europe, and her image still appears on thousands of websites. She said in interviews that she had a deeply unhappy childhood. She may have ended her own life, although her husband was at one time charged with her murder. We don't think she had BDD. Her symptoms were not typical and in many ways her behaviour was an extreme version of body modification and self-mutilation, which was reinforced by male attention.

Another person who carries out an extreme version of body mutilation is a woman known as Orlan, who usually represents her body modifications as 'art'. For one operation, she had silicone implants put into her cheeks and forehead to give herself 'horns'. This was intended to make her uglier and raise questions about the nature of beauty. The operations are videoed as 'body art', and amputated parts of her body are sold to the public. Examples of extreme body modification into animals include two men living in the USA, known as 'Tigerman' and 'Lizardman'. No cosmetic surgeon will assist such individuals to transform their bodies, so lay individuals carry out such surgery without anaesthetic.

Additional problems that may coexist with BDD

People with body image issues often have other problems as well. This can make the body image problem harder to treat, and it might be difficult to separate the problems from each other.

Depression

The most common additional condition to that of body shame is depression, especially in individuals with BDD. Everybody feels down from time to time, but the feeling usually passes fairly quickly and doesn't interfere too much with the way we live our lives. When most people say 'I'm depressed' they mean that they are feeling low or sad, or perhaps stressed, which are normal human experiences. However, when health professionals talk of depression, they are using the term in a different way. They are referring to a condition that is different from the normal ups and downs of everyday life. This is the type of depression we shall be discussing: it is more painful than a normal low, lasts longer and interferes with life in all sorts of ways.

Depression nearly always occurs after the onset of a body image problem. This suggests that the feeling of depression comes on as a result of the frustration caused by body shame. Often, individuals with body shame do not have a full-blown clinical depression but experience mood swings, irritability and a sense of frustration. If you suffer from depression, you might also find it helpful to read our book called *Manage Your Mood* in this series. After years of social isolation, individuals with body image problems often have low self-esteem relating to areas other than their appearance. If this is a problem, then we would also recommend the book *The Compassionate Mind Workbook* by Chris Irons and Elaine Beaumont, published by Robinson.

There are several ways you can monitor the severity of your depression and whether it improves with treatment.

The most common questionnaire for measuring the severity of depression is the PHQ-9, which you can find easily with an internet search. Each item is scored between 0 and 3, and the range is a total score of 0 to 27. If you score 9 or more then you are likely to have depression. Higher scores reflect greater severity.

HAVE I GOT DEPRESSION?

So how do you know if you are experiencing depression or just going through a period of feeling low? Depression can be diagnosed only by a health professional, but to meet the criteria for a diagnosis you must have been feeling persistently down, or lost your ability to enjoy your normal pleasures or interests, for at least two weeks. The symptoms should be significantly distressing or seriously interfere with your normal activities. The lowered mood should vary little from day to day, and not usually change according to circumstances. However, it's not unusual for people who have depression to find that their mood is worse in the morning. There is a lot of variation from one individual with depression to another, especially among adolescents. In some cases, anxiety and agitation can be more prominent than the depression, or the depression might be masked by irritability, excessive use of alcohol or a preoccupation with your health. Typical symptoms

> of depression include feeling tearful or irritable; being socially withdrawn or inactive; having poor concentration; experiencing disturbed sleep or appetite; and being very negative in your thinking and brooding a lot on the past.
>
> You can learn more about how to tackle depression in Chapter 8 of this book.

Social anxiety disorder (social phobia)

Most people with BDD or body shame have varying degrees of anxiety in social situations and worry what others think about them. Both problems can involve feeling intensely self-conscious. Social anxiety disorder (or social phobia) consists of excessive anxiety in situations where you feel you might be scrutinised or judged by others. People with social phobia fear they will do or say something that will be humiliating or embarrassing. They may fear that other people will see them blush, sweat, tremble or look anxious. They try to avoid participating in meetings, talking to strangers or people in authority, eating or drinking in public, dating or being the centre of attention.

Social anxiety disorder is diagnosed when social anxiety significantly interferes with a person's life and stops them from doing things that they would like to do. When it is persistent and chronic, it is often linked to low self-esteem and depression. It may be diagnosed in addition to BDD or an eating disorder, when the concerns are not only about appearance. For example, the person is not only worried about how they look to others but also about their performance and how they come across (for example, if they are being boring or if their hands are shaking). Effective treatment of social anxiety often helps reduce body image problems, although some people will require specific treatment of body image disorder.

For more information and advice, read *Overcoming Social Anxiety and Shyness* by Gillian Butler. A common questionnaire to monitor the severity of social anxiety that you can find on the internet is the Social Phobia Inventory (SPIN).

Obsessive-compulsive disorder (OCD)

OCD is a condition involving recurrent intrusive thoughts, images or urges that the person finds distressing or disabling. These typically include thoughts about contamination; harm (for example, that a gas explosion will occur); aggression or sexual thoughts; and an excessive need for order. The person often becomes very concerned with avoiding thoughts and situations that might trigger the obsession or compulsion. Actions such as obsessive washing or checking might have to be repeated over and over again until the person feels comfortable or certain that nothing bad will happen. For more details see our book *Overcoming Obsessive Compulsive Disorder*, also in this series.

DO YOU HAVE BODY DYSMORPHIC DISORDER?

Sometimes the symptoms of OCD and BDD overlap – for example, a person may believe that their skin is contaminated, and this may lead to washing compulsions or compulsive skin-picking. Others who are preoccupied with perfection and symmetry in their home extend this to their appearance and their clothing. Such people do not believe their feature to be defective or ugly, but might feel a need for their hair to be exactly symmetrical, or their make-up to be perfect or 'just right'.

Autistic spectrum condition

Autism is not an illness but someone on the autistic spectrum may think and act in a way that is different to most of the population.

- They may find it more difficult to understand the minds of others, and to communicate or interact with others.
- They may find things like bright lights or loud noises overwhelming or stressful.
- They may get upset about unfamiliar situations and social events.
- They may be more rigid in their thinking and repeat certain behaviours to soothe themselves.

There are many well-known individuals, from Elon Musk to Albert Einstein to Leonardo da Vinci, who had or have autism. The problem is that being different, especially during childhood or adolescence, may lead to being teased or bullied, and vulnerable individuals may then develop BDD.

Generalised anxiety disorder (GAD)

Generalised anxiety disorder (GAD) is a condition characterised by persistent worry that is difficult to control. However, people with GAD often describe themselves as 'having been a worrier' all their life, and seek help only when their condition has become severe and uncontrollable. For a diagnosis of GAD to be made, the anxiety should occur most of the time and not be focused only on body image. In most people with GAD, the worries are most commonly about relationships, health or money. People usually experience some of the following feelings most of the time:

- restlessness, or feeling keyed up or on edge
- being easily fatigued
- difficulty concentrating or mind going blank
- irritability
- muscle tension (for example, headaches)
- sleep disturbance.

GAD can also cause a number of physical symptoms and interfere with your ability to function normally. It is a very common problem, either alone or in combination with depression and body image problems. For more information, see another book in this series, *Overcoming Worry and Generalised Anxiety Disorder*, by Kevin Meares and Mark Freeston.

Health anxiety

Health anxiety consists of a preoccupation with a fear or belief that you have a serious disease. Some people have both BDD and health anxiety, and the two conditions may overlap. Such individuals have usually misinterpreted normal blemishes or sensations as evidence of an illness. They may compulsively check the relevant feature and seek repeated reassurance from health professionals that they have not got what they fear. They may follow a special diet or take measures to protect the area on their body. They will have a lasting suspicion or belief that not only is the feature ugly or defective but that they must be suffering from an illness despite medical investigations and reassurance. However, the degree of illness (for example, acne) will often be mild and will not require the treatment or measures that are being used. The first treatment is cognitive behavioural therapy that is specific for health anxiety, and sometimes anti-obsessional medication. You can read more in Rob and David's book, *Overcoming Health Anxiety*, also in this series.

Alcohol and substance misuse

Sometimes people 'cope' with body image problems by excessive use of alcohol, illegal drugs such as cannabis or stimulants like cocaine. However, the alcohol or drugs then become the problem, as cannabis and stimulants increase paranoia and depressed mood, and decrease motivation. Individuals will usually need to stop drinking or using illegal drugs before embarking on treatment, as these interfere with therapy. Regular use of substances such as cannabis or ecstasy may also trigger the onset of BDD.

Consuming excessive amounts of alcohol or binge-drinking are other forms of avoidance – they make you emotionally numb, and reduce unpleasant thoughts and feelings about the way you look in the short term. Other signs indicating a possible drinking problem are if you:

- have often been unable to remember what happened the night before because of your drinking
- often feel embarrassed about what you did because of your drinking
- are often late for college or work or are taking days off because of hangovers
- have frequent arguments with your partner about your drinking
- do not fully participate in family life because of your drinking
- have convictions for drink-driving
- often get into fights when you drink
- find yourself having sex with someone you don't particularly like
- use alcohol as a way of coping with feeling stressed or bad
- cannot control the amount you drink at any one time.

For more information on alcohol and drug problems, see our book *Manage Your Mood*, published by Robinson.

QUESTIONNAIRE: HAVE I GOT A DRINK PROBLEM?

One way of helping you decide whether you have a drink problem is the CAGE questionnaire for your current drinking:

- Have you ever felt you should Cut down on your drinking?
- Have people Annoyed you by criticising your drinking?
- Have you ever felt Guilty about your drinking?
- Have you Ever had a drink first thing in the morning to steady your nerves or to get rid of a hangover?

If you answer 'yes' to two or more of these questions (or have more than 21 units a week if you are a man, or 14 a week if you are a woman), you need to reduce your drinking.

Olfactory reference disorder (ORD)

Olfactory reference disorder (ORD) is a condition in which an individual is preoccupied by body odour, bad breath or farting, which is not noticeable to others. It is sometimes regarded as part of BDD. Such individuals may be using perfume to hide the presumed odour. They frequently shower excessively, brush their teeth, change their clothes, and ultimately avoid public and social situations where they think their body odour will be noticed. Some people seek frequent reassurance about their body odour. Others go to great lengths to avoid being around people and may become housebound. We have seen some people with BDD who are also preoccupied with their body odour. This blended easily with their preoccupation with aspects of their appearance. For example, if you believe you look hideous, it is not surprising if you also believe that you smell disgusting. The best treatment is cognitive behavioural therapy and medication.

Schizophrenia

People with schizophrenia may have a distorted body image and may make dramatic changes in their appearance (for example, bizarre use of make-up, sunglasses or unnecessary clothes). They may 'hear' voices commanding them to act in a particular way or have other unusual experiences. They may be inaccurate in their body size estimations, feeling that parts of their body are unusually small or that their body size has changed. They may also feel that they are no longer at home in part of their body or that their body is torn apart.

Emotionally unstable personality disorder (EUPD)

People with an emotionally unstable personality (also called a borderline personality) usually have unstable and intense relationships. They have great difficulty being alone and fear being abandoned. They have a poor sense of their own identity, with a feeling of worthlessness and emptiness. They have frequent mood swings and have difficulty tolerating unpleasant feelings. They may be easily hurt, and this leads to frequent expressions of anger. They may cut or harm themselves (e.g. take an overdose) or carry out other impulsive behaviours (e.g. spending excessive amounts of money, binge-eating, drinking or taking illegal substances). They may lead chaotic lives, and having symptoms of BDD is a very common feature of an emotionally unstable personality. However, it is often regarded as part of the disorder – if you hate yourself, it is not surprising you also hate your appearance. Treatment usually needs to focus on the features of EUPD. The therapies include dialectical behaviour therapy, mentalisation-based therapy and compassion-focused therapy.

Celebrities with body image problems

Many celebrities have been ashamed of their bodies or may have had BDD. Note that in most of these examples there is a discrepancy between how others rate their appearance (or whether it is important to them) and how the person rates themselves.

Andy Warhol, who died in 1987, probably had BDD. A leading figure in the pop art movement, who became famous for his paintings of Campbell's soup cans and coloured photographic images of Marilyn Monroe, Warhol was very self-conscious and preoccupied by 'redness' on his nose. In his autobiography he revealed:

> *I believe in low lights and trick mirrors. A person is entitled to the lighting they need . . . At one time, the way my nose looked really bothered me – it's always red – and I decided that I wanted to have it sanded. . . . I went to see the doctor and I think he thought he'd humour me, so he sanded it and when I walked out of St Luke's Hospital, I was the same underneath but had a bandage on. . . . If I didn't want to*

look so bad, I would want to look 'plain'. That would be my next choice.

Carl Withers, who became his lover in 1952, confirmed in a magazine interview that Warhol 'was incredibly self-conscious and had such a low opinion of his looks, it was a serious psychological block with him'.

The late US pop singer, Michael Jackson (1958–2009), had many emotional problems and repeatedly underwent cosmetic surgery, so he ended up looking abnormal and denying he had had cosmetic procedures. There was a lot of speculation that he probably had BDD (as well as many other emotional problems). He had an abusive childhood at the hands of his father – who repeatedly called him ugly – and suffered from acute acne as a teenager. In later years, he led an isolated life and frequently covered his face using a surgical mask when out in public.

Judy Garland, Hollywood film star and mother of Liza Minnelli, was known to be very insecure and ashamed about her body. One biography states:

Deaf to all those who were now calling her pretty, blind to the evidence of her own eyes, Judy peered into the mirror and saw reflected back not the attractive young woman everyone else saw, but the comical hillbilly of her film Pigskin Parade. The silhouette of the pudgy girl she once had been was burned on her retina and there it would remain. Completely colouring her existence, the ineradicable conviction that she was ugly affected virtually every thought she had, every move she made and every relationship she entered into.

PIT STOP

Let's stop and think about what you have just been reading. Can you summarise the key ideas you have taken on board? What is sticking in your mind? Maybe write it down. If you have any questions, jot those down too. You can return to them once you have had a chance to digest the information.

What is sticking in my mind from my reading so far?

1.

2.

3.

3

How BDD develops

This chapter summarises what is known about the 'causes' of body image problems and what makes a person vulnerable to experiencing one. Although it can be important and useful to have some understanding of how you have come to develop a problem, we do not want to encourage you to look endlessly for reasons or causes. When you fall down a hole, you don't need to know the exact route by which you arrived at the bottom in order to climb out again. Usually there are fairly obvious triggers for body image problems (for example, being teased during adolescence) or vulnerability (for example, being abused as a child). If there is a family history of a mental disorder such as depression or anxiety, genetic inheritance could also be a factor.

Possible causes

We do not know the exact 'cause' of any body image problem. However, we hope in this chapter to help you identify some of the pieces in the jigsaw and recognise that *understanding* your body image problem is part of the solution.

Also note that there will be several pieces of the jigsaw that are 'unknown' and that it is impossible to 'get to the bottom of it all'. Before we help you achieve an understanding of your body image problem, it's worth thinking about how our minds work in evolutionary terms. We want to acknowledge Professor Paul Gilbert for these insights, particularly his work on compassion-focused therapy.

All human beings could be said to have a design fault in the brain. There is a lot of evidence that we share an 'old brain' with reptiles and other mammals. It is responsible for our emotions and drives. These help us to be safe, to find food and to reproduce. We also have the benefit of a well-developed 'new brain', which gives us considerably more sophisticated abilities. We talk more about the new brain and how it relates to the old brain below. It is important therefore to develop a good understanding of the motivation behind your behaviour.

The three main systems in our 'old brain' are:

1. The threat system. This is designed to motivate us to detect and respond to threats in our lives, and creates the 'fight or flight' response. We then feel the emotions of anxiety, shame and anger. The threat system has become dominant in body image problems.
2. The drive system. This is designed to motivate us to be interested in, and take pleasure from, obtaining important resources (e.g. food, sex, social approval). It enables us to survive, to experience pleasure and to feel excited. Some people try to cope with their body image problem by keeping themselves busy

and achieving things with their drive system. When this system is eventually overwhelmed by the threat system (as often occurs), they may feel depressed and lack any drive at all.
3. The compassion system. This is designed to motivate us to connect with others and to understand ourselves. It helps to balance the other two systems, giving us a feeling of wellbeing and contentment. This system may also be overwhelmed by the threat system in body shame and, if it is, you may struggle to self-soothe and connect with others. This is the basis of the compassion-focused therapy developed by Paul Gilbert and colleagues, which helps people to balance their threat and drive systems.

For now, we will focus on the threat system. To begin to understand anxiety, let's scroll back thousands of years and imagine the inhabitants of the African savannah; those who survived had a good threat system that kept them safe when there was danger, such as a lion in the vicinity. You will probably recognise the response they will have experienced: feelings of anxiety and panic, coupled with the body automatically preparing to fight, flee or freeze. The threat system works rapidly to give the best chance of safety and survival. There is no time to take unnecessary risks. To survive, you need a good, functioning threat system.

In body shame, the threats are not external (a lion, a mugger, a vehicle out of control); they are internal, in our minds, and come from the 'new brain', which is well developed and responsible for our ability to problem-solve, to plan, to use language and to be creative. It is both invaluable — enabling us to figure out how to get to the moon or create a work of art — and our Achilles heel, as it allows us to imagine threats. Thus a tricky loop can appear between the 'new brain' and the 'old brain': the new brain might try to be rational and convince the old brain that the way you see yourself in your mind's eye is not a threat; unfortunately, the old brain is designed to keep you safe, and when you are anxious it tends to dominate ('better safe than sorry'). So when you 'imagine' a threat, it activates the system in just the same way as a real external threat would. That's why it feels as if you have two parts to your mind: your anxious old brain and your rational new brain. The key issue is that all humans need a good threat system to survive — feelings of anxiety or disgust are a normal response, which you can't get rid of. You will be learning to understand the context in which your threat system is being activated, and the processes involved, so that you can try to distance yourself and act against the way you feel.

Factors that make up a body image problem

When considering possible causes for the symptoms of your body image problem, it is usually helpful to think of three groups of factors. Those that:

1. have made you vulnerable to developing symptoms (for example, childhood abuse, trauma, genetic inheritance and unknown factors)

2. have triggered your symptoms (such as experiencing acne or being disfigured, or living or working in an environment that places exceptional pressure to 'look' a certain way)
3. have helped maintain your symptoms (for example, the way you react, with particular patterns of thinking and acting).

We will discuss the third group of factors – that is, the patterns that maintain your body image problem – in Chapter 5. It is not only within your ability to change them but doing so is the cornerstone of self-help and CBT. In this chapter, we will examine the first two factors.

As we outlined in the previous chapter, there are many different types of body image problem, and no one can be sure exactly what causes them. What we can safely say is that a body image problem is usually the result of a mixture of psychological and biological factors and life experiences since birth. A good understanding of the development of your body shame can help you to take a more sympathetic, compassionate view of yourself. Your efforts to overcome it will then be more effective.

In some cases, long-term parental neglect and a deep sense of being unloved from childhood may be important factors. Likewise, a person might be teased by their peers over a long period, or a trauma such as a car crash occurs and a person is left with a disfigurement.

Bullying is not uncommon in schools, particularly during adolescence. Bullies tend to pick on the thing that singles someone out or makes them different from their peer group. Unfortunately, appearance is the thing that is most apparent to others. Many people who have body image problems can recall being picked on in a way that made them feel vulnerable and alone.

Bullying also occurs in relationships, and this can be more subtle. Someone who knows another person well tends to know about their insecurities, and may pick on things that they know to be the most hurtful. Unfortunately, this can sometimes be taken as confirming evidence – for example, that the person is fat or ugly or has a big nose – when in fact they look perfectly normal.

Bullying does not have to be sustained, or a hurtful remark made intentionally. One very thoughtless comment can haunt someone for years – a ghost from the past – and sustain a body image problem many years later. Often, when challenged, the person who said it will have had no idea of the lasting preoccupation that this comment has triggered, and will be amazed at the upset caused by something that to them seemed inconsequential.

When you consider possible causes of body image problems, it's important to remember that life experiences all interact with one another. Imagine that the cause of a body image problem is like a cocktail in a glass. The ingredients of the cocktail will be different for each individual, and they will also mix and interact in different ways.

What makes a person vulnerable to BDD?

Vulnerability to a body image problem could be due to three types of factors, which may overlap:

- physical conditions, including medical, biological and genetic causes
- personality or psychological traits, and
- life experiences.

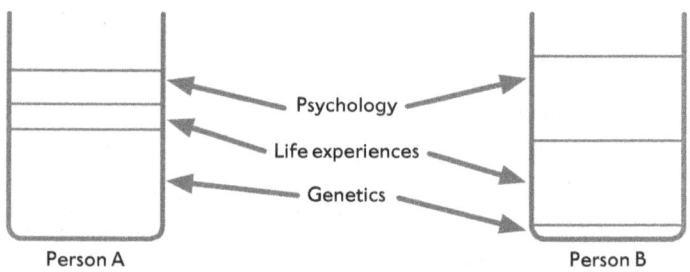

Person A   Person B

Genetic factors

A mental health problem can sometimes run in families. For instance, if you have a close relative who has had BDD, depression, an eating disorder, autism or obsessive-compulsive disorder, you could be at increased risk of experiencing a body image problem at some time in your life. However, having a genetic factor does not mean that you will inevitably develop a body image problem. Similarly, it is possible to develop a body image problem without any evidence of genetic risk, so there is no point in worrying that you may be at greater risk than other people.

Psychological factors

Certain aspects of your personality can make you more vulnerable to developing a body image problem. For example, you might be a perfectionist, or excessively shy and reserved. Such traits, in combination with one or more triggers, can make you more vulnerable to developing a body image problem.

There is good evidence that people with BDD have a highly developed eye for detail, but their ability in what's called 'global processing' is not as good. What this means is that your brain may automatically pay more attention to details in your appearance and not 'step back' and take in your appearance as a whole. This sheds an important light on why you might see yourself differently in the mirror to those people around you who care about you.

People with body image problems might also be more aesthetically sensitive than the average person. According to a small study that compared people with BDD with others suffering from post-traumatic stress disorder (PTSD), depression or obsessive-compulsive disorder, people with BDD were much more likely than the other three groups to have had an education, training or occupation in art and design. At present, it is unclear whether being more aesthetically sensitive makes you more vulnerable to developing BDD or is a consequence of developing BDD.

Other studies suggest that healthy people might be slightly positively biased (or 'wearing rose-tinted glasses') when it comes to rating their own attractiveness, compared with how others rate them. This tendency can be beneficial, as such individuals are more likely to have happy relationships and to be working successfully and doing the things in life that are important to them. In contrast, people with a body image problem seem to have lost their rose-tinted glasses and have no positive bias when rating their own attractiveness. People with body image problems can appear to have problems with their perception – for example, in perceiving their body size to be larger than it really is in anorexia – but the problem lies more in their emotional reaction to their appearance, the degree of importance they attach to appearance and the way they judge themselves. We shall discuss these psychological factors in Chapter 5.

Life experiences that may make you vulnerable during childhood or adolescence include emotional neglect, rejection, bullying and sexual abuse, all of which can lead to a sense of being worthless or unloved. Traumatic experiences, such as accidents resulting in scars, or a skin condition such as acne or eczema, can lead to a lot of attention being focused on appearance. For others, the importance of appearance might be positively linked with success during childhood (e.g. comments such as 'You were wonderful on stage and you looked so good', rather than 'Your performance was excellent'). Alternatively, a particular body part, or a person's height or weight, might have been highlighted. Early dating success, and other adolescent experiences where the importance of appearance is at a premium, could also play their part.

Social factors

Most cultures value appearance. Less 'attractive' leading female television or movie stars are in the minority, and several recent TV reality shows have focused on 'unattractive' women who undergo a radical transformation. In addition, we are bombarded by advertisements telling us that physical attractiveness is necessary for success, and that we need cosmetic products and surgery to achieve the appearance we want.

Some cultures seem to place greater emphasis on the importance of looking attractive. For example, cosmetic surgery in Brazil is very common and out of proportion to the wealth of the country. Equally, in Western cultures gay men seem to feel that they are under increased pressure to look attractive. At the other extreme, fundamentalist Islamic states may protect some women against developing body shame, as wearing a veil ensures that such women do not reveal themselves other than to their husband or family. Arab cultures do not generally value physical attractiveness as much as Western cultures do. This is because many people in Arab countries believe that beauty may make certain individuals vulnerable to the evil eye and misfortune is blamed on envy. Other cultural aspects can be relevant in individual cases. For example, a Puerto Rican woman was intensely distressed by a small facial scar that she received in an accident. This was because, in her community, a scar was inflicted as a punishment for adultery.

Apart from cultural factors, immediate peers and family can have a big influence on the importance of appearance to an individual. For example, research has shown links between a daughter's recollection of her mother's earlier attitudes to her own body and the daughter's own current body image. In addition, having a more attractive sibling may encourage a person to rate their own attractiveness unfavourably.

Medical conditions

There are many medical conditions that can alter someone's appearance, such as polycystic ovary syndrome (which leads to weight gain and excessive body/facial hair growth), or an underactive thyroid (which might lead to weight gain, forgetfulness, excessive tiredness, a hoarse voice, slow speech, constipation, feeling cold, hair loss, dry rough skin, irregular periods and infertility, as well as symptoms of anxiety and depression). There are also many medical treatments that alter personal appearance (for example, there may be facial wasting after antiretroviral treatments for HIV, or 'moon face', altered body shape and skin thinning after use of steroids).

However, a change in appearance does not inevitably lead to a body image problem. Body image problems are more closely related to how much you believe that others will notice your abnormality, the importance you attach to appearance and the unfavourable comparisons you might draw with a former self.

'Brain chemical' factors in BDD

Biological explanations focus on the role of chemicals such as serotonin in body dysmorphic disorder. These chemicals are part of the nervous system and allow one nerve to communicate with another. Serotonin plays a part in many aspects of normal human functioning, including appetite, sexual desire, anxiety and mood, so it is not unique to BDD. An imbalance of serotonin is not therefore necessarily a cause of BDD.

Lately there has been a lot of scientific interest in the relationship between the gut microbiota and various emotional disorders. Our guts are regarded as our 'second brain', so that when you feel anxious, you can feel it in your guts. Equally there are billions of bacteria and viruses that live symbiotically in your guts and can influence your brain by the chemicals they produce or directly via the nervous system. It's possible that various emotional disorders may be associated with bacteria that do not look after your brain. In future we may know how to optimise our gut microbiota in order to influence our brain and body functioning, but for the moment the advice is to minimise ultra-processed (junk) foods, and to eat plenty of fibrous foods (for example, artichoke, asparagus, onion, garlic, wholemeal flours, beans and pulses) and probiotics such as kefir, kimchi, kombucha, and live yoghurts and cheeses.

Medication that helps to enhance activity in nerves that use serotonin can ease symptoms of BDD or depression; we will look at such drugs in detail in Chapter 13. However, just because drugs that help BDD or depression act on nerves that contain serotonin, it does not mean that a deficiency of serotonin necessarily causes BDD. This is like saying that if aspirin improves headaches, then headaches are caused by a deficiency of aspirin. The changes in serotonin are likely to occur because your mind is trying to cope by dampening down your anxiety. Drugs that address the imbalance in serotonin may help in BDD (and depression or anxiety) by enhancing the function of serotonin nerve cells in the brain. If your BDD or mood improves, then it may help you to cope better and to face up to and deal constructively with any difficulties you may have. In summary, trying to unravel the biology of BDD is a complex business, and statements that BDD is caused by an imbalance of serotonin or other chemicals in the brain are simplistic nonsense.

In general, any biological changes observed in the brain of a person with BDD can be reversed, using either psychological treatment or a physical therapy. If a person overcomes his or her BDD (by whatever method), the brain will switch off the biological changes that may occur in reaction to the BDD and the system will return to normal. There is unlikely to be any permanent structural damage in someone who recovers from BDD, and the use of medication does not tell us anything about the cause of BDD.

What can trigger a body image problem?

A body image problem usually occurs as an understandable response to specific events and in a particular context. Many of the triggers in a body image problem are long-term difficulties that may drain someone emotionally and psychologically over time. The most common triggers for a body image problem are:

- being teased or bullied about being different – for example, your height, being chubby, your skin, or your legs being thin
- being aware of a change in your appearance, such as developing acne or a skin condition
- being involved in an accident and developing a scar.

Sometimes a body image problem such as BDD seems to occur out of the blue, without any identifiable trigger or social factors. In this case there could be more biological factors at work. There are a very few medical conditions that might aggravate or mimic BDD. If your medical history suggests a possible physical cause or if you are not getting better with conventional treatments, such causes should perhaps be investigated despite their relative rarity. For example, a thyroid problem could be linked to BDD.

Understanding the psychological causes of a body image problem

Mental suffering is extremely common, so much so that it is almost part of the human condition. This fits with the Eastern or Buddhist philosophy that 'life is suffering'. Such an approach views the problem as not being inside (like bad genes or faulty thinking) but on the outside. In other words, it's normal to feel sad when bad things happen or when something is missing in your life.

This is not to say that there are no biological factors in body image problems. There are several types of body image problems, and even when there are strong biological influences, the way you react to your body shame still influences the severity of the symptoms. The way you respond (for example, by being withdrawn and inactive and brooding) could determine the severity of your symptoms.

Even if a doctor recommends that you take medication for BDD or another problem such as depression, there is nothing to stop you improving your symptoms by also using the approaches described in this book. This will involve developing a more compassionate and caring view of yourself, acting as if you truly believe you have nothing to be ashamed of in your appearance, and doing more of the activities you are avoiding.

In summary, the assumption behind body shame is that we are a product of our genes and what we have learned since we were born. The way we think and act is shaped by our experiences, though some people are more vulnerable to body shame through greater biological risk or personality traits. Throughout this book, we emphasise the importance of context. For instance, lots of 'bad' events may occur, especially in childhood – from emotional and physical abuse and neglect to lack of boundaries or learning about the importance of appearance. If we experienced unpleasant events when we were younger, we tend to avoid anything similar and anything that reminds us of them when we are older. If you were teased or not loved during childhood or adolescence, it would not be surprising if you grew up believing yourself to be ugly. You would also be adversely affected if you learned from people in your family not to show your emotions or if you were punished inconsistently or not given any boundaries.

Much of our development occurs without our being aware of it, and we are exposed to literally millions of moments of learning. It is utterly impossible to unravel or organise them into a causal order. Therefore, therapies that promise to 'get to the bottom of it all' and discover the cause of your body image problem in childhood are often unhelpful. In fact, such therapies may sometimes make things worse by encouraging you to brood. It is better to focus on the here and now and what is maintaining your symptoms.

If you do have very low self-esteem and are very self-critical, you may view your actions as a way of protecting yourself (or even punishing yourself before others can punish you), and making sure you are not hurt or not criticised by others. In this book, we will be examining if this really prevents bad things from happening or whether it makes it more difficult to achieve what you really want to achieve in life. For example, Sabine, whom we introduced above, was highly critical of herself to try to avoid being shocked by other people's comments. Unfortunately, the result was to increase her own dissatisfaction and isolation.

Identifying your triggers and vulnerability

Please add your own thoughts in response to the questions below.

Biological factors

Are there any possible genetic or biological risks? For example, do you have a family history of mental disorder? Did you have a persistent skin problem like eczema or acne? Were you born with a visible difference in your appearance? Have you regularly taken an illegal substance? Do you live on junk food? Is your sleep chaotic (for example, going to bed very late and getting up late)?

_____

_____

_____

_____

Psychological factors

Are there aspects of your personality that make you vulnerable? For example, have you always had low self-esteem, been a perfectionist, had an anxious temperament, or been someone with a particular appreciation of art and beauty?

_____

_____

_____

_____

Life experiences

Did you have any bad experiences like bullying or neglect when you were younger that might have made you more vulnerable and less able to cope well with stress now? Did your parents or culture emphasise the importance of appearance? Does success in your work depend on what you look like (e.g. modelling or acting)?

_____

_____

_____

_____

In Chapter 5 we'll ask you to consider in more depth early life experiences that may have contributed to you developing BDD.

Triggers

Have there been social or personal problems in your life, like the break-up of a relationship or an accident such as a car crash? Have there been any major changes in your role in life?

_____

_____

_____

_____

By writing down the factors that might have made you vulnerable to your body image problem you are building an understanding view of the 'history' behind it. We hope this will help you to be less critical of yourself for having a body image problem and will help put your problem in context.

What if I can't identify any factors in the cause of my body image problem?

Don't worry if you can't identify particular factors that make you vulnerable to developing a body image problem. It can sometimes be difficult to be certain of the causes, especially if a problem developed from a young age. As yet, we do not fully understand all the causes of body image problems. Constantly searching for a reason might seem like a good idea if you think that you need to find the reason before you can fix the problem. This approach usually works with physical problems: if you have a chest pain caused by a lack of oxygen to your heart because of a blockage in an artery, then a doctor can do the right investigations to find the blockage and bypass the blocked artery with a graft. However, this approach does not work if you have an emotional problem, because the more you try to stop feeling bad by searching for an elusive 'root cause', the more you focus on how bad you are feeling. As a result, you are likely to end up making yourself feel worse.

Inevitably, you will read or be told different things by different therapists or doctors. The more opinions you seek and the more books and websites you read, the more your doubts will increase. Some experts may emphasise the role of brain chemicals, while others may empathise with your childhood experiences. Change involves learning to tolerate uncertainty and accepting that you will never know the 'exact' combination of factors that might be relevant for you. Some of the 'causes' are probably in the unknown category and, even if you did know the exact order of events, you probably couldn't do anything effective about them. Just say no to any therapy that offers to find the route you took into the hole. Instead, insist on a proven psychological treatment for a body image problem that helps you get out of the hole!

PIT STOP

Let's stop and think about what you have just been reading. Can you summarise the key ideas you have taken on board? What is sticking in your mind? Maybe write it down. If you have any questions, jot those down too. You can return to them once you have had a chance to digest the information.

What is sticking in my mind from my reading so far?

1.

2.

3.

4

Setting yourself on the right course

This chapter is designed to help you define your problem and monitor the severity of your body image problems and their impact on your life. Identifying and rating the current severity of your body image problem at the outset will give you a reference point against which you can measure your progress. You may find it helpful to make additional copies of the questionnaires provided, to help you to measure your progress. They are designed to help you define the nature of the problem and its effect on your life. Some of them can be completed weekly to determine whether or not you are making progress.

Severity of your body image symptoms

The following questionnaires have been designed for you to use weekly or fortnightly.

1. **Body image questionnaire** (see Appendix 3): This is the questionnaire you answered in Chapter 2. It is

designed to measure the severity of your BDD symptoms and can be used as an outcome measure. This is the weekly nine-item version in which the items are scored from 0 (least impaired) to 8 (most impaired). There are other, longer, versions of the questionnaire, but this version is the one adopted for use in NHS talking therapies.

The score is achieved by summing all the items. Items 1, 2 and 4 are reversed (that is, if you circle '8' then this is a score of zero, circling '7' is scored as '1', and so on). The total scores range from 0 to 72, with a higher score reflecting greater impairment and symptoms of BDD. Individuals who score 40 or more are likely to have a diagnosis of BDD.

2. **Appearance anxiety questionnaire** (see Appendix 3): This is designed to monitor the frequency of processes (e.g. overthinking, self-focused attention) and the way you cope (e.g. social avoidance, appearance checking). Each item is scored on a 5-point Likert scale (0 = not at all to 4 = all the time) and a total score is obtained by summing all the items (the range is 0 to 40). There are two groups of items (or factors): an avoidance subscale (items 1, 3, 5, 7, 9, 10) and a threat monitoring subscale (items 2, 4, 6, 8).

Rating the severity of your depression and anxiety

Rating the severity of your depressive symptoms at the start and then at regular intervals will help you to monitor your progress and assess whether or not what you are doing is effective. Even if you decide not to use any self-help techniques, or decide to take medication, it is still important to monitor your progress, so you should still do these exercises. You can then report back to your doctor and decide whether to try an alternative approach. You can also use the Hospital and Anxiety Depression (HAD) Scale in Chapter 8 and Appendix 3 to monitor depression and anxiety.

Focusing on what's important to you

As a result of your BDD you will have become overly focused on your own appearance, other people's appearance, appearance in the media, the role of appearance in our culture, and so on. The aim of the next exercise is to boost your understanding of your values and what you want your life to stand for. This will enable you to engage in a life that has a better balance and is less dominated by concerns about appearance. Once you clarify your valued directions, you can start acting towards them with greater drive and determination.

We have adapted the 'valued living questionnaire' from acceptance and commitment therapy. There are various prompts for each area to help you write down a brief statement. You don't have to fill in every area – just leave an area blank if you think it is inappropriate for you. After writing down your statements, you may want to clarify them with a friend or therapist. Be careful not to write down values that you think you should have just because others will approve of them. Write down only what you know to be true for yourself. It is probably a valued direction if you acted on it consistently before you experienced your body image problem. If you have had a body image problem for many years, you may struggle with this exercise, but you should persevere because it is very important.

Note that values are not goals – they are more like compass points, and they need to be lived out by committed action. Goals are part of this process. With values, you never reach your destination because there is always something more you can do to work towards them. If your valued direction in life is to be a good parent, then your first goal might be to spend a few hours just hanging out with your child and playing with them. Other goals might be to get your child through school or college. It might take some time to discover all of your values, so here are some prompts to help you:

- Imagine what aspects of life you would be engaging in if you were not feeling ashamed of or preoccupied with your appearance at this moment. We understand that you might feel upset at the things you seem to have lost, but this exercise will help you chart your course on the journey you wish to take.
- Brainstorm all the activities/interests you can think of and consider which might be close to your valued directions.
- Remind yourself of what you used to value or aspire to when you were younger. Have any of these values simply been 'squashed' by your body image problem?

- Consider whether a fear of what other people will think, or a fear of failing, might be holding you back from pursuing your valued directions.
- Consider a role model or hero and the values they hold.
- Have a chat with a trusted friend (or therapist) who knows you well and see what they would guess your values to be.
- Be prepared to experiment and 'try on for size' living consistently with a given valued direction to see how it 'fits'.

Valued directions form

UNDERSTANDING YOUR VALUES	
Area	**Valued direction**
1. **Intimacy** What is important to you in how you act in an intimate relationship? What sort of partner do you want to be? If you are not involved in a relationship at present, how would you like to act in a relationship?	
2. **Family relationships** What is important to you in how you want to act as a brother/sister; son/daughter; father/mother or parent-in-law? If you are not in contact with some of your family members, would you like to be, and how would you act in such a relationship?	

3. **Social relationships** What is important to you in the way you act in the friendships you have? How would you like your friends to remember you? If you have no friends, would you like to have some and what role would you like in a friendship?

4. **Work** What is important to you in your work? What sort of employee do you want to be? How important to you is what you achieve in your career? What sort of business do you want to run?

5. **Education and training** What is important to you in your education or training? What sort of student do you want to be? If you are not in education, would you like to be?

6. **Recreation** What is important to you in what you do to follow any interests, sports or hobbies? If you are not following any interests, what would you ideally like to be pursuing?

7. **Spirituality** If you are spiritual, what is important to you in the way you want to follow a spiritual path? If you are not, would you like to be and what do you ideally want?

8. **Voluntary work** What would you like to do for the wider community? For example, voluntary or charity work, or political activity?

9. **Health/physical well-being** What is important to you in how you act for your physical health?

10. **Mental health** What is important to you generally in how you look after your mental health?

11. **Any other values that are not listed above**

Now define your own valued directions in life. There is a blank form in Appendix 3, or you can print out a version from https://overcoming.co.uk/715/resources-to-download.

As we see it, the real purpose of overcoming BDD is for you to become free to live your life more fully. Now you have clarified your valued directions, you can use this information to help guide your recovery and reclaim your life.

The next step is to get specific on your problems – the ways your BDD is impacting you – and to set yourself clear goals for recovery.

Listing your problems

Building a list of your problems helps in a number of ways. First, it helps you to break down your body image problem into specific areas to tackle. It also gives you a chance to rate these problems overall now, so that you can re-rate them later to help measure your progress. Here are Sabine and Rusha's lists of problems:

SABINE'S PROBLEM LIST

Severity rating: 0–10 (10 being most severe)

1. Feeling very preoccupied and ashamed about my skin, leading me to worry about it most of the day and to spend approximately four hours applying make-up if I have to leave the house.

   Rating: 10

2. Feeling depressed, leading me to spend as much time as I can at home and not keeping on top of my bills and domestic chores.

   Rating: 8

3. Frequently checking in the mirror/reflective surfaces and comparing my skin to people in the media, leading me to feel envious towards people with far better skin than me.

   Rating: 7

> **RUSHA'S PROBLEM LIST**
>
> *Severity rating: 0–10 (10 being most severe)*
>
> 1. Being preoccupied and anxious about the shape of my nose bothers me for at least six hours a day and makes me want surgery.
>   **Rating: 10**
>
> 2. Frequently checking in the mirror and comparing to old photographs and to other people's noses.
>   **Rating: 8**
>
> 3. Feeling down most of the time. I don't really want to see any of my friends or colleagues, and tend to avoid them.
>   **Rating: 7**

Now make your own list of problems and rate the severity of each one.

Describing your goals

Next, you need to write a description of your goals relating to the problems that you have described and the values you have identified. Start with short-term goals, which are easier to tackle, and set yourself a realistic timetable by which you intend to move on to the next set of goals.

Try to make your own SMART goals. They should be Specific, Measurable, Achievable, Relevant and Time-bound (i.e. achieved by a particular date).

It's sometimes hard, as we have forgotten what is normal or healthy. To help generate ideas for healthy alternative behaviours, consider the following questions:

- What did you do before you had a body image problem?
- If you had a twin who was the same as you in every respect but without a body image problem, what would they do?
- What would a healthy role model of yours do?
- What would you do if you were following your relevant valued directions?

You will need to ask yourself these questions for goals in the short, medium and long term. You can then monitor your progress towards your goals on a scale of zero to 10, where zero is no progress at all towards the goal and 10 means the goal has been achieved and sustained. Your goals should relate to your valued directions in life and tackle what you have been avoiding.

Here are Sabine and Rusha's progress rating forms for their short-, medium- and long-term goals:

SABINE AND RUSHA'S PROGRESS RATING FORMS

Sabine's goals   *Progress rating: 0–10*
                     (10 being completely achieved)

Short term
1. To cut down the number of foundations I use to one over the next couple of weeks.
2. To invite a friend round for coffee at least once a week, starting this week.

Medium term
1. Stop excessively comparing my skin to other people's. I'd like this to reduce and then stop over the next month.
2. Allow my friends to take photographs with me in them and to put them up on social media without me checking or avoiding them. Two months.
3. Start dating within the next couple of months.

Long term
1. To routinely see my friends out of the house within three months.
2. To only think about my appearance for no more than about half an hour in a typical day. I'd be pleased if I get to this within three to six months.

Rusha's goals   *Progress rating: 0–10*
(10 being completely achieved)

Short term
1. Start having more conversations with people using the camera rather than just the audio on my phone. Do this with my mum once a week from this week.
2. Stop researching cosmetic procedures. Do this from today.

Medium term
1. Get my level of thinking about my appearance to less than an hour a day.
2. See my friends at least once a week. For this to be regular within three months.
3. Get back to working face to face every day.

Long term
1. To regularly attend evening class, book group and tennis within four months.
2. Find a new relationship. Not sure how long this will take, but I'm going to aim for the next year.
3. To no longer be self-conscious and self-focused on my nose – aim for six months.

EXERCISE: NOW WRITE OUT YOUR OWN GOAL LIST

My progress rating: *0–10 (10 being completely achieved)*

Short term

1.

2.

3.

Medium term

1.

2.

3.

Long term

1.

2.

3.

Now that you have your problems and goals written down, the next chapter is about understanding the processes that are maintaining your problems. Once you understand these better, you can start changing them and move towards your goals.

PIT STOP

Let's stop and think about what you have just been reading. Can you summarise the key ideas you have taken on board? What is sticking in your mind? Maybe write it down. If you have any questions, jot those down too. You can return to them once you have had a chance to digest the information.

What is sticking in my mind from my reading so far?

1.

2.

3.

5

What keeps your BDD going? Building your 'vicious flower'

Any attempt to solve a problem is only as good as the definition of what the problem is. If you have BDD, one of the big challenges is that it often seems very clear that your appearance, or at least one or more aspects of your appearance, will look and feel like the problem. This chapter is about looking at things from the perspective of 'what if' your problem is a body image problem (rather than a problem with your appearance). That would mean you are experiencing shame and anxiety that is maintained by your behaviour and overthinking. This chapter is about taking a fresh look and defining these processes more clearly. By the end of the chapter, we hope you will have built your own 'vicious flower' of your BDD – a cluster of vicious circles that help you clarify what's keeping your problem going. This then shows you what needs to change for you to break free from BDD.

Here's the template for the vicious flower. We'll explain below how to fill it in and deepen your understanding of how your BDD works.

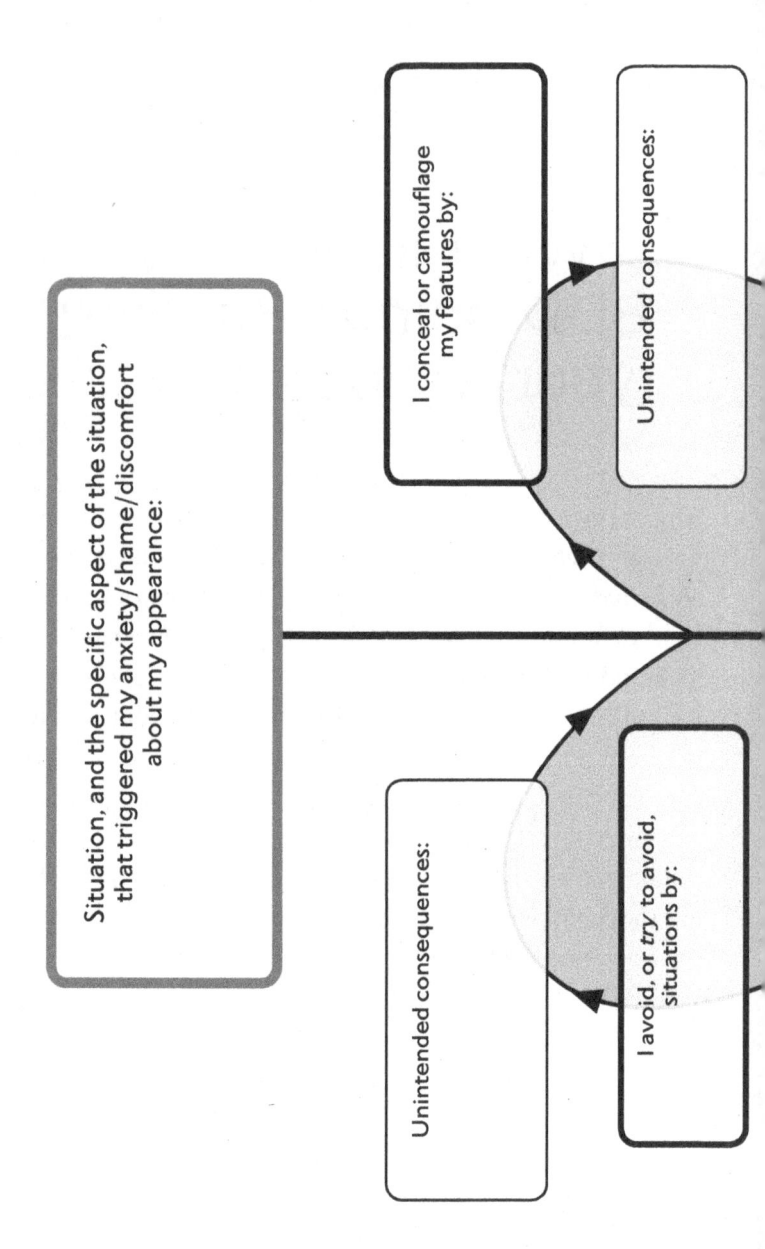

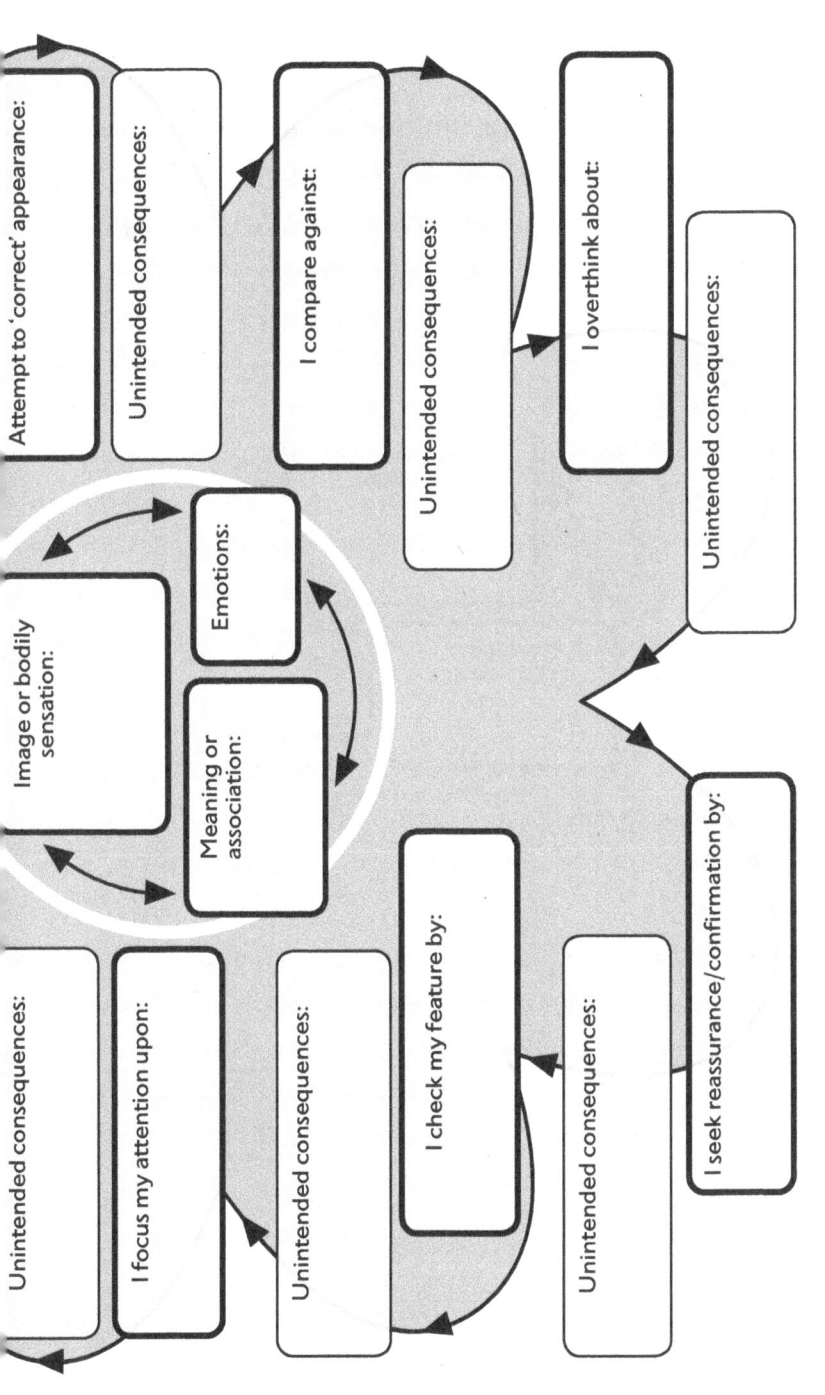

The centre of your vicious flower: how your mind processes your body image

Let's start with the heart of your vicious flower, which aims to capture the way your mind currently constructs your body image.

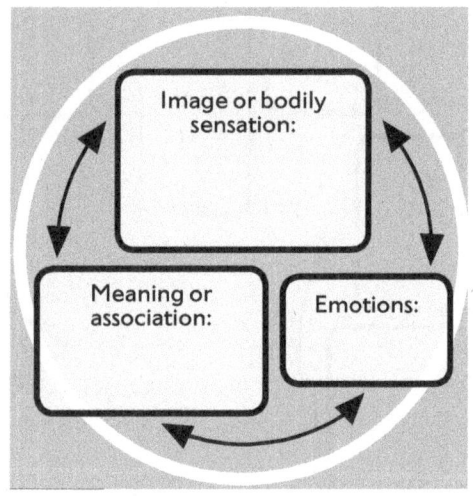

Images

Images are pictures or felt impressions of how you look that just pop into your mind. They may be triggered when you are more anxious in social situations or be there permanently. Images are not just pictures in your mind but can also be felt *physical sensations* or impressions you have of how you appear to others. A key issue is the sense of uncertainty about these images and the way they seem to change. The beliefs about being ugly may be fixed, but the image or felt impression of how you look can vary. This drives your need to check in reflective surfaces and take selfies to know exactly how you look. This in turn undermines your confidence in exactly how you look, and feeds the preoccupation and distress with your features.

People with body image problems usually experience such images from an observer perspective – that is, as if they are looking back at themselves. When we say an image, we mean a 'felt impression' of how you feel you look. This commonly occurs as a picture in your mind but can also be a physical sensation or smell. Someone with a body image problem believes that the picture in their mind is an accurate representation of how they appear to others. However, this is questionable, as such pictures might be linked to bad experiences and are like ghosts from the past, which have not been updated. Thus, if you have been teased or bullied, and learned from your tormentors that you were ugly or defective, then that memory becomes ingrained and influences you in the present.

Pictures often reflect and reinforce your mood. For example, if you are very anxious, you might have mental pictures of being humiliated in the future. However, treating images as reality can create many problems. Change involves recognising that you are just seeing a picture in your mind and that this is not current reality.

SELF-PORTRAIT

Can you draw yourself based on the picture in your mind or how you think you appear to others? Once you have drawn your self-portrait, discuss it with someone you trust and ask whether they view you in the same way?

Meaning or association

When you are ashamed of your body, you may think negatively about your appearance by comparing and rating yourself against others unfavourably. You might judge yourself as 'ugly', 'abnormal', 'not right', 'too fat', 'too masculine' or 'too feminine', or 'not muscular enough'. You may think that others will view you as inferior, flawed or defective. This may make you feel you will be rejected and alone all your life, or that your suffering will carry on for ever.

You probably believe that you are extremely noticeable and that others are looking down on you. It might be just your features that you think others are looking down on, or you might assume that the whole of you is being condemned or humiliated.

For some people, their appearance becomes the single most important aspect in defining them as individuals, and they hold attitudes such as 'I am my nose' or 'My skin defines who I am.' If you hold such an attitude, and are satisfied with your appearance, then you may be worried and anxious about losing your looks. If you are dissatisfied with your appearance, then you are more likely to brood on how helpless you are to do anything to change it.

We hope to show you that your appearance is only part of who you are, and that, even if you are visibly very different from other people, this does not mean you can or should define yourself by your defect.

Many people have their first taste of being really worried about their appearance when they are teenagers. This is not only a time of considerable change in appearance, but also a time when humans are biologically programmed to become more aware of being physically attracted to others and wanting others to be physically attracted to them. For some people with body image problems, it seems as if their attitude to their appearance has not been updated since they were much younger. Many still treat their appearance every day as if looking their best is as important as it would be on a special occasion, job interview or first date. Part of recovery is becoming more flexible in the standards you set for your appearance, and on most days prioritising other aspects of your life.

QUESTIONNAIRE: IDENTIFYING EARLY EXPERIENCES THAT MAY BE RELEVANT TO THE DEVELOPMENT OF YOUR BODY IMAGE PROBLEM

1. Are there any early experiences you can remember that may have contributed to your developing unhelpful patterns of thinking and acting about your appearance? These might be experiences of teasing, bullying, humiliation, sexual abuse, or what you learned from your parents or peers. These links may not necessarily be about your appearance but something that you learned about yourself that made you think you were different or abnormal. To begin with, simply list any memories that come to mind.

_____

_____

_____

_____

WHAT KEEPS YOUR BDD GOING?

2. The second way to identify relevant memories is to use your experience of the picture in your mind or the felt impression you have of yourself. Try to think of a recent time when you felt upset about your appearance. What was the situation? Where were you?

_____

_____

_____

_____

3. What was happening at the time?

_____

_____

4. How did you feel emotionally?

_____

_____

5. What was the picture or felt impression in your mind? Can you draw yourself or describe the impression you had of yourself?

_____

_____

_____

_____

_____

_____

_____

6. Did you have any bodily sensations? Where in your body did you feel them (e.g. tightness in your skin)?

_____

_____

7. How old were you when you first experienced that picture or felt impression of your feature? Please describe your experience in the first person, present tense (e.g. 'I am about six years old and playing in a school playground. A boy who is quite popular with other girls just comes up to me and tells me I look ugly').

_____

_____

_____

_____

8. What was the most upsetting meaning that this experience had for you? The meaning might influence your views about yourself (e.g. 'I am ugly and I'll be alone all my life') or how you think others will behave towards you (e.g. 'People will always humiliate me').

_____

_____

9. Can you remember the first time you had this meaning in your mind?

_____

_____

There may be several painful experiences that have all contributed to the views you have of yourself and others. Try to repeat this questionnaire for the most important experiences.

Emotions

Linked to your image is a feeling of shame or anxiety. You might feel anxious before checking in the mirror, hoping you might know exactly how you look or that you will see something different from how you think you look in your mind's eye. However, after you look in a mirror you may feel worse. You might feel shame as you rate your feature as ugly. During a long session in front of a mirror, some people might experience feeling disconnected from their bodies and a sense of being very unreal. Some might become angry or feel more shame for wasting so much time.

Anxiety is usually triggered by a sense that you are in danger. The threat might be real or imagined, and may be from the past (for example, a memory), present or future. When anxiety dominates the picture, your mind will tend to think of all the possible bad things that could occur ('catastrophising') and will want to know for certain that nothing bad will happen in the future. This leads to people worrying about how to solve non-existent problems. The natural desire is to escape or avoid situations that are anxiety provoking. Anxiety can produce a variety of physical sensations, including feeling hot and sweaty, having a racing heart, feeling faint, wobbly or shaky, muscle tension (for example, headaches), upset stomach or diarrhoea.

If, however, you are becoming despondent about the future, you may feel down or emotionally 'numb', or feel that life has lost its fun. These are core symptoms of depression.

Others may frequently feel hurt and angry because they feel they are being unfairly treated and humiliated when they don't deserve it, or don't deserve to be born the way they are. They may become irritable or lash out.

If you are feeling stressed by a conflict in a relationship, or you have been depressed, withdrawn, inactive and brooding on the past, it will probably make you more self-focused and more preoccupied with how you look, creating a further vicious circle. Anything that improves your mood and decreases other stresses is likely to improve your body image.

Body shame

At the core of BDD is body shame. The first step is to define what we mean by body shame. It consists of a mixture of different emotions. Typically, someone experiences disgust directed against the self. Disgust or revulsion is an emotion that means literally 'something offensive to the taste'. With disgust, there is a reflex closing of the muscles around the mouth. When disgust is directed against the self it is called shame, and when it is directed specifically against your own body, it is called body shame.

Shame about your appearance can be broken down into 'external' and 'internal' body shame. External shame means believing that others think you are unattractive or ugly. This usually leads you to feel anxious in social or public situations. People have learned that it is humiliating or painful to be rejected and therefore try to avoid it. Human beings are social animals. We want to be part of a group, even if we feel under constant scrutiny. External shame is therefore based on what you believe other people think about you.

Internal shame is what you think about yourself. It occurs if you rate yourself negatively, sometimes even feeling a sense of disgust about all or part of yourself. You feel unattractive or ugly to yourself, and feel you must limit the damage to yourself either by avoiding or giving in to others. However, what matters is the sense of not meeting your own standards and being something less than you want to be. Often people continue to feel damaged and spoiled in some way long after the specific events that caused the shame have passed.

Internal and external shame often go together, but not always. Thus, someone may rate themselves as ugly according to their own standards but know that others are not bothered by it. Equally, someone may believe that others think they are ugly but not care about their opinions.

Shame is not something we are born with. It is something we probably learn over time. Positive feelings about ourselves usually come from parents and peers when we are loved and given compliments. Thus, from a young age, children develop a sense of pride when they know others feel positively about them, and this enables them to feel positive about themselves.

Putting the petals on your flower: your responses and coping strategies, and their 'unintended consequences'

There is a metaphor to describe people who are trying to cope with BBD, through no fault of their own. Imagine you are blindfolded and placed in a field with a tool bag. You're told that this is what life is all about and that your job is to run around this field with the blindfold on. Now, what you don't know is that there are some deep holes in this field. So you start running around and enjoying life. However, sooner or later you fall into a deep hole. You can't climb out and you cannot find an escape route. You feel inside your tool bag for something you can use to get you out. The only tool is a shovel. So what do you do? You start digging. It seems so obvious because you are stuck and can't get out. Soon you notice you're not out of your hole, so you try digging faster, but you're still in the hole. So you try big shovelfuls, you try throwing the dirt far away from you, and so on, but you're still in the hole.

Does this relate to your experience of trying to solve your BDD? You might be seeking help from this book or going to a therapist in the hope that you can find a bigger or better shovel to help you feel better. Well, the fact is that you can't dig your way out. However, if you let go of the shovel, you can feel around to see whether there is anything else to help you out – a ladder, for example. Remember, you are blindfolded, and you won't be able to find the ladder or anything else until you drop the shovel. From the perspective of this book, your shovel represents the attempts you are making to control or escape from the way you feel about your appearance.

Looking at your actions compassionately

It is important to remember that, like falling down a hole in the example above, having a body image problem is completely understandable. Yes, life is unfair but it's not your fault – you've fallen down a hole. You have the ability to get out but, before you started to read this book, you did not know what to do, and you did what you did because it seemed natural. We are not saying that the situation is hopeless but, and this is very important, your solutions – trying to avoid or control the way you feel about your appearance – are not working. All they do is make the situation worse and make you feel more stressed and depressed. Remember, working out how you fell into your hole is not going to get you out of it. Some therapies unintentionally provide you with a bigger shovel.

As noted above, only when you stop shovelling can you feel around for something to help you out – like a ladder or rope. This may seem like a leap of faith, but if you don't accept the uncertainty, the situation is guaranteed to get worse.

Unintended consequences: effects of safety-seeking behaviours on others

Many of these safety behaviours also have an effect on others around you. Examples include:

- Frequently seeking reassurance. This can leave another person feeling frustrated and impotent when they are unable to have a lasting effect (if any) on how you feel.
- Other people thinking you are obsessed with yourself, and finding this boring or unattractive.
- Your worries placing restrictions on socialising, reducing your friends' or partner's pleasure at seeing you, and increasing your sense of isolation and conflict.
- Your worries about your looks increasing feelings of jealousy, placing strain on a relationship.
- Your worries about your looks restricting physical intimacy.
- Wearing particular types of clothes to hide a feature, which might provoke comments.
- Keeping your head down and avoiding eye contact, leading others to assume that you are not interested in them. They will then back off and you are more likely to think there is something wrong with you.
- Being distracted by your worries about your looks,

causing you to seem aloof or uninterested. This in turn may lead people to be less warm towards you than they would otherwise be.

All these examples show how a safety behaviour can leave you trapped in a cycle, where the behaviour you have put in place to protect you becomes the problem in two different ways. First, it preoccupies you and prevents you attending to what is really happening. Second, it stops you developing a positive and helpful way of behaving with other people.

Unintended consequences: when problematic solutions seem to work

It may seem to you that digging your way out of a hole works because you are doing something with the tools you have and stopping bad events from happening. It is therefore likely that you will avoid or escape from unpleasant thoughts and situations in the future because such behaviour has been 'reinforced'; it has apparently been successful. However, as we have already pointed out, if you cope by avoiding or escaping from unpleasant thoughts or situations, the technique becomes unworkable for a number of reasons:

- Your 'solutions' of avoidance and escape will make you feel worse and more depressed as you come to realise that they are not going to work and you begin to worry more about problems.
- Avoidance often prevents you from finding out whether something is true or not. For example, if

you never ask a person why they appeared to ignore you, you will never find out if it was because they dislike you or whether, for instance, they were not wearing their contact lenses or were busy worrying about a problem of their own.

- Avoidance and escape have unintended effects on the people around you. Your friends and family might stop trusting you and end up taking on your responsibilities. This in turn could create a vicious circle in which you feel incapable of doing certain things.
- Avoidance stops you from doing what is important to you. For example, you want to be a good parent, or a person to whom your friends and family can turn for support. When you can't do these things you will inevitably feel more depressed. You might spend more time focusing on yourself and beating yourself up. Your behaviour then has an effect on the people around you. Others may be critical or unsupportive, and you will probably become more depressed – in a vicious circle.

While you focus on your negativity, you totally buy into the content of your thoughts as if they were facts. These thoughts are just mental chatter, not objective evidence. In general, the aim should be to 'understand' these thoughts, not so that you can question whether they are true or not, but to consider how you react to them.

Here are some examples of the sorts of strategies people with BDD use and their unintended consequences:

My pre-occupation	Example of safety behaviour	Unintended consequence
Nose too big	Change posture to avoid being seen side-on	Increases self-consciousness, strengthens belief that people will notice and think negatively
Nose too big	Pressing nose with hand to try and re-shape	Increases focus of attention, nose feels red and sore (swollen and bigger)

Avoidance behaviours

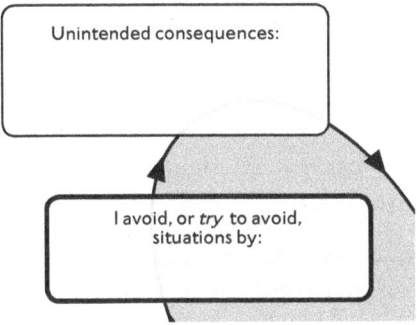

Avoidance is a very common way of trying to cope with many emotional problems. Unfortunately, it is powerful in maintaining problems and can have numerous negative effects on your life. Here are some examples of common avoidance behaviours in BDD:

- avoiding public and social situations
- avoiding leaving the house
- avoiding going to a family or social gathering
- avoiding going to school or university
- avoiding going to work
- avoiding going to a doctor to be examined
- avoiding dating or being intimate
- avoiding being outdoors or in bright lighting
- avoiding having a haircut
- avoiding shopping for clothes
- avoiding using a public changing room or going swimming
- avoiding being seen near people you regard as attractive
- being careful about choice of lighting
- being careful about choice of certain mirrors
- using alcohol or drugs to alter your mood.

Sometimes avoidance can include trying to suppress distressing images, thoughts and memories in your mind. Other people may avoid looking at a bodily feature, in mirrors or the shower, because it triggers distress and/or a time-consuming ritual such as bodily checking.

Action

Now write in your vicious flower an example of an avoidance behaviour you use, and the unintended consequences that feed your preoccupation and distress.

Self-focused and/or threat-focused attention

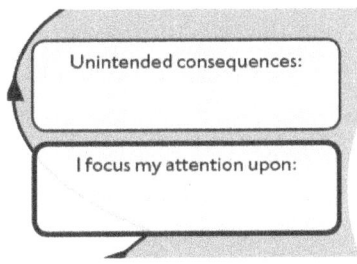

When you are ashamed of your body, you become more focused on your own thoughts and feelings. This makes you more likely to assume that your view of the way you look, and the picture in your mind, is reality. This in turn interferes with your ability to make simple decisions, pay attention or concentrate on your normal tasks or what people around you are saying. When this problem is severe, it may make you feel more paranoid. Your view of the world now depends on your thoughts and how they chatter away, rather than your experience. In other situations, you may be so focused on comparing yourself to others that you fail to take in the context and find it difficult to concentrate on what people are saying or their body language.

When you have a picture in your mind of the features that you feel look ugly you become self-focused, as you have to monitor exactly how you look when you don't have a mirror. It's as if your features are like a dangerous tiger that has to be watched very carefully. Once a threat is on your mind, you will find that this has an impact on what you notice in the world; you develop a bias in your attention, and you become more aware of the way you look. In contrast, someone without a body image problem tends to be focused on what they see in their surroundings or on a task (like talking to the person in front of them), rather than looking back at themselves and constantly monitoring how they think they are coming across.

Attentional bias happens all the time in everyday life. For example, when a woman becomes pregnant, she starts to notice other pregnant women and babies everywhere. It is not that there are more pregnant women and babies – she is just more aware of them. Another common example occurs when you or someone you know is about to buy a certain type of car. Suddenly it seems as if there are many more of that type of car on the roads. If you were to concentrate now on how your big toes feel, after a minute or so you might start to feel a sensation you were not aware of before.

A person with a spider phobia will notice a spider in a room far more readily than someone without that kind of fear. Similarly, someone with BDD may find that their mind is 'on the lookout' for signs of being judged negatively or being treated differently because of their appearance. This is part of the reason you might find that you are prone to jumping to conclusions about people judging you negatively.

People with BDD are a lot more aware of a feature (or any changes that occur in their appearance) than someone without a body image problem. This 'attentional bias' is a result of their over-concern about their appearance, and also contributes to its maintenance, since their personal world can seem flooded with information about the importance of appearance, reinforcing their own sense of the exaggerated importance of appearance. If you have experienced this, you will know that, because your own fears are related to threats about certain features, you are very likely to want to focus on those features. In this way, a vicious circle is set up, whereby the more preoccupied you are with your features, the more you focus your attention on them, further fuelling your preoccupation.

Another situation where self-focused attention occurs is in front of a mirror. We know from research that people with body shame are more likely to focus on their felt impression and on certain features that are viewed as defective compared to people without a body image problem. Furthermore, when individuals without body shame look at themselves in a mirror they tend to focus more on features that they consider attractive.

Action

Now write in your vicious flower an example of your 'self-focused' or 'threat-focused' attention and its unintended consequences.

Comparing

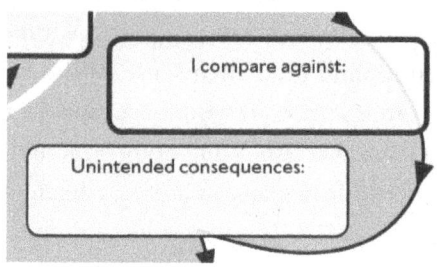

In day-to-day life, comparing is a process that may be either aversive or gratifying. It is very common in the population, and especially in BDD. It is usually automatic and involuntary. It can get quite complicated! The first type of comparing is 'social comparison'. This can be upward comparing (that is to a person whose appearance or character you rate as better), or downward (that is to a person whose appearance you rate as worse) or lateral (i.e. to people you rate as having similar features). In the animal kingdom, this might be motivated to know your place and avoid aggression or conflict; thus a puppy may roll over and avoid conflict with a larger dog. There is also 'temporal comparison' – that is, comparing a feature to how you think you used to look or how you could look in the future. There is also 'counter-factual comparing'. This is a type of fantasy – for example, thinking 'if only' your feature could look differently. There is also 'criterion-based comparing'. This is comparing to how you expected to look, for example after a cosmetic procedure. Lastly there may be 'dimensional comparing', where you focus on comparing other attributes to compensate for your feature that you do not like.

The problem in BDD is that people frequently compare specific features instead of considering their overall appearance. This adds to the attention bias and the way you define yourself through a particular feature. Comparing means more time is spent thinking about your appearance, and this adds to your preoccupation. It also contributes to the self-focused attention and a heightened awareness of the perceived defect. Satisfaction is worse after upward comparing and reduces confidence in your appearance. This in turn adds to the distress. Social media is especially problematic as there are unlimited images to compare yourself against. When meeting others, it reduces your ability to connect with them socially. In general, it just feeds the overthinking, checking and safety-seeking behaviours to verify or camouflage the perceived defect.

It may be difficult to understand the motivation about comparing. You may be trying to improve the certainty about how you look – for example, 'So I can be clear about what is wrong with my appearance.' It reminds you to take care – for example, 'So I don't forget how ugly I am.' You might feel it keeps you safe from rejection and humiliation – for example, 'So I know my place.' Lastly, it may be trying to motivate you to improve your appearance – for example, 'So I can work out how I might improve my appearance or conceal my flaws.' For many people, comparing is such a habit, and it may be difficult to understand the motivation.

Here are some of the common unhelpful consequences of comparing:

- fuels your preoccupation
- contributes to self-focused attention
- strengthens your attention on specific feature(s), resulting in a heightened awareness of the perceived defect
- reduces confidence in your appearance
- contributes to a biased view of the appearance of others, and an unrealistic ideal
- reduces connection in social situations
- feeds the overthinking, checking, avoidance and safety-seeking behaviours to verify or camouflage the perceived defect(s).

Action

Now write in your vicious flower an example of you comparing your appearance and the unintended consequences.

Overthinking: brooding and worrying

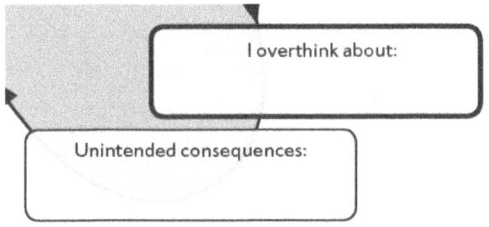

Some people cope by trying to 'put right', or make sense of, past events or their appearance by overthinking, brooding or constantly mulling the problem over. Technically this is called 'ruminating' as it describes what cows or sheep (ruminators) do when chewing the cud. If this sounds familiar, you are probably trying to solve abstract problems that cannot be solved, or to analyse a question that cannot be answered. This usually consists of a lot of 'Why?' questions. 'Why am I so ugly?' or 'Why did I get that surgery?' Another favourite is the 'If only . . .' fantasy, as in 'If only I had not seen that surgeon . . .'. You might be using 'mental' cosmetic procedures in your imagination to think how you could look. Alternatively, you may be a bully and making judgements and criticising yourself. Brooding invariably makes you feel worse, as you never resolve the existing questions and may even generate new questions that cannot be answered.

The process of worrying is a variation on the same theme, in which you try to solve non-existent problems. These usually take the form of 'What if . . .?' questions. Examples include 'What if my partner leaves me?' and 'What if I get called names in front of others?'

You may also find yourself brooding on why you look the way you do or why you had a particular cosmetic procedure. This brooding process may reduce your distress for a brief period, so you get a pay-off because brooding seems to 'work'. Then the next time you feel bad, you will have trained yourself to brood or avoid activity again. Unfortunately, in the long term this will make you feel more depressed. All the time spent alone means that you miss out on what is important to you in life and prevents you from having any positive experiences. The belief that you are ugly or unlovable is therefore strengthened, as you are unable to test out or disprove your negative expectations. The most important thing about brooding and worrying is that it feeds your preoccupation and distress with your appearance.

Self-attacking thoughts

These are self-critical, self-attacking thoughts. Your mind can be made up of different parts, which may be in conflict (e.g. one part may want to eat some chocolate and another part tells you that would be stupid when you want to lose weight). When you attack yourself, one part of your mind may tell you, for example, 'You are so ugly compared with him' or 'You look like an alien and deserve to be humiliated.' Such thoughts tend to make you fall into submission and you can end up feeling very small.

WHAT KEEPS YOUR BDD GOING?

People with BDD problems tend to put themselves down about:

- their appearance
- having an emotional problem and not being able to 'pull themselves together'
- having done something that may have worsened their appearance
- the consequences of having a body image problem, such as not having a partner.

Here are some examples of what we mean:

- George, who was preoccupied with the idea that his eyes were too big, attacked himself for being 'a freak'.
- Harry viewed himself as a 'total idiot' because he believed that pushing certain areas of his face, initially in an attempt to improve his appearance, had made his looks worse.
- Sarah thought she must be unlovable because she didn't have a boyfriend, although it was really her BDD that meant she tended to stay at home, making it very difficult for her to meet men.

Brooding or self-attacking can lead to a number of unintended consequences, such as:

- feeling more distressed about your appearance
- feeling more depressed
- thinking more about bad events from the past
- believing thoughts in which you put yourself down
- being more pessimistic about the future

- being less able to generate effective solutions to problems and less confident in the ones you do generate
- becoming more withdrawn and doing less of what is important to you
- becoming more likely to be ignored and criticised by others.

When most people brood, it makes them feel worse and they are more likely to avoid getting involved in life. Any counselling that encourages you to search endlessly for reasons why you have a problem can also encourage you to brood.

By contrast, 'worry' is overthinking about possible things that could go wrong in the future (including excessive planning and preparation), which will make you more anxious. Many people with body image problems therefore use a mixture of brooding and worrying, depending on their mood.

Action

Now write in your vicious flower an example of you brooding or worrying, and the unintended consequences.

Reassurance or confirmation

Because of your high levels of distress and preoccupation with your perceived flaws in your appearance you may at times want to speak to someone about it. Seeking emotional support for your distress, especially as you push through discomfort to break free from BDD and reclaim your life, is something we encourage. However, some sorts of discussion may not be so helpful:

- repeatedly asking for reassurance that your perceived flaw is not as bad as, or is less noticeable than, you fear
- asking someone to check your appearance to see if they can see changes
- asking someone to look at your perceived flaw to confirm that they can see the problem
- asking someone to look at your perceived flaw in order to discuss what might be done to improve it
- repeatedly debating, arguing or persuading about having a cosmetic procedure.

Action

Now write in your vicious flower an example of you seeking reassurance or confirmation, and the unintended consequences.

Concealing and camouflage

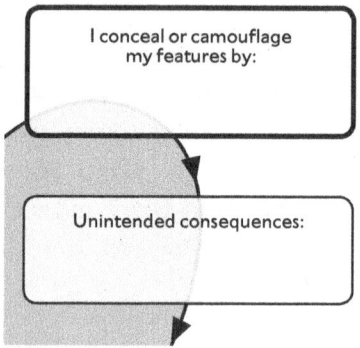

A very common response to feeling ashamed of a part of your body is to try to hide it or make it less noticeable. This might temporarily reduce your feelings of embarrassment and allow you to feel less anxious that people might judge, reject or ridicule you. However, it can prevent you from testing out your fears about other people's responses, maintain your own shame and self-disgust, fuel your preoccupation, and increase your self-consciousness. A common example of an 'unintended consequence' we hear about is people worrying that their concealer is wearing off soon after they have applied it, leading them to feel self-conscious and having the urge to check and reapply. Other types of concealment include:

- covering up or altering the shape (padding out) of body parts using clothing
- styling hair to cover up a flaw, draw attention away from a flaw, or until hair is 'just so'
- using make-up to conceal flaws, or applying it until it is 'just so'
- retouching make-up repeatedly throughout the day
- making frequent trips to beauty salons or hairdressers
- changing posture or covering a feature with your hand
- avoiding bright lights.

Action

Now write in your vicious flower an example of your own action to conceal or camouflage your perceived flaw, and the unintended consequences.

Checking behaviours

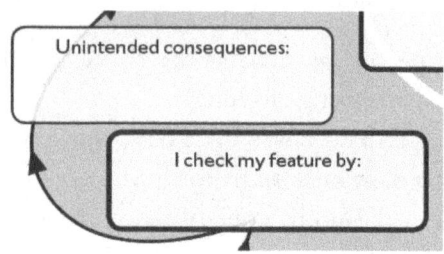

Checking is another common 'safety-seeking behaviour', which is intended to increase certainty about how one looks and reduce anxiety, but usually leaves people feeling worse and prevents them from testing out their fears. For instance, you might be:

- repeatedly checking your appearance in a mirror
- repeatedly checking your appearance in other reflective surfaces
- measuring body parts to see 'how bad they are'
- seeing if your camouflage is hiding the perceived defect
- feeling your skin with your fingers
- taking photographs of yourself
- examining photographs.

Action

Now write in your vicious flower an example of something you avoid, and the unintended consequences.

Attempts to 'correct' appearance

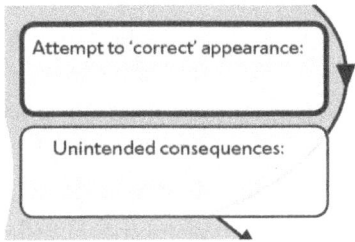

A common behaviour that can be part of maintaining BDD is trying to 'correct' a flaw that you see in your appearance. Common examples include:

- picking your skin to make it smooth
- retouching your hairstyle throughout the day
- cutting or combing your hair to make it 'just so'
- doing 'DIY' cosmetic surgery or dermatological treatments
- 'aesthetic' treatments like Botox or fillers
- having dermatological treatments
- dental procedures
- looking for and trying out new beauty products
- researching or seeking cosmetic surgery
- carrying out specific exercises to change the shape of your perceived flaw(s)
- pushing, hitting or squeezing parts of your body.

This list is by no means exhaustive. Part of the reason we say this is because the cosmetic and aesthetic industries are constantly evolving, and new 'treatments' will become available.

As ever, consider the function of 'correcting', and pay close attention to any unintended or undesirable consequences. We've known many people who have run up thousands of pounds of debt as a result of having cosmetic procedures, causing them considerable stress. We've known several others who feel great resentment that their family have refused to support needless interventions. Others have found that picking their skin to make it smoother has left them paralysed by a cycle of picking, redness, scabs, healing, and picking again. You will be able to break out of these sorts of vicious circles, and understanding how your own circles work can help you see more clearly what you need to change.

Action

Now write in your vicious flower your own example of correcting, and the unintended consequences.

It's worth reflecting on what you think might happen to someone with a relatively healthy body image who practises a number of these activities on a regular basis. We tried this once for just a few hours, and we soon started to become preoccupied and dissatisfied with our own appearance. Thus, a further vicious circle has been set up, as the unintended consequence of safety behaviours is to increase preoccupation and distress.

All methods of escaping from a situation or checking how you look are safety-seeking behaviours. A message we shall return to over and over again is that safety behaviours maintain your worry. They prevent you from testing out your fears, allow the worry to persist and make the problem worse in the long term. Clearly, you have to stop all your safety behaviours if you are to overcome your body image problems successfully.

Building your own vicious flower

A vicious flower is a model you can use to help think through the effects of your current methods of coping. Essentially, a vicious flower is several 'vicious circles' – solutions that aren't working, that help maintain your preoccupation and distorted perception of your appearance. This visual illustration of how a body image problem is being maintained can be very striking. Many people are surprised to see just how much is 'going on' in the maintenance of their body image problem.

We have provided examples below and also provided a blank vicious flower for you to fill in yourself (you can find this on pages 430–1 or in Appendix 3), although it's sometimes easier to draw your own on a blank sheet of paper so that you can have as many 'petals' as you wish. Once you have filled in or drawn your own vicious flower, you can return to it as you progress through the rest of this book. You might add a new petal if you identify a new safety behaviour, but we hope that most of your time will be spent pulling the petals off your flower by facing things you have been avoiding, retraining your attention and dropping unhelpful safety-seeking behaviours.

Marie's Vicious Flower

Situation, and the specific aspect of the situation, that triggered my anxiety/shame/discomfort about my appearance:

Going to a coffee shop in town

I conceal or camouflage my features by:
When I could, I put my phone up against my head to try to conceal my nose

Unintended consequences:
I felt self-conscious because I knew this was not my usual behaviour

I avoid, or *try* to avoid, situations by:
Not letting people see my face from side-on so they wouldn't be so shocked

Unintended consequences:
I felt awkward and uncomfortable. More conscious of the people around me, and annoyed when I couldn't avoid them

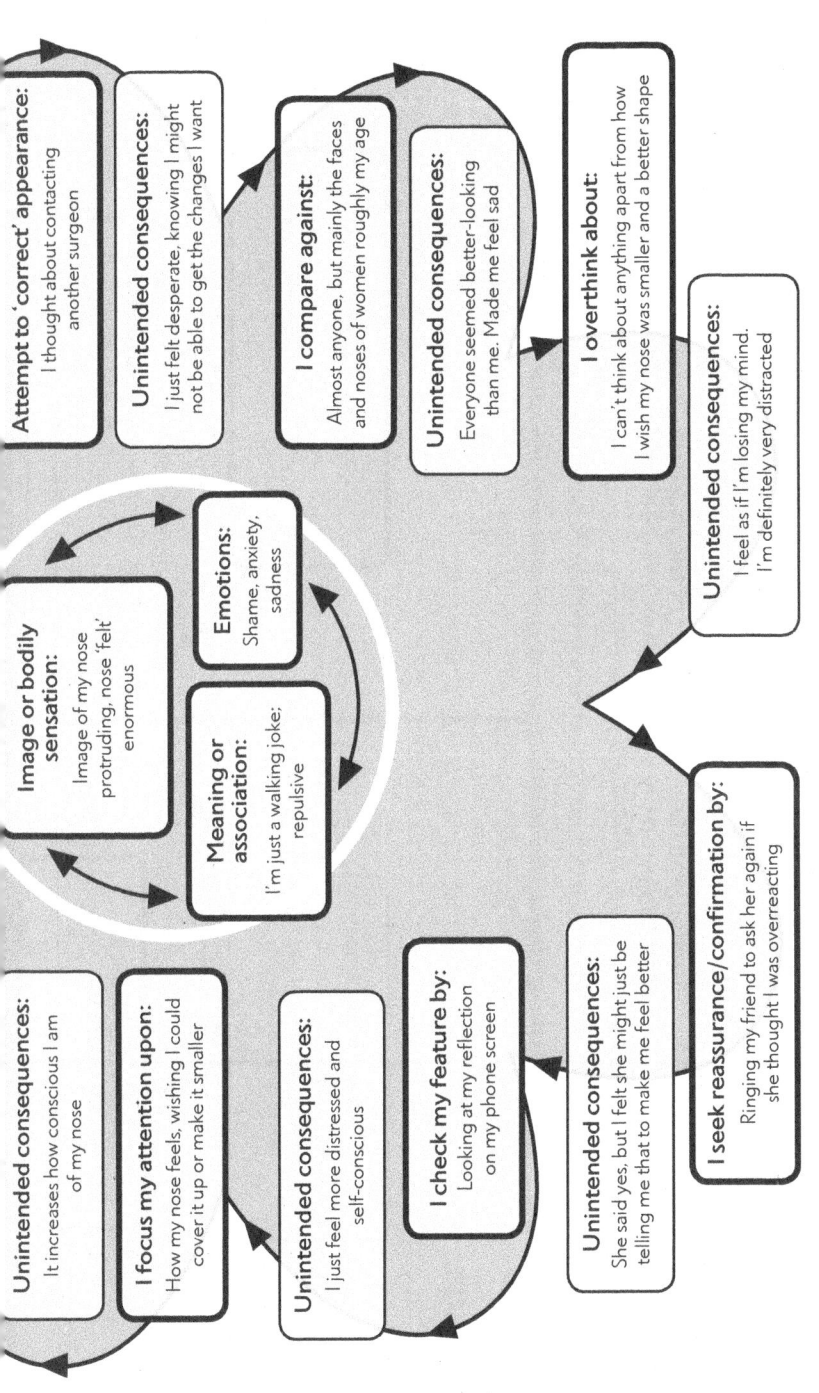

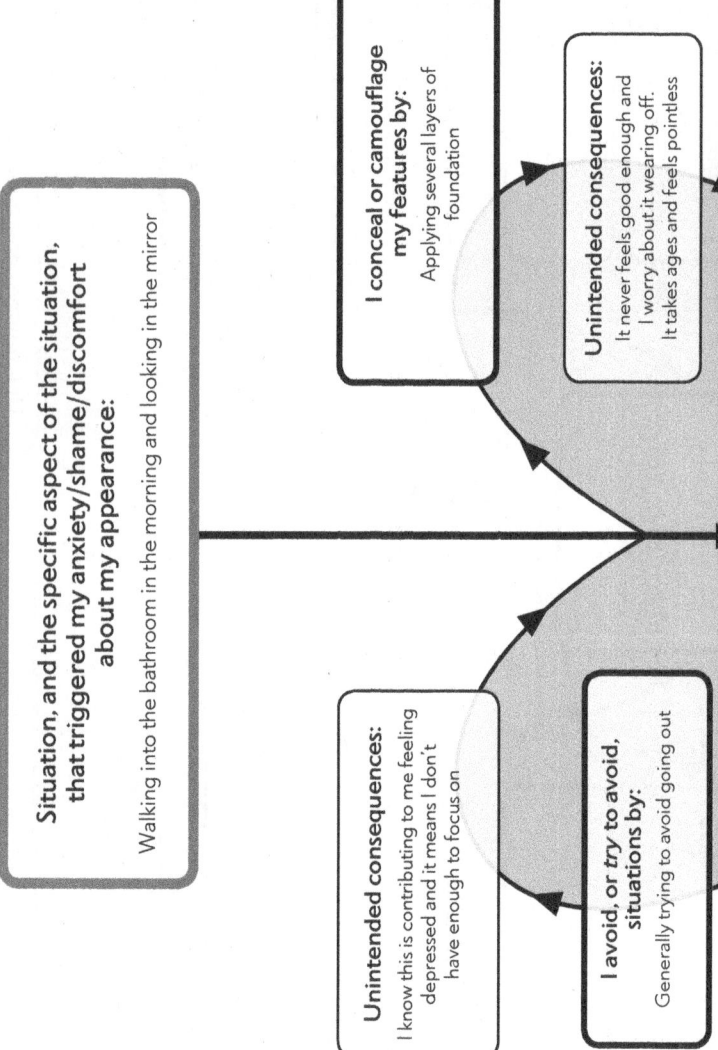

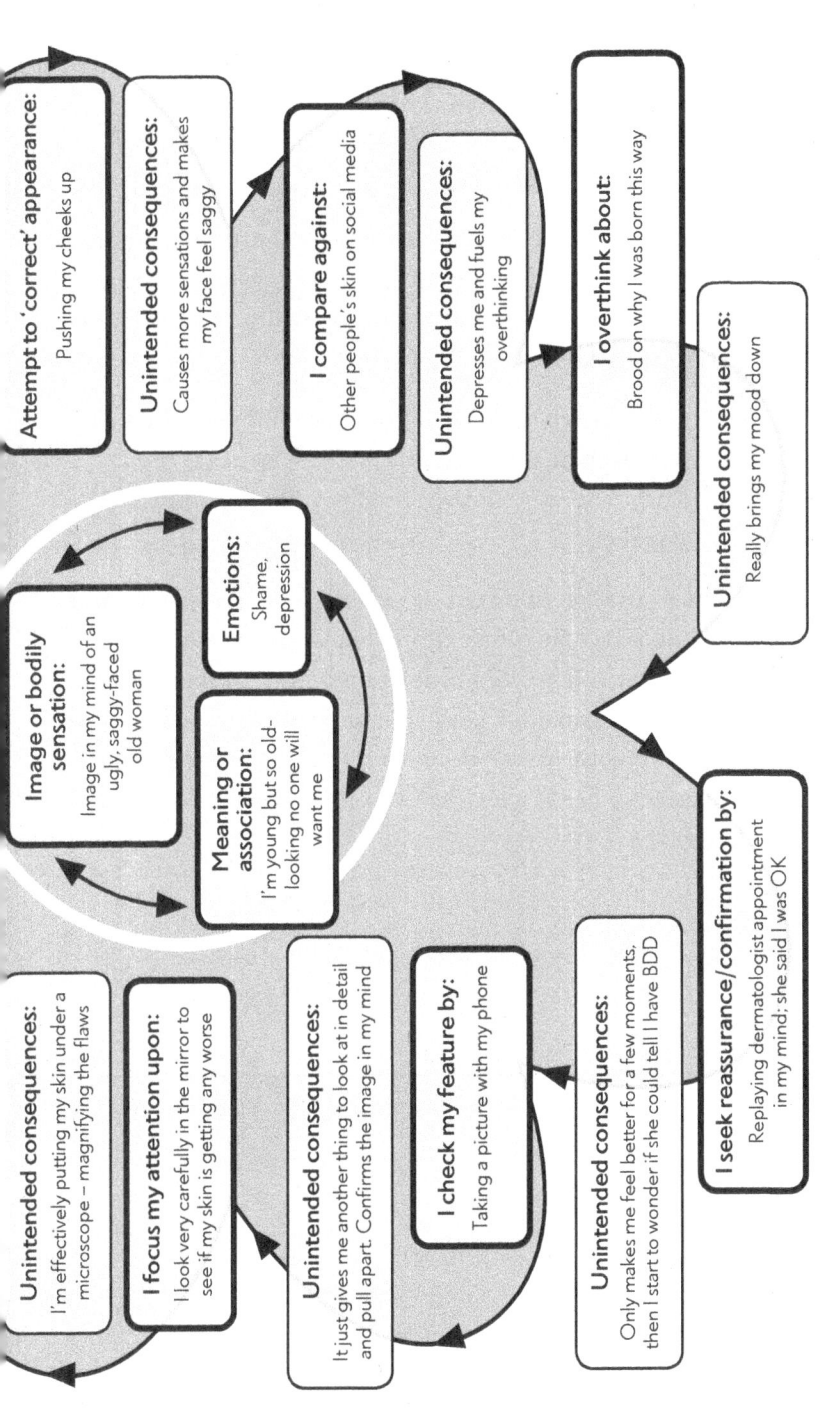

Building alternative explanations: Theory A versus Theory B

The essence of overcoming a body image problem using the various techniques outlined throughout this book is to gather evidence to see 'which theory fits the facts'. Doing the various tasks will allow you to:

- find out whether what you fear will happen does in fact happen, and
- learn new ways of behaving by acting against the way you feel.

You will also be finding out whether the results of your experiment best fit your existing explanation for your body image problem (e.g. your problem is your appearance) or an alternative explanation (e.g. your problem is excessive preoccupation with your appearance). In body image problems there are two broad alternatives to be tested: Theory A and Theory B.

THEORY A AND THEORY B

Theory A
I have a problem with the way my hair looks. My solution is to take every possible step to avoid being humiliated and rejected.

The evidence for this theory:
I go by the way I feel I look in the mirror and the felt impression in my mind's eye.

If this is true, then I have to act by:
I have to keep acting by hiding my hair, avoiding people and relationships, and to keep checking.

If this is true what this says about the future:
It means a life of misery and being unable to live life to the full. I shall be alone all my life.

Theory B
I have a body image problem with being excessively preoccupied by my hair, and am worried about being humiliated and rejected; my 'solutions' (driven by Theory A) have become my problem and feed my preoccupation.

> **The evidence for this theory:**
> The evidence for this is that I was bullied when I was younger and am stuck in the past. The image in my mind changes so it can't be right.
>
> **If this is true, then I have to act by:**
> Testing out my fears and resisting the urge to camouflage and check in mirrors. It is important not to avoid situations or activities, and to embrace life.
>
> **If this is true, what this says about the future:**
> It means I can live a full life and perhaps develop a relationship and meaningful friendships.

Try thinking of your own body image problem in terms of two competing theories. Remember that only one theory can be correct – they can't both be true. In the space below, write under 'Theory A' how you have viewed the problem, and how it has led to you using avoidance and safety behaviours. Then write against 'Theory B' another way of looking at your experience that would enable you to test out your alternative.

WHAT KEEPS YOUR BDD GOING?

EXERCISE: THEORY A AND THEORY B

Theory A

_____

_____

_____

The evidence for this theory:

_____

_____

If this is true, then I have to act by:

_____

_____

If this is true, what this says about the future:

_____

_____

> **Theory B**
>
> _____
>
> _____
>
> _____
>
> **The evidence for this theory:**
>
> _____
>
> _____
>
> **If this is true, then I have to act by:**
>
> _____
>
> _____
>
> **If this is true, what this says about the future:**
>
> _____
>
> _____

If you have a body image problem, you will probably have been following Theory A for many years. However, in order to determine whether Theory B might be the correct explanation for your problems, you will have to act as if it were correct (even if you don't believe it), at least for a time while you collect the evidence.

This may seem rather scary. But think of it like this: if, after, say, three months, you remain unconvinced, you can always go back to Theory A and carry on with your current solutions. Remember the image of the hole and the spade? You might believe that the risk of being humiliated or being rejected through testing out Theory B is too high to risk dropping your shovel to see if there is in fact a ladder there. However, if you don't let go of the shovel, then you won't ever know if there is anything else there to take hold of. If there's nothing there, you can always go back to your shovel, but if you don't test out the alternative theory, all you will ever have is your shovel – and all you will do is dig yourself further into the hole, causing yourself more distress and limiting your life even more.

PIT STOP

Let's stop and think about what you have just been reading. Can you summarise the key ideas you have taken on board? What is sticking in your mind? Maybe write it down. If you have any questions, jot those down too. You can return to them once you have had a chance to digest the information.

What is sticking in my mind from my reading so far?

1.

2.

3.

6

Thinking about thinking

This chapter aims to help you improve how you think about your body image. As you'll see, this includes updating some of the meanings and associations that affect the way you feel you look. You'll remember this is at the heart of your BDD, represented by your 'vicious flower' from Chapter 5. It will also focus on some of the maintaining processes, or 'petals' of that vicious flower, such as self-focused attention, over-thinking and comparing. You'll notice that these are mainly 'mental' factors. Other, more observable 'behavioural' processes, such as camouflaging, concealing, and checking and avoidance, are covered in the next chapter. As we've said before, your understanding of your own BDD is the most important guide to overcoming it, so do keep your vicious flower to hand. We will first discuss the centre of the flower, which is the felt impression of how you look, the meaning you attach to your felt image and the shame that you experience.

Updating unhelpful associations and meanings: the 'triple column' method

This is a 'pen and paper' strategy for taking another look at distressing or unhelpful experiences. The aim is to describe the meaning you attached to an experience when it happened, and then to look at the experience as an older, wiser person and generate an alternative way of understanding the situation. To help yourself do this, use the table below and consider the following questions:

- What would be the effect of a kinder, more compassionate way of looking at the situation?
- How would you help a child, close friend or loved one look at the situation?
- What is a more balanced and non-extreme point of view?
- How would someone you respect look at the experience?

Early experience	Meaning	Alternative meaning

A male client, Rajiv, who suffered from BDD, recalled the first time he felt really ashamed about his appearance. This was when he was being hit by a bully at school. One of the bully's friends made a comment during this upsetting experience that he remembered very well: 'Stop hitting him, it won't make him any better-looking.' At the time Rajiv thought 'I'm being hit because I look disgusting', and later concluded, 'I must always look good to avoid people hurting me.' This rule drove a considerable degree of his preoccupation with his appearance. If he focused on the memory, Rajiv would get an image of a bully standing over him, hitting him, with a crowd of people standing around him, watching. He reported that he had the distinct impression that the onlookers were enjoying the spectacle, a bit like a Victorian freak show.

Rajiv considered alternative meanings using the triple column method first, and then went on to imagine himself as an older person explaining to his younger self that he was being bullied simply because he was shy and had moved from another school. He explained that the comment from the bully's friend was the only comment of its type he'd ever been on the receiving end of in his life. As such, it was a rare, unusual event, not the norm for his life and therefore not something from which to draw general conclusions.

Avoiding placing excessive importance on your appearance

Many people with BDD place an unhelpfully large amount of importance on appearance and tend to over-identify appearance with their 'self'. That is, they define their self according to the appearance of the feature(s) they find ugly. Imagine you are preoccupied by your nose. In simplistic terms, this can be presented as your self as a walking nose. You define yourself by your nose. The danger is that such a philosophy has great potential to make you extremely self-conscious and preoccupied by your nose, with an enormous sense of shame. It can mean you become excessively critical of your nose, leading you to scrutinise it in great detail. This is of course a body image problem in terms of the felt impression of how you look in your mind's eye. So a key issue will be to ignore the felt impression and refocus your attention on the world around you, and to act on your values despite the felt impression.

You are too complex to measure or rate globally

You may hear therapists express the importance of self-acceptance. This does not mean resigning yourself to being ugly. It means the following:

- As a human being, you are a unique, multifaceted individual.
- As a human being, you are ever changing and developing.

- You may, to some degree, be able to measure specific aspects of yourself (e.g. how tall you are), but other things are harder to place a value on (e.g. how kind you are).
- It is in the very nature of being human to be fallible and imperfect.
- Because you are a complex, unique, ever-changing individual, you cannot legitimately be rated or measured as a whole person.

To overcome disturbing feelings such as shame and anxiety about your appearance, it helps to regard your feature(s) as only one aspect of you, rather than defining you. (For example, you are more than your nose!) Naturally, it's foolish to deny that some people and indeed some aspects of 'society' place an overly large importance on appearance, but you don't automatically have to go along with them. This means accepting the whole of yourself without judgement and recognising that you are a unique, fallible, human being like everyone else.

Big I, Little i: You are made up of a huge number of characteristics

Consider the 'Big I, little i' illustration above. This is one way of showing that each and every one of us is made up of a huge number of parts, and that appearance (and the feature you are preoccupied by) is only a part (or even a few parts) of who we are.

PRACTICAL EXERCISE

Take a pack of sticky notes and a large wall or door (or another person, if they're prepared to help out). Write down on a note a characteristic that you, as a whole person, possess and stick it on the wall, door or willing volunteer. Keep doing this, trying to think of all aspects of yourself, until you run out of characteristics (or notes!). This can be a very memorable illustration of how multifaceted you are.

Actions speak louder than words

Actions speak louder than words, so one of the most powerful ways of building your 'strength of belief' in your alternative beliefs is to act as if you already really believe the alternative. The way you act or behave has a big impact on your thinking. So, if you deliberately act against your negative beliefs, you are simultaneously eroding them and building up your new beliefs. This strategy is extremely helpful, so practise it often.

Here is a questionnaire to help you get acting 'as if':

QUESTIONNAIRE: ACTING 'AS IF'

1. Write down the new belief or attitude that you wish to strengthen (e.g. 'I have a feature that others do not notice or believe to be that abnormal. The problem is that I have a felt impression of it looking ugly and am extremely self-conscious').

_____

_____

2. Now consider, if other people in your life could see positive changes in you, what do you think they might notice? How would you be behaving differently if you truly believed in your new way of thinking about yourself, others and/or the world? Think of people you know who seem to hold the kind of attitude that you wish to strengthen in yourself. How do they behave in ways that reflect that way of thinking? Write down how you can act 'as if' you believe in your new healthy belief:

3. Where and when could you act in the ways you have described above?

Learning to de-fuse your unhelpful thoughts and beliefs

A fundamental process that maintains the way you feel about your body is 'thought–event fusion'. Thus, if you feel ugly or have the thought that you will be alone all your life, then that becomes very real to you. Rating yourself as ugly and the future as being hopeless is treated as a fact in the same way as 'the sky is blue'. Sometimes other people reinforce this tendency (for example, friends or relatives who say 'I'd be depressed too if I went through what you did').

While you focus on your negativity, you don't notice the process by which your thoughts and reality are becoming fused. Instead, you totally buy into the content of your thoughts as facts. These thoughts are really just mental chatter, rather than objective evidence that everyone can agree with. When the way you feel about your body is very rigid, we understand you won't believe the alternative meanings. However, it may be more helpful to consider your relationship with your thoughts and how you react to them. If you have fused your thoughts with reality and believe them to be true, it's not surprising that you want to escape from them or from the feeling of being ugly. Thus, in order to escape unpleasant thoughts and feelings, you might start to put in place things that seem to be protective, but that actually make your life much harder. Look back at Chapter 5 and your 'vicious flower' for examples.

Labelling your thoughts and feelings

Another strategy for unhelpful thoughts is to label the thought or feeling by saying it out loud and writing it down. For example:

- 'I am **having a thought** that I am fat.'
- 'I am **having a memory** of being bullied as a child.'
- 'I'm **having the feeling** of my face sagging.'
- 'I'm **making a rating** of myself that I am ugly.'

As an alternative, some people find it more helpful to distance themselves from such thoughts by labelling them as products of their mind – for example, 'My mind is telling me I am ugly.'

> I am having a feeling of (describe)
>
> _____
>
> _____
>
> _____
>
> I am having memories about (describe)
>
> _____
>
> _____
>
> _____
>
> I am making a rating about (describe)
>
> _____
>
> _____
>
> _____

Labelling your thoughts may feel awkward at first, but with practice it will help you to accept your thoughts or feelings without buying into them. Some people find it helpful to speak their thoughts out loud in a funny voice or the voice of a cartoon character. Again, this can help you to distance yourself from your thoughts and de-fuse them from your 'self'.

The aim of all these exercises is to acknowledge the existence of such thoughts and label them for what they are. It's usually best not to challenge their content, as they are strongly bound up with past memories and in body image problems that are often rigidly held. As you progress, you'll discover that you can experience unpleasant thoughts and feelings and still do what's important for your life, despite their presence. If you keep doing this, they will slowly fade.

Keeping a record of your thoughts

Try making a list of all your recurrent body image thoughts and feelings, label them for what they are, and put a tick in the relevant box each time they occur. Such thoughts are more likely to appear in difficult situations. It can be helpful to monitor them just to see which ones turn up in particular situations and try to bully you. We don't want you to do this repeatedly – just to see what happens over a few days. You will soon start to develop different ways of looking at your thoughts and not buying into them, brooding, comparing or paying attention to what your mind is telling you. Here is David's chart as an example:

DAVID'S THOUGHT MONITORING CHART							
I have thoughts that:	Mon	Tues	Wed	Thurs	Fri	Sat	Sun
1. I will be alone all my life	✓✓ ✓✓ ✓	✓✓ ✓✓ ✓✓ ✓✓ ✓✓	✓✓ ✓✓ ✓✓ ✓	✓✓ ✓✓ ✓✓ ✓✓ ✓✓ ✓			

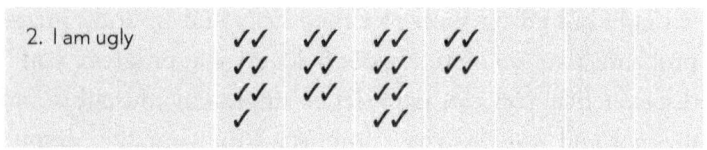

A blank thought-monitoring chart (similar to David's), which you can photocopy, can be found in Appendix 3, or you can print a copy from https://overcoming.co.uk/715/resources-to-download. Note that the purpose of monitoring your thoughts is not to challenge their content, or to control or reduce their frequency – just to acknowledge them and to thank your mind for its contribution. If your thoughts are very frequent (and in some people this may be a thousand or more times a day), you might find it easier to use a tally counter and transfer the total to your chart at the end of each day. (You can purchase a tally counter online. You will easily find a supplier if you type 'buy tally counter' into an internet search engine.) You can also note the situations in which the thoughts most commonly occur, in order to see if there is a pattern. It would be useful to know if there is such a pattern so that you can predict what thoughts will turn up and ensure that you are better prepared for them.

Watching your thoughts pass by

You have gathered by now that what we want you to develop is a sense of distance from your thoughts and feelings. This means not buying into them but being aware of them as a passive observer.

This is best illustrated by closing your eyes and bringing to mind, say, a bowl of fruit, then watching it without influencing it in any way. It's okay if your attention strays away from the orange or if the image changes (for example, the orange falls off the top of the bowl). You should merely be aware of the changing content of your attention without influencing the content in any way. This may not be easy at first, but it's worth persevering. The technique of distancing your thoughts can also be used just to notice your intrusive thoughts and not to engage with them.

Another analogy for watching your thoughts is to imagine them as cars passing on a road. When you are depressed, you might focus on particular 'cars' that tell you that you are a failure and life is hopeless. You cope either by trying to stop the cars or by pushing them to one side (if you're not in danger of being run over, that is!). Alternatively, you may try to flag the car down, get into the driving seat and try to park it (that is, analyse the idea and sort it out until you feel 'right'). Of course, there is often no room to park the car and as soon as you have parked one car another one comes along . . .

Distancing yourself from your thoughts means being on the pavement, acknowledging the cars and the traffic but just noticing them and then walking along the pavement and focusing your attention on other parts of the environment (such as talking to the person beside you, noticing other people passing you and the sights and smells of the flowers on the verge). You can still play in the park and do what is important for you despite the thoughts. In other words, such thoughts have no more meaning than passing traffic – they are 'just' thoughts and are part of the rich tapestry of human existence. You can't get rid of them. It's just the same as when you are in a city and there is always some slight traffic noise in the background and you learn to live with it. Notice these thoughts and feelings and acknowledge their presence, then get on with your life.

AN EXERCISE IN DISTANCING

In this exercise, you will need to get into a relaxed position and just observe the flow of your thoughts, one after another, without trying to figure out their meaning or their relationship to one another. You are practising an attitude of acceptance of your experience.

Imagine for the moment sitting next to a stream. As you gaze at the stream, you notice a number of leaves on the surface of the water. Keep looking at the leaves and watch them drift slowly downstream. When thoughts come, put each one on a leaf, and notice each leaf as it comes closer to you. Then watch it slowly moving away from you, eventually drifting out of sight. Return to looking at the stream, waiting for the next leaf to float by with a new thought.

> If one comes along, again watch it come closer to you and then let it drift out of sight. Allow yourself to have thoughts and imagine them floating by like leaves down a stream. Notice now that you are the stream. You hold all the water, all the fish and debris and leaves. You need not interfere with anything in the stream – just let it all flow. Then, when you are ready, gradually widen your attention to take in the sounds around you. Slowly open your eyes and get back to life.

The importance of practising tolerance of uncertainty

An intolerance of uncertainty is an important process in many people with body image problems. Most people have a sense of uncertainty of exactly how they look, but if you have BDD, then this is a potential threat, and you feel you have to know exactly how you look. Others want a guarantee that nothing will change for the worse, or that they will not be rejected or humiliated. Not knowing how bad you look is worse in terms of anxiety than knowing you look as bad as you fear. An example is a person who wants to know for certain how they look and repeatedly checks in mirrors. This is the ultimate insurance policy and usually means thinking that, if you try hard enough and carry out sufficient checking, then you can feel more certain. The reality is that trying harder to get certainty generally increases doubts and feelings of uncertainty. It is not surprising that intolerance of doubt and 'need' to be sure can be significant obstacles to progress. This can drive overthinking and ruminating. To overcome your body image problems, we will want you to tolerate your doubts and the feelings you may experience in your body; instead, follow your hopes and dreams, and live according to the kind of person you truly wish to be (despite not knowing how exactly you look).

Reducing your tendency to jump to conclusions

In Chapter 5 we saw that many people with BDD are prone to 'jumping to conclusions' that people are thinking negatively about them. One way of learning to combat this bias is to practise using an 'interpretation pie chart'. Here's how you do it:

- Identify your interpretation (those teenagers were laughing to ridicule me because of my big ears).
- Rate your belief (0–100 per cent).
- Make a list of all possible alternative causes of the event you believe is a result of your appearance.
- Put your appearance concern(s) as the last cause on the list. When the list is complete, divide up a pie chart into rough percentages – start at the bottom of the list!
- Re-rate your belief.

You can repeat this for past and possible future experiences, to give yourself practice in holding in mind that there could be more than one explanation for other people's apparent responses to you.

Here's an example:

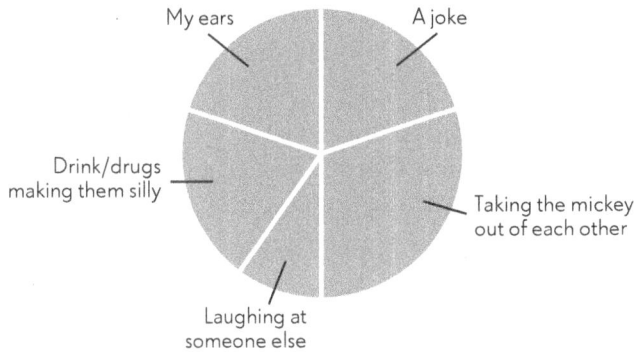

Teenagers laughing

Overcoming attentional biases

Up to now we have been discussing the centre of the flower, which is the felt impression of how you look, the meaning you attach to your felt image and the shame that you experience.

We are now going to move on to the way you cope, or the petals of the flower.

In Chapter 5, we described how various attentional biases influence your awareness of your feature. Being self-focused means being on the outside looking in at yourself from an observer perspective, and very aware of your thoughts and feelings. Being externally focused means being on the inside looking out at the world around and what you see or hear or smell. People with body image problems are frequently self-focused, and monitoring their felt impression or picture in their mind. You may want to know exactly how you look and therefore how likely you are to be humiliated (although whether this is very accurate or not is a different matter). Or you may be trying to avoid the gaze of someone who you think is being critical.

In the right situation, it can be productive for your attention to be focused inwards – for example, when you are trying to solve a particular problem or come up with a new theory of relativity. (However, we have never yet met anyone who has had a 'Eureka' moment when they are preoccupied with their appearance.) Spending a lot of time going over problems in your mind serves only to stimulate stress on your mind and body. Refocusing your attention onto the outside world gives your brain a rest and allows you to take in what the world has to offer.

Overcoming a body image problem will mean broadening your attention to take everything in, not just focusing on your features, and refocusing your attention away from your inner world.

It is important to recognise that biased perception is very likely to lead to biased conclusions. For example, if you constantly live in your head and monitor your impression of how you look, you will feel uglier. Excessive self-focus will also mean that your appearance is much more likely to be on your mind, and this fuels the number of hours a day you will be preoccupied. (One of us once tried it for ourselves by looking in a mirror for half an hour and focusing on the parts we didn't like. We then left the mirror but kept our attention on monitoring how we looked. It was an awful experience and interfered in our ability to function.) Once you recognise that your solutions are part of the problem you can helpfully correct for this bias in your mind. Imagine riding a bicycle that tends to veer to the right when you point the handlebars straight ahead. What would you do to make the bicycle go straight (before you had a chance to fix it)? You would correct for the bias towards the right by steering slightly towards the left. You can do the same in your mind: so, if you know that you assume that your features are ugly or likely to lead to humiliation, you can correct your thinking by deliberately acting as if you look OK and are safe from attack.

The second example is recognising that trying not to notice something, as an attempt to correct this bias, is doomed to failure. (It's like trying not to think of a pink elephant – try it.) However, you can improve the extent to which you focus on other things. The key question is whether focusing your attention inwards helps you to achieve the goals and valued directions you want.

In summary, most people find that being self-focused causes them to dwell more on the ghosts from the past and to feel more preoccupied, which in turn makes them feel worse and likely to do less and become more self-focused.

The alternative direction is to be less on the 'outside looking in' at yourself and more on the 'inside looking out' at the world and doing what is important to you despite what your mind is telling you.

Monitoring your self-focused attention

In any given situation, especially when you are feeling more anxious or withdrawn, you can estimate the percentage of your attention that is being focused on:

1. yourself (e.g. monitoring how you appear to others or how you feel)
2. your tasks (e.g. listening or talking to someone, or writing)
3. your environment (e.g. the hum of traffic in the background).

The three must add up to 100 per cent, and the ratio is likely to vary in different contexts. When you are very self-focused, about 80 per cent of your attention might be on yourself, about 10 per cent on the task you are involved in and 10 per cent on your environment. Someone without a body image problem might normally focus about 10 per cent on themselves, 80 per cent on the task and 10 per cent on the environment. This is an important observation because it means you can train yourself to be more focused on tasks and the environment and less on yourself.

EXERCISE: RATING YOUR ATTENTION PERCENTAGES

1. How self-focused are you? Over the next few days, use a copy of the chart below to make a note of different situations (e.g. being in front of a mirror, reading, talking to someone of the opposite sex of the same age) and then rate the percentage of your attention that is on:

   - yourself (0–100 per cent)
   - your task (0–100 per cent)
   - your environment (0–100 per cent)
   - total percentage (remember the three above must add up to 100 per cent)
   - degree of distress (0–100 per cent).

2. Try to compare the same situation with a different percentage of attention on yourself. For example, compare talking to someone you know well:

   (a) being very self-focused (for example, 80 per cent of attention on self or your felt impression)

with

   (b) concentrating on what you are saying and really listening to your friend (for example, 80 per cent attention on the task).

3. How does your degree of distress compare in (a) and (b)?
4. What effect does your change in attention focus have on your friend? Do they find you warmer and friendlier?

MONITORING SELF-FOCUSED ATTENTION CHART						
Date	Situation	% attention on self	% attention on task	% attention on environment	Total (100%)	Distress (0–100%)

There is also a blank copy of the chart in Appendix 3, or you can print out a version from https://overcoming.co.uk/715/resources-to-download.

Adjusting your attention

We hope we have convinced you that it would be helpful to reduce your self-focused attention. When this is difficult, you can use specific exercises that have been proven to help people focus their attention better on the outside world. Think of these exercises as helping you to build the psychological muscle that places your attention on the world around you, rather than on yourself.

Task-concentration training

The first technique is called 'task-concentration training' (TCT). It was devised by the psychologist Sandra Bögels in the Netherlands. This technique requires practice within progressively more challenging situations.

The technique is that every time you notice that your mind is self-focused (say, above 50 per cent) then you should immediately refocus your attention onto the task or the environment.

Practise being absorbed in a particular task (e.g. having a conversation) and, when you notice your attention is drawn towards yourself, deliberately refocus your attention away from yourself onto something else around you. Similarly, if you tend to focus all the time on how you feel, refocus attention outside yourself on some practical task in hand or on the environment around you. Every time you notice your mind's endless chatter and focus on how you feel, refocus your attention back on to the task or your environment. As a guide, try to aim for self-focused attention in most contexts to be reduced to 30 per cent or less.

If you are alone and have no specific task to do, you will need to refocus on your environment and make yourself more aware of:

- the various objects, colours, people, patterns and shapes that you can see around you (e.g. fabrics, decor, cars on the street, trees, litter)
- the sounds that you can hear (e.g. the hum of a heater, the sound of traffic, a clock ticking)
- what you can smell (e.g. scent of flowers, traffic fumes, fresh air, fabric softener)
- what you can taste (in the case of food or drink)
- the physical sensations you can feel from the environment (e.g. whether it is hot or cold, whether there is a breeze, the hardness of the ground beneath your feet).

This training is done in a graded manner for specific situations. For example, if you experience marked anxiety in social situations, you can practise the exercise starting with easier situations (e.g. listening to someone telling you about their holiday) and moving on to the most difficult situations (e.g. being at a party with strangers). This exercise is normally combined with the exercise in exposure and dropping safety behaviours from Chapter 7 (see page 184). You should also keep a record of each exercise on the 'Monitoring self-focused attention chart' from this chapter (see page 156) (a blank version can be found in Appendix 3, or you can print out a version from https://overcoming.co.uk/715/resources-to-download).

EXERCISE: FIRST LISTENING EXERCISE

You and another person (e.g. a relative or friend, or a therapist) sit facing away from each other (so that there is no eye contact). The other person tells you a two-minute story (e.g. about their holiday). You must concentrate on the story (task) and summarise it afterwards. You should estimate the percentage of your attention that was directed towards yourself, towards the task and towards the environment. Then both of you should estimate the percentage of the story you were able to summarise. The exercise is repeated until the concentration directed towards the task is at least 51 per cent (more than half the total).

EXERCISE: SECOND LISTENING EXERCISE

You and the other person now turn your chairs so that you make eye contact. The other person tells you another two-minute story. As in the first listening exercise, you have to concentrate on the story and summarise it afterwards. You should then estimate the percentage of attention directed towards yourself, the task and the environment. Then both of you should estimate the percentage of the story you were able to summarise. Typically, you may become more self-focused because of the eye contact with another person, and, as a result, memorise less of the story than in the first exercise. Think about how this relates to everyday life. The exercise is repeated as before until the concentration directed towards the task is at least 51 per cent.

EXERCISE: THIRD LISTENING EXERCISE

The other person tells you another two-minute story. Try to distract yourself while listening by looking at your appearance in a mirror (and then try to concentrate again on the story). As in the first listening exercise, estimate the percentage of attention directed towards yourself, the task and the environment. Then both of you should estimate the percentage of the story you were able to summarise. Typically, you may become more self-focused while thinking about your feature, and, as a result, have gaps in the summary of the story at the moments where you thought about the problem. Think about how this relates to problems in your everyday life. Repeat the exercise as before, until the percentage of concentration directed towards the task is at least 51 per cent.

EXERCISE: FOURTH LISTENING EXERCISE

The other person tells you another two-minute story, which involves worries about being judged on the feature that most concerns you.

All four exercises need to be repeated until at least 51 per cent of your attention is focused on the task. The effect of the more complex elements in the later exercise means that most people will become more self-focused as a result, but are able to refocus on the task after some practice.

EXERCISE: SPEAKING EXERCISES

The speaking exercises are practised in the same way as the listening exercises. This time, you tell a two-minute story to the other person, while concentrating on the task (speaking and observing whether the other person listens and understands what they are being told). The other person listens. The speaking exercises are repeated in the same way as in the second, third and fourth listening exercises (above) until your attention on the task is greater than 51 per cent.

EXERCISE: NON-THREATENING SITUATIONS

Practise focusing your attention in non-threatening, everyday situations. An example is walking through a quiet park. You should pay attention to all aspects of the park (what you see, what you hear, what you smell) as well as to each one of your own bodily sensations while walking.

Another example is to listen to music, first to each instrument separately, then to all the instruments at the same time. Focus your attention first on one instrument, and then on all aspects of the music together.

EXERCISE: THREATENING SITUATIONS

Draw up a list containing approximately ten social situations in which you are anxious. Arrange these situations in a hierarchy, with the first item being the least fear-inducing. This exercise can be combined with the exposure exercise on page 192, and repeated until the attention you place on the task is greater than 51 per cent.

Your goal is to employ task concentration in each situation and quickly refocus attention to the task

> after being distracted by fear of being rated. The exercises are built up hierarchically, since in very fear-inducing situations the feelings will absorb most of your attention. As a result, directing your attention to the task is more difficult. It takes practice to train your brain to stay focused on the world around you and away from thoughts and feelings related to your appearance.

Understanding your motivations for being self-focused

If you are excessively self-focused, and you are having difficulty in switching your attention externally, it can be helpful to explore (a) the contexts in which you tend to be self-focused; (b) the pay-off you think you get from being self-focused; and (c) the motivation for being self-focused. For example, some people might use the picture of themselves as a portable 'internal mirror' that can be easily carried around with them. Thus, you might want to check your appearance internally so you can know exactly what you look like at all times (and especially when there is no external mirror available). After you have completed the exercises on the following pages it will be helpful to discuss what you have written with a trusted friend or therapist.

RECORD OF ATTENTION TRAINING

Rating scale

−3: entirely focused on your own thoughts and feelings or the impression you have of yourself

0: attention divided equally between being self-focused and externally focused

+3: entirely externally focused on a task (e.g. listening to someone) or the environment (e.g. what you can see or hear)

Date	How self-focused I have been generally today (−3 to +3)	How long the training lasted	Number of sounds I used	Any other comments

Spot when, where and how often you brood

The first step is to monitor yourself to see at what times of day and in which places and situations you brood, and how often you do it. You can do this with a tally counter or a simple tick chart for whenever you ruminate (use the chart below; a blank version can be found in Appendix 3, or you can print out a version from https://overcoming.co.uk/715/resources-to-download). This awareness will help you to change your behaviour.

BROODING AND WORRYING SELF-MONITORING CHART

WEEK BEGINNING

Write in your most common brooding and worrying thoughts, and tick the relevant column each time you have that thought, or add the total from your tally counter.

	Mon	Tues	Wed	Thurs	Fri	Sat	Sun
I brood about:							
I brood about:							
I worry about:							

I worry about:						
I attack myself about:						
I attack myself about:						

Understand your brooding, self-attacking thoughts

Now you have understood how difficult brooding is to stop, and how powerful these thoughts can be when they are pulled by emotions. However, they can also be very harmful and we are now going to show you ways in which you can begin to escape the power of brooding.

Your goal will be to stop engaging in the content of your brooding or worries, and not to respond to the incessant demands. As soon as you have noticed yourself brooding or worrying, refocus your attention outwards, onto the real world. Choose to do something that you value and that is consistent with the goals that take you closer to a long-term reduction in preoccupation with your appearance. Then monitor the effect of this change. This means having a realistic plan or timetable for the activities you are avoiding and what is important in your life rather than doing what you feel. Eventually you will be able to stand back and observe your thoughts, not buy into them, and act in a valued direction in your life.

Assumptions about ruminating and worrying

Sometimes people brood because they feel they have a good reason to do so. If you are struggling to stop brooding or worrying, it may be helpful to understand your motivations about brooding (or *your* thoughts about your thoughts). Here are some examples of the motivations that people with body image problems give:

- 'I can prepare myself for the worst.'
- 'I can figure out where I went wrong and I won't make the same mistake again.'
- 'If I don't, it will let people who have hurt me off the hook.'
- 'It means I don't have to think about the bad things that are happening now.'

People can hold positive motivations about worrying (e.g. 'I must worry in order to think through all the things that could possibly go wrong'), as well as recognising the negative consequences ('If I worry, then I will go crazy and I won't be able to think straight'). Not surprisingly, this brings on more anxiety and depression. Feeling anxious and depressed will pull you back into brooding and being self-focused. Learning to distance yourself and break free from your emotions is tough and requires a lot of practice.

EXERCISE: WHAT IS YOUR MOTIVATION FOR BROODING OR WORRYING?

Do you sometimes think that brooding or worrying could help you? Do you feel as if you need to prepare yourself for being humiliated or something bad happening? Try to write down your assumptions about the benefits of brooding or worrying, e.g. 'If I brood, then I can prepare myself for the worst.'

1. _____

2. _____

3. _____

Now ask yourself:

- Does this assumption about brooding help me in my goals?
- Can this rule about brooding or worrying be made more flexible?
- Does my assumption help me to follow the directions in life that I want to follow?
- Is the cost of brooding or worrying too high?
- While I hold this assumption about my brooding or worrying, do I become more preoccupied and act in ways that are unhelpful?
- For how long am I going to carry on with my solution?

> Now decide whether holding such assumptions about your brooding is really helpful. Then write down some alternatives you can try.
>
> 1. _____
> 2. _____
> 3. _____
> 4. _____

Assumptions about self-attacking thoughts

People who are critical of themselves (feeling, for example, that they are ugly, weak or pathetic) might also have reasons for allowing themselves to be bullied by their minds. It is often helpful to ask yourself, 'What is my greatest fear if I give up criticising and bullying myself?' Criticism can also act as a warning ('If I don't tell you how fat you are and you don't lose weight, then nobody will love you'). Sometimes self-criticism can be triggered by a memory or be linked to your identity. Examples of assumptions behind self-criticism in depression are:

- If I don't put myself down, then I'll be arrogant.
- If I don't get in first with criticism, someone else will.
- I attack myself so I can improve myself.
- I attack myself so I get the humiliation I deserve.

- If I don't criticise myself, I'll forget how bad I look and won't cover up properly.

This sort of reasoning is probably an important factor in maintaining long-standing depression and low self-esteem. You might like to consider the costs and benefits of keeping up such a strategy.

EXERCISE: SELF-ATTACKING THOUGHTS

BENEFITS OF SELF-ATTACKING

What do you think is your motivation or the assumptions behind your self-attacking thoughts?

1. _____
2. _____
3. _____
4. _____

COSTS OF SELF-ATTACKING

- Does self-attacking make your preoccupation and mood worse?
- Does it help you achieve the goals you have set yourself?
- Does it help you stick to your valued directions in life?

- Is self-attacking something you would teach a friend or relative in a similar position? If not, why not?

YOUR PERSONAL COSTS OF SELF-ATTACKING

What do you think are the personal costs of your self-attacking thoughts?

1. _____
2. _____
3. _____
4. _____

Having identified what you believe to be the costs and benefits of self-attacking, you could talk these ideas through with a friend or health professional to see whether self-attacking helps or whether there is an alternative to your strategy. You might want to consider whether an alternative compassionate approach might help you to achieve the goals you want in life. Compassion is putting yourself in another person's shoes and being able to understand their emotional experience and be moved by it. It means being non-judgemental, and sensitive to the distress and needs of your mind. Thus, it is very understandable for your mind to want to try to protect you and prevent you from, for example, being arrogant or being rejected. However, there are other ways of achieving the same goal. It may be helpful to talk to someone about an alternative that does not lead you to feel more distressed and to miss out on life.

Comparing

Another repetitive thinking pattern in body image problems is to compare your feature with someone else's and then judge yourself against that feature. Comparing is fairly common in people without body image problems (especially in women), but it occurs more frequently in people with body image problems. People typically compare the feature they don't like with the same feature in someone else of the same age and sex. They may compare themselves with airbrushed models in the media or people they meet in everyday life. There is nearly always an upward comparison with people who have the same feature that is considered more attractive. Alternatively, you may compare your feature with the way the same feature looked in the past, or to an ideal that you hold in your mind.

Spot when, where and how often you compare

The first step is to monitor yourself to see in what contexts (times of day, activities and situations) you compare and how often you do it. Being more aware of when you are comparing will help you change your behaviour. Self-monitoring, using a tally counter, can increase your awareness of your comparing tendency, as it may be occurring many hundreds of times a day.

COMPARING SELF-MONITORING CHART

WEEK BEGINNING

Write in your most common comparing thoughts and tick the relevant column each time you have that thought, or add the total from your tally counter.

	Mon	Tues	Wed	Thurs	Fri	Sat	Sun
I compared my:							
I compared my:							
I compared my:							

Identifying your motivation for comparing

The motivation for comparing is usually to know where you stand in relation to someone else, as a form of threat monitoring (e.g. 'I have to know where I stand in case I am humiliated'). This usually leads to safety-seeking behaviours such as keeping your head down and trying to camouflage your 'defect'. This makes sense if you are an animal – for example, a puppy will roll over in front of a larger dog and be submissive; this strategy is highly effective in avoiding a conflict and preventing the puppy being harmed. However, when you 'roll over' this is another example of treating the body image issue as an appearance problem and has a number of unintended consequences.

Here are some common motivations for comparing:

- To improve certainty about how you look – e.g. '*So I can be clear about what is wrong with my appearance.*'
- To confirm beliefs about your appearance – e.g. '*So I don't forget how ugly I am.*'
- To keep yourself safe from rejection and humiliation – e.g. '*So I know my place.*'
- To improve your appearance – e.g. '*I can work out how I might improve my appearance or conceal my flaws.*'
- Habit – sometimes it can be difficult to understand your motivation as you may have started some time ago and now your brain does it almost automatically.

What is important is to question how helpful it is to compare your appearance. What's the effect? Would you recommend it to a friend? Or teach it to a child? To deepen your understanding of the effect of your comparing, use the tables below. First read the completed sample table below, then fill in the blank table in the exercise that follows it with examples from your own experience. Instead of comparing, we would encourage you to broaden your attention to all the sights, sounds, smells and textures around you, or focus on the whole of a person's appearance rather than just a part – and to fully listen to what another person is saying.

EXAMPLE EXERCISE: A, B, C, D, E OF COMPARING

Activating event

Describe a recent typical situation in which you compared your feature? What were you doing at the time?

I went for a walk with some friends.

Behaviour

Who or what did you compare yourself with?

I kept looking at the skin on my friends' faces.

Immediate **C**onsequences

Was there any pay-off from comparing? Did you think it prevented something bad from happening?

I wanted to know whether my partner had been lying to me in saying that my skin didn't look any worse than any of my friends' skin. It temporarily felt like I was answering an important question.

Unintended <u>C</u>onsequences

What effect did the comparing have on the way you felt?

I felt humiliated and betrayed.

What effect did it have on how self-focused you became on a scale between −3, which is totally focused on what you were thinking, to +3, which is totally focused on environment or tasks?

−2 I felt self-conscious.

What effect did the comparing have on your valued directions and the time you can devote to what is important in your life?

I was very distracted and didn't really engage with my friends as much as I wanted.

What effect did the comparing have on the people around you?

I think my friends might have been upset at me seeming a bit distant.

Did you do anything to excess as a consequence (e.g. drink more, use drugs, binge-eat, purge)?

No.

Overall, how helpful was it to compare?

Not at all.

Alternative **D**irections

What alternative direction could you find that is consistent with your goals and valued directions? What could you do instead of comparing?

I need to practise focusing away from skin into conversation and the world around me.

Effect of alternative directions

What effect did following your alternative direction have?

When I tried this it was very hard to resist comparing, but I do think it's going to make me less self-conscious and better company.

Is there a pattern to the situations that are typically linked to comparing that you could change? For example, can you do anything to prevent such situations occurring? Do you need to unfollow that influencer? Can you put old photographs away, etc.?

I really need to practise refocusing my attention and stop comparing when I'm watching TV and film.

EXERCISE: YOUR A, B, C, D, E OF COMPARING

Activating event

Describe a recent typical situation in which you compared your feature? What were you doing at the time?

Behaviour

Who or what did you compare yourself with?

Immediate Consequences

Was there any pay-off from comparing? Did you think it prevented something bad from happening?

Unintended Consequences

What effect did the comparing have on the way you felt?

What effect did it have on how self-focused you became on a scale between −3, which is totally focused on what you were thinking, to +3, which is totally focused on environment or tasks?

What effect did the comparing have on your valued directions and the time you can devote to what is important in your life?

What effect did the comparing have on the people around you?

Did you do anything to excess as a consequence (e.g. drink more, use drugs, binge-eat, purge)?

Overall, how helpful was it to compare?

Alternative **D**irections

What alternative direction could you find that is consistent with your goals and valued directions? What could you do instead of comparing?

Effect of alternative directions

What effect did following your alternative direction have?

Is there a pattern to the situations that are typically linked to comparing that you could change? For example, can you do anything to prevent such situations occurring? Do you need to unfollow that influencer? Can you put old photographs away, etc.?

In this chapter, we've encouraged you to work on some key safety-seeking behaviour, and we will look at more in the next chapter. Often it is more realistic to start off with 'disrupting' and 'stopping more quickly' than to be able to 'stop it'. Your brain will, at first, want you to go back to your old ways in order to maintain 'homeostasis' – what it believes to be your 'regular' state. To help yourself on the road to recovery, consider the following suggestions:

- Keep recording with your tally counter or frequency chart of the behaviour (including mental actions like comparing and self-attacking).
- For a trigger situation, experiment with focusing your attention on wider aspects of people and places – using all your senses.
- Seek out increasingly varied/challenging situations.
- Expect good days, bad days and setbacks.
- Be patient, persevere, and keep learning about what mental and psychical behaviour worsens your BDD or helps you recover.

PIT STOP

Let's stop and think about what you have just been reading. Can you summarise the key ideas you have taken on board? What is sticking in your mind? Maybe write it down. If you have any questions, jot those down too. You can return to them once you have had a chance to digest the information.

What is sticking in my mind from my reading so far?

1.

2.

3.

7

Taking action

This chapter focuses on you doing things in life that are important to you so you can reclaim your life and break free from BDD. This will involve entering situations or doing activities that you are avoiding because of feelings like shame and anxiety. This is potentially the most important component in you treating your problem 'as if' it's Theory B (even if you don't believe it) and your feelings of being ugly are a body image problem that is influenced by memories and bad experiences (look back at Chapter 5 if you need a reminder of Theory A versus Theory B).

Your starting point, and the most important guide, in taking behavioural steps towards overcoming your BDD is your understanding of how your problem works. The vicious flower you completed in Chapter 5 is your guide. If you understand the extent to which avoidance and safety-seeking behaviours maintain your problem, then a strategy of exposure and response prevention (ERP) will seem far more like common sense. Exposure is like a form of mental/behavioural physiotherapy – exercise, training and practice to help correct an existing problem. You counter your avoidance and overcome fear by facing feared and avoided situations. At the same time, you stop or 'drop' safety-seeking behaviours like checking, concealing and so on – pulling off the other petals in your flower.

Take note, though: the (BDD) devil is in the detail!

In our experience, there are some pitfalls when you are facing your fears as part of overcoming BDD that are especially important to avoid:

- Increasing behaviours like checking and concealing, to try to feel more comfortable or less vulnerable.
- Using 'subtle' avoidance such as only going out in low light or going out but avoiding certain kinds of people.
- Trying too hard to 'see' if people are looking at you, making comments, treating you differently – the problem is that we humans tend to find trouble if we go looking for it, leading to very faulty conclusions.
- Staying very 'self-focused' (e.g. by keeping your head down), which will keep you feeling self-conscious.

These are only a few examples; what is important is to understand the principle that, because your mind is so accustomed to trying too hard to keep you safe, you will need to help it to keep acting against maintaining your BDD.

The principles of exposure

Exposure therapy is popularly described as 'facing your fears'. However, it is more than that. It means:

- Planning to face your fears deliberately and repeatedly. It's a separate process to your BDD being triggered as part of day-to-day life.
- Not using compulsions or safety-seeking behaviours – this is the 'response prevention' part. If you have BDD, this is extremely important.
- At a high enough level of discomfort, and for long enough, experience tolerating and pushing through the distress. This recognises that your discomfort may not reduce when you do a particular session exposure (this is not essential for recovery), but it gets easier when you repeat it again and again.
- Doing it as part of testing out your expectations. In this sense, exposure is a 'behavioural experiment' when you are testing your expectations, for example assessing whether your experience best fits with Theory A or Theory B.

How might this work with BDD?

- Rusha, who fears being ridiculed because of the shape of her nose, avoids being seen close up and in bright light. For her, exposure might mean sitting in a brightly lit restaurant without monitoring what angle she is seen from. This would help her test her expectation that she would be unable to tolerate the feelings of anxiety, as they will go on for ever, and whether she will be humiliated.
- For Sabine, who is preoccupied with her skin, repeatedly deliberately approaching social situations

without comparing could help her to see whether Theory A (that she has a skin problem) or Theory B (that she has a body image problem and is excessively self-conscious about her skin) fits the facts best.

By acting as if Theory B is true, you will learn that you can tolerate your anxiety *provided that* you are not doing something to seek safety (such as checking your appearance or monitoring other people's reactions), and are testing out your expectations and seeing if Theory B fits with the evidence.

Exposure and behavioural experiments

We will refer to deliberately facing your fears as 'exposure' for short, rather than 'exposure and response prevention (ERP)' or a 'behavioural experiment'. The term 'exposure' originates from behaviour therapy, and 'behavioural experiment' from cognitive therapy. However, these are just two sides of the same coin. One is learning to tolerate, or 'push through', the feelings of anxiety (or disgust) in a planned manner, and the other is testing your expectations about the way your problem works – namely, 'Do the results of the task best fit with Theory A or B?' (for example, Theory A is that your feelings of anxiety will go on for ever, and that others will be disgusted by you; Theory B is that this is a body image problem, and a fear and worry about others being disgusted). Some therapists will use the term 'exposure', and some will use 'behavioural experiment'. It just depends what tribe they belong to.

Courage

Being *willing* to experience feelings of anxiety and revulsion is crucial. We don't want you to act as if you are on a roller coaster, clinging on to the handrail for dear life, gritting your teeth and desperately willing it to be over. We want you to develop the courage to approach uncomfortable thoughts, feelings and memories. Of course, courage does not just come out of the blue; when you approach difficult situations, you will feel anxious. You cannot have courage and not feel anxious.

Safeness

Exposure is more effective if you feel 'safe'. You can feel safe if you can be compassionate towards yourself – for example, can you be understanding, soothing and encouraging to yourself in approaching difficult situations? If you struggle with this and can be very self-critical, it may be helpful to feel connected with a person you trust who is understanding, soothing, tolerates distress and encourages you when you do the exposure. If no such person is readily available, you may – as do some other people – find using an imagined warm and caring figure to be helpful.

'Graded' exposure

Many people have heard that they must do exposure *gradually*. However, this is no longer believed to be the case. Focusing on 'grading' your exposure can reinforce the idea that emotional distress can be harmful or counterproductive, or that somehow graded exposure is kinder. Many people find it difficult to choose a 'lower distress' place to start, leaving them feeling stumped as to where to begin. However, you don't need to start with an 'easier' target – remember that compassion is a drive to relieve suffering; it's not about avoiding discomfort.

Yes, exposure is often done in a graded manner, with a series of steps (called a 'hierarchy'), so that you face your less intimidating fears first and confront the most difficult last. But grading your exposure is just a means to an end, and new research suggests that jumping around the hierarchy in different situations is more effective than slavishly sticking to doing easy things then moving up the hierarchy in a very gradual way – for example, doing something easy, then something very slightly more difficult, and so on, which could take years. Remember the following key points about emotions:

- Distressing emotions (such as shame, anxiety and disgust), though uncomfortable, will not harm you.
- If you approach your fears too gradually, you'll only reinforce the idea that this discomfort is potentially harmful or should be avoided because it is too uncomfortable.
- The rationale is learning to *tolerate* anxiety, so elevated fear should be maintained and this does not usually occur at the lower levels of an anxiety hierarchy. The aim is *not* to wait until the fear reduces. This is an older view of exposure by habituation, as it does not always reduce.

- You need to turn your thinking 'upside down': the more you try to avoid anxiety or disgust in the short term, the more of it you're likely to have in the long term.
- Interpreting your anxiety or disgust as a natural reaction – your mind and body trying to prepare you for a challenge or a perceived threat – will help you to feel better.

With any exposure, it really is crucial that you stick with the anxiety, otherwise you run the risk of strengthening the idea that anxiety is harmful. If you find the anxiety is persisting for longer than two hours, then it may be that you are performing a subtle safety behaviour, or not fully engaging in the exposure, in which case it might be best to seek professional help to make progress.

One useful way of remembering what exposure and response prevention means is the acronym 'FEAR':

> **F**ace
> **E**verything
> **A**nd
> **R**ecover.

Now let's look at the key steps of exposure for BDD.

Develop a list of exposure tasks

A list of tasks is the basis of a step-by-step plan that you can carry out to do exposure. Ensure you understand the rationale and purpose to the exposure. Make a list of your tasks for exposure – the things you tend to fear or avoid because they activate your shame. These may be activities, situations, people, words, objects or ideas – the range of forms will depend on your particular fear. Decide on when you will do the task, where you will do it, what resources you will need and how it can be repeated in different contexts. Choose tasks that relate to what you avoid and what you value. Most importantly, the tasks need to be done without safety-seeking behaviours (e.g. keeping your head down), and while being fully engaged with the people and environment around you.

Remember: It's important to plan your approach.

Face your fears

The critical point about your exposure list is that you do not stick slavishly to starting at the bottom and working your way up. It is more effective to jump around and consistently focus on trying to tackle the more difficult tasks.

- Set a particular time frame, which you then keep to, like a set of instructions.
- Decide which targets you will take from the hierarchy and, for each one, deliberately face your fear.
- Choose targets that are challenging but not overwhelming.
- Power through the easier targets if they are not sufficiently anxiety provoking. You may need to ask a friend to come up with suitable tasks that are more challenging.

- The hierarchy will ideally include things that you wouldn't normally do (for example, leaving the house and entering a social situation having spent only a few minutes preparing your appearance).

The nature of an exposure task will depend upon your problem and some of the avoidance you defined in Chapter 4. As noted in the list above, it is important to plan a particular time frame, which you then attempt to carry out, like a set of instructions. This is an example of a hierarchy: a set of steps up a ladder to your biggest fears. You can measure the amount of distress by using a rating scale of 'SUDs'. SUD stands for standard units of distress, whereby 0 is no distress at all and 100 is overwhelming distress. Using a table like the one shown in the example below, you can give each trigger a rating in the second column according to how much distress you'd expect to feel if you experienced that trigger and didn't perform a compulsion. For example, you may rate being intimate as causing as 90 SUDs out of 100. Another individual might rate going swimming as 99 SUDs out of 100, and so on.

Try to group the activities you fear into different themes (intimacy, social situations, etc.) and, within the themes, to put them in order of how much distress you would feel if you experienced each trigger.

We have included an example of a completed hierarchy for you here; there is a blank copy for you to complete in Appendix 3, or you can print out a version from https://overcoming.co.uk/715/resources-to-download). Remember you need to have a good Theory B completed (see Chapter 5) to determine whether the results of the exposure best fit Theory B.

Exposure to feared triggers

Here's an example of a completed hierarchy of exposure chart:

HIERARCHY OF EXPOSURE TO FEARED TRIGGERS	
Trigger (object, place, person, situation):	**Estimated distress (0–100)**
Asking an attractive man out on a date, without my hat and without checking beforehand	100
Going to an interview	90
Sitting and having a meal in a brightly lit fast-food restaurant	80
Asking for directions in the street on a brightly lit day	70
Going for a walk around the local park on a busy day without my hat	70
Going for a walk around the park on a quiet day without my hat	65
Sitting and having a meal in a dimly lit restaurant	60
Standing, profile on, in a long queue in shop	60
Having a friend to my home for coffee and deliberately allowing them to see me from the side	50

Make exposure long enough

Face your fear long enough for you to learn that you can do it and to test out your prediction. For example, when you enter a swimming pool, don't rush in so that your body is under the water – sit around a bit, or stroll up and down the side and smile at others before getting into the water. Distress will decrease only when you give it a long enough time and learn that bad things do not happen.

Make exposure challenging enough

Sometimes people fear that too much anxiety can be harmful. As we noted above, it's true that exposure may be done in a graded manner, via a series of steps (called a 'hierarchy'), so that you face your less intimidating fears first and confront the most difficult last. But grading your exposure is just a means to an end, and the sooner you can reach the top of your exposure hierarchy the better. Remember that anxiety, though uncomfortable, will not damage you. If you approach your fears too gradually, you'll only reinforce the idea that anxiety is potentially harmful or should be avoided because it is too uncomfortable. As we saw a little earlier, in dealing with a body image problem you have to turn your thinking 'upside down': the more you try to avoid anxiety in the short term, the more of it you're likely to get in the long term.

So try to make sure that your exposure is challenging and potent, both in terms of the trigger you are facing and the length of time for which you expose yourself to it. Face your fear long enough for you to *tolerate* the anxiety or disgust. Exposures do not *have to be* long; sometimes quite a short exposure time may be effective. What is more important is that there is change in the level of anxiety or confirmation of alternative understanding of the problem (Theory B). This means that there is sufficient time to be surprised and mess up Theory A.

When you drop your safety behaviour (for example, using make-up) you might feel 95 SUDs (standard units of distress); this is understandable. You are learning to tolerate the anxiety and to test out your expectations – this means finding out whether your experience best fits with Theory B. The longer you stick with it, the more you are learning that you can tolerate it.

Always ensure that the predictions you make are judged on objective information – for example, what someone says or how they behave towards you, and if possible that there are others who can be objective. It doesn't help if your prediction is that people will think that you are ugly, as you can't read their minds. It is more helpful to observe their behaviour and go by what they say and do. In this situation, you need to be especially careful to ensure that you do not use any safety-seeking behaviours – for example, if you keep your head down, have poor eye contact and say very little, then you're less likely to be aware of how they act towards you, and people are more likely to assume that you are not interested in them and to avoid you. You in turn may interpret this as evidence that you are ugly. Try to practise having appropriate eye contact and smiling. Try to make a conscious effort to stand upright and look straight ahead. If you smile, strangers are more likely to respond positively; when you have your head down, hurrying past, you are more likely to be self-focused and get information about your surroundings from what your mind is telling you. Maintain good eye contact. This is a signal to show you have an interest in others, that you are listening, and whose turn it is to speak in a conversation. Trying to avoid the gaze of others will always be viewed negatively. You are signalling that you do not want to engage in any kind of contact with the other person.

Try to engage in conversation whenever you can. It is harder to do if you are focused on how you look and how people are responding to you, rather than listening and being involved in what people are saying. Anxiety tends to heighten the temptation to 'self-monitor' so it is harder to focus on what is going on around you. Asking people about themselves, what they do for a living, whether their children go to the local school, and similar questions, are all ways of initiating a conversation. Similarly, topical subjects are things that other people will have a view about. The result of the latest big football match, an ongoing soap storyline, news headlines and the price of petrol are all areas that people will have a view on.

If you are doing exposure in front of a mirror that you have avoided, then do not make predictions about how ugly or unattractive you think you are. Rating yourself as 'ugly' or 'unattractive' is an evaluation that others may or may not agree with. We know that such ratings are usually based on ghosts from the past and that various emotions will bias your rating. Stick to objective information like the colour of your eyes, your height and weight, which is objective. We will discuss more in the section on mirrors (page 203).

Keep a record of your predictions and whether they occurred or not on your record sheet (page 192).

Make exposure frequent enough

- Repeat the exposure as often as possible in different situations.
- Daily exposure is an absolute minimum until the anxiety is becoming less in the same or similar situations. Ideally, aim for several times a day in different activities and situations.
- Leaving long gaps between exposure means fears will return.
- Think about how you can incorporate exposure into your everyday life so that it is easier to carry it out on several occasions every day.
- Try to generalise your exposure tasks across different contexts (e.g. in unfamiliar places, at different times of the day).

Drop safety-seeking behaviours during your exposure

Exposure also needs to be done without using a safety-seeking behaviour. Remember, safety behaviour is something within a feared situation that aims to prevent a catastrophe and reduce harm. Safety-seeking behaviours in body image problems include a broad range of ways of escaping, and trying to cope – for example, keeping your head down, comparing, using excessive make-up, wearing bulky clothes, keeping your hand up to your face, checking in a mirror or brooding in your head. However, safety-seeking behaviours may have several unintended consequences. They may prevent you from finding out that what you are predicting is not true. They also tend to make you more self-conscious, more preoccupied with your appearance and more distressed, as you then have to monitor whether your safety behaviour is working. Lastly, they may make you appear cold and unfriendly in social situations.

If you are not sure if what you are doing is a safety-seeking behaviour, ask yourself what the aim is before you carry it out. If the aim is to reduce what you think is potentially harmful to you, or the degree to which you would be able to control the harm, then it is a safety-seeking behaviour.

Remember to act according to your values or your best interests (Theory B), not according to how you feel and your desire to escape (Theory A). It may be helpful to act as if you are not afraid even if you feel frightened.

Focus your attention on the environment around you

Make sure that when you do exposure you are externally focused on the world around you, and fully aware of what you can see, hear and smell. This will help you to feel less self-conscious, which in time will help you to feel more comfortable in social situations.

Use self-compassion

It's helpful to 'engage fully' with the exposure compassionately. This means:

- using courage to approach the difficult situations that are anxiety provoking
- noticing your thoughts and images, and if there is anything new coming up that can be tested as part of Theory B
- practising being understanding and sympathetic towards yourself
- encouraging yourself in a soothing, kind tone
- it can be helpful to label the emotion – for example, 'OK, these are my feelings of . . . (e.g. fear, anxiety, shame)
- tolerating your feelings; this means just doing the exposure without condemning, judging, blaming or pitying yourself, or biting your tongue until you get through it; this is especially important if your exposure is reactivating an old memory, which has been traumatic for you; the goal is just to fully accept the memory with the anxiety – don't engage with any of the intrusive ideas; however, 'accept' does not mean resigning yourself to being ugly or that your anxiety will go on for ever, it just means not judging and not fighting it

- not using alcohol or, as required, medication such as alprazolam, to dampen your anxiety, as this will become a safety behaviour.

If the aim is to help you achieve your task so you can move on and do something more challenging without the behaviour, then this is enhancing your exposure and is a means towards an end.

Monitor your exposure tasks

Monitor your exposure constantly, so that you can learn from how you respond and see your progress. This is essential whether you're working on your own or alongside a therapist. If you see a therapist, you can use this information to help keep them updated on how you got on with the exposure that you negotiated in the previous session. You should also monitor whether you responded with any repetitive behaviours. To help you do this, we have provided a suitable form entitled 'Exposure record form', below; a blank copy of this form is included in Appendix 3, or you can print out a version from https://overcoming.co.uk/715/resources-to-download.

EXPOSURE RECORD FORM

Exposure task	Level of discomfort	Duration of discomfort	Coping strategies	Testing your expectations	Next steps
Write out the date and what you actually did:	0–10 at the start and when it was at its maximum?	How long did the maximum level of anxiety last for?	What helpful things did you do to tolerate your anxiety? Did you use any unhelpful ways of coping (for example, any safety behaviours)?	What did you learn about how your body image works? Did your experience strengthen Theory B?	How might you progress from here – for example, repeating, extending or developing this exercise, or moving on to an alternative task?
	Start: Maximum:				
	Start: Maximum:				
	Start: Maximum:				

TAKING ACTION

A completed example is shown below.

EXPOSURE RECORD FORM

Exposure task	Level of discomfort	Duration of discomfort	Coping strategies	Testing your expectations	Next steps
Write out the date and what you actually did:	0–10 at the start and when it was at its maximum?	How long did the maximum level of anxiety last for?	What helpful things did you do to tolerate your anxiety? Did you use any unhelpful ways of coping (for example, safety behaviours)?	What did you learn about how your body image works? Did your experience strengthen Theory B?	How might you progress from here – for example, repeating, extending or developing this exercise, or moving on to an alternative task?
Leave the house without my make-up, in bright daylight and meet a friend for lunch.	Start: 8 Maximum: 9	20 mins	I called my mum for some moral support.	I was very nervous and this was tough to get through, but felt like a huge step.	Practise with more people in more situations.
Going out to the supermarket with only foundation.	Start: 6 Maximum: 8	5 mins	I made sure to really focus my attention externally.	Staying focused on my surroundings was definitely better. Supports Theory B.	Try the same thing with only a small amount of foundation.
Going out to the local pub without any make-up on.	Start: 9 Maximum: 9	30 mins	I went into the toilet to check.	Showed me how much more self-conscious checking in the mirror makes me.	Resist mirror checking.

If you do a safety-seeking behaviour, then re-expose yourself

If you can't resist doing a safety behaviour, you must redo the exposure so that you always finish with exposure. For example, if you put your hand up to your face to hide your skin, and keep your head down to avoid any eye gaze, then re-expose yourself. This means taking your hand down and smiling at the other person.

Detach and observe your intrusive or unhelpful thoughts

Just 'notice' or 'be aware of' any unpleasant images or thoughts that are self-attacking, judging or blaming that might occur during exposure. This is especially important if your exposure is reactivating an old memory that has been traumatic for you. The goal is just to accept the intrusive thoughts and feelings. Just distance yourself from them and do not buy into their content. Wait for the anxiety to fade by itself. The issue here is acceptance and not trying to control or escape from the anxiety. We will discuss this in more detail shortly.

Monitor your exposure tasks and predictions on a form

Monitoring your exposure enables you to re-rate your distress at the end of exposure and see whether you overestimated the degree of distress that would occur or for how long it would last.

As noted above, this is also essential when you are seeing a therapist so that they can monitor whether you are doing the exposure negotiated in the previous session.

Checking and mirrors and reflective surfaces

For people with body shame, mirrors and other reflective surfaces, or taking selfies on a phone, can present a real problem. Mirrors or reflective surfaces are commonly used as a safety behaviour, to check on how you appear. If this is a problem for you then the first step is to see how often you are checking in a mirror and to increase awareness of when you are checking. If you are not aware of when you carry out a repetitive behaviour, you cannot resist it. This can be monitored with a record sheet like the one below.

Frequency of checking

DATE	Mon	Tues	Wed	Thurs	Fri	Sat	Sun
I check in a mirror for a long duration (e.g. applying make-up, grooming)							
I check briefly in a mirror or reflective surface (e.g. window)							

OVERCOMING BODY DYSMORPHIC DISORDER

I check by looking at a feature directly without needing a mirror							
I check the 'picture in my mind' or memory of how I last looked							
I check by feeling my skin with my fingers							
I check my feature using a camera on my phone							
I check the feeling of elasticity or amount of fat by pinching my skin							
I check by measuring my feature							
I try to convince others about how unattractive my feature is							
I ask others to confirm the existence of my defect							

I seek reassurance about whether my feature has got worse			

I seek reassurance about whether my feature is camouflaged (for example, by make-up)			

Some people check in a mirror thirty, fifty or hundreds of times a day; in such cases it is best to use a tally counter and then to carry over the total to a chart. Both of these methods will give you a baseline for how often you are checking, so you can see in future whether this is decreasing over time. It will also make you more aware of when you are checking so that you can resist it in future. There are of course many different ways of checking: it might include long checks in front of a mirror doing something like styling or cutting your hair, plucking your eyebrows, picking spots, applying make-up or trying to do mental cosmetic surgery. Or it may be brief glances in shop windows or your phone screen. Alternatively, you may be doing internal checking of the picture in your mind or memory of how you last looked. If your feature (for example, your thighs) can be examined directly, you might not need a mirror to check. Add a tick or click on your tally counter whenever you do any of these checking activities.

The next step is to try to understand more about your motivation for checking and the pay-off you obtain in the short term, as well as the unintended consequences in the long term.

AN A, B, C, D, E OF UNDERSTANDING YOUR CHECKING: WORKED EXAMPLE

Activating event

Describe a recent typical situation in which you were checking the feature (for example, looking in the mirror or a reflective surface, or pinching your skin). Did you experience a picture in your mind or memory before the checking started? Was there uncertainty in how you felt you looked?

I was lying in bed in the morning, thinking about having to go out to college.

Behaviour

What did you actually do? What was your mind telling you as you checked? How long did it last?

I started touching my skin with my fingers, and then got out of bed to look in the mirror.

Immediate **C**onsequences

Was there any pay-off from checking? For example, did you avoid anything that was uncomfortable? Did you briefly feel more certain about how you do look? Did you feel you were doing something to improve your appearance?

I did feel less uncertain, and less like I might be ignoring something important.

Unintended <u>C</u>onsequences

What effect did the checking have on the way you feel?

I very quickly started to worry that my skin was too spotty and scarred.

What effect did the checking have on how you act? What effect did it have on the time you can devote to what is important in your life?

I spent a long time – about forty minutes – checking my skin in the mirror and feeling my skin for bumps.

What effect does checking have on the people around you?

My dad was annoyed/worried that I was checking again.

Did you do anything to excess as a consequence of checking (for example, drink more, use drugs, binge-eat, purge)?

No.

Overall, how helpful was it to give in to your urge to check?

Not at all.

Alternative **D**irections

What alternatives could you do that are consistent with your goals and valued directions instead of checking?

I could focus on getting ready and making sure I've had breakfast, so I'm prepared for college.

Effect of alternative directions

What effect did following your alternative direction have?

This was hard to do because I was initially quite distracted and self-conscious, but I can see that this could get easier.

Is there a pattern to the situations that are typically linked to checking? For example, can you do anything to prevent such situations arising?

I could probably try to avoid lying in bed 'thinking', and get up straight away instead.

EXERCISE: AN A, B, C, D, E OF UNDERSTANDING YOUR CHECKING

Activating event

Describe a recent typical situation in which you were checking the feature (for example, looking in the mirror or a reflective surface, or pinching your skin). Did you experience a picture in your mind or memory before the checking started? Was there uncertainty in how you felt you looked?

_____

_____

_____

_____

Behaviour

What did you actually do? What was your mind telling you as you checked? How long did it last?

_____

_____

Immediate **C**onsequences

Was there any pay-off from checking? For example, did you avoid anything that was uncomfortable?

Did you briefly feel more certain about how you do look? Did you feel you were doing something to improve your appearance?

_____

_____

_____

Unintended Consequences

What effect did the checking have on the way you feel?

_____

_____

What effect did the checking have on how you act? What effect did it have on the time you can devote to what is important in your life?

_____

_____

_____

What effect does checking have on the people around you?

_____

_____

_____

Did you do anything to excess as a consequence of checking (for example, drink more, use drugs, binge-eat, purge)?

_____

Overall, how helpful was it to give into your urge to check?

_____

Alternative **D**irections

What alternatives could you do that are consistent with your goals and valued directions instead of checking?

_____

_____

Effect of alternative directions

What effect did following your alternative direction have?

_____

>
>
> ———————————————
>
> ———————————————
>
> Is there a pattern to the situations that are typically linked to checking? For example, can you do anything to prevent such situations arising?
>
> ———————————————
>
> ———————————————

Motivation for checking

Examples of the motivation that people with body image problems give for checking include:

- I hope that I don't look as bad as I think I look.
- How long does the hope last for? What happens after that?
- I have to know what I look like before I do anything.
- Do you ever notice that it's actually quite hard to 'know' how you look? Does checking actually help with this knowing?
- I have to know for certain how I appear in public.
- For how long do you feel certain you know what you look like? Then what happens?
- I believe that if I stare long enough, I might see a different image.

- How does this help you reduce your preoccupation? How often does this work? If you do see a different image, how long does this help for?
- If I resist looking in the mirror, then I will feel worse.
- Does checking make you feel better in the long term? Does it always make you feel better even in the short term? Does the discomfort of resisting checking really last if you refocus, move on and don't dwell on it?
- I need to see what I don't like about myself.
- How does this help you reduce your preoccupation? Is it consistent with treating your problem 'as if' it's Theory B? Has this strategy really helped you up until now?
- If I don't look then I might forget about how ugly I am.
- What are the costs of continuing to attack yourself as ugly? How does this fit with treating your appearance concerns 'as if' they are part of a psychological problem of being over-ashamed, over-anxious and excessively preoccupied? Could you still take good care of your appearance if you were less preoccupied?

Some of these assumptions can be tested in an experiment. For example, compare two different time frames of checking – once a day and twenty times a day – to see whether this leads you to be more or less certain about how you look. Does increasing the checking make you more preoccupied and distressed?

In general, what do you notice is the effect of mirror checking on your concerns about your appearance?

_____

_____

Using a mirror in a healthy way

For many readers, mirror use will be an important target for change. The key is to think of a mirror as a 'functional' object – there to help us with taking care of our bodies and appearance, but not a tool for excessive scrutiny and assessment. We would encourage you to develop the following goals with mirrors:

- Use mirrors at a slight distance, or ones that are large enough to incorporate most of your body.
- Deliberately focus attention on your reflection in a mirror rather than an internal impression of how you feel.
- Only use a mirror for an agreed function (e.g. shaving, putting on make-up) for a limited period of time.
- Use a variety of different mirrors and lights rather sticking to one that you 'trust'.
- Scan your body and focus attention on the whole of your face or body rather than specific 'defects' or in any detail. (People without body image problems tend to focus their attention on features that are considered to be more attractive. This is an alternative strategy.)

TAKING ACTION

- Try not to make any judgements about your appearance. Just be aware of any intrusive thoughts and images about being ugly without buying into them. Take the position of an observer of passing traffic rather than trying to control the traffic and believing what enters your mind must be true.
- Do not use mirrors that magnify your reflection.
- Do not use your phone screen or take 'selfies' to check or scrutinise your appearance.
- Do not use ambiguous reflections (for example, in windows, the backs of CDs, cutlery or mirrors that are dusty or cracked).
- Do not use a mirror when you have the urge to check, but try to delay the response and do other activities until the urge has diminished.
- Do not 'swing' from excessive mirror checking to avoiding mirrors – it's important to learn to resist the urge to check or scrutinise while in the presence of your own reflection.

For some people, it is more important to monitor how long the mirror gazing lasts; in some cases a single use of the mirror can last several hours. Here the criteria used to finish a check may be problematic. Thus, someone may finish mirror gazing when they feel 'comfortable' or 'just right'. In fact, we know from research that sometimes people with body image problems stop looking in the mirror as much because they feel distressed or frustrated, as much as anything else.

Instead of using 'internal' reasons for finishing (e.g. when it feels right), focus your attention and concentrate on the environment around you and what you see. This means finishing using the mirror when you still feel anxious, acting against the way you feel. This goes against the grain when you believe you have to be guided by your feelings or 'sixth sense'. The problem is that you are receiving a false signal of danger and you have now got used to it. The goal is to finish using a mirror, or grooming or combing your hair, when you can 'see' that it looks 'good enough'.

As an experiment you might want to alternate between using a 'just right' feeling and 'just doing it' without using internal criteria.

If you can reduce the amount of make-up or grooming, then this will tend to significantly reduce the amount of time in front of a mirror. It is also worth remembering that when women reduce the amount of excessive camouflage on their face, they may well receive comments from others that they look different. This is not the same as being 'ugly'!

Mirror avoidance

Some people may avoid 'unsafe' mirrors. Avoiding mirrors altogether is an unrealistic goal and will cause problems in the long term. Deliberate mirror exposure is sometimes necessary in people who are avoiding all or certain mirrors. It can be done as graded exposure with varying degrees of light, how close you stand to the mirror or the amount of your body that is exposed. If your problem is with your whole body then a swimming costume can be worn if someone else is present. When looking in the mirror it is important to describe your appearance objectively (the colour of your eyes, your complexion, height, build etc.). Observe and describe, but do not 'rate' or value these features. Scan the whole of your body and do not focus attention on a specific 'defect' or detail. Look at the person in the mirror as if it were a stranger, and try to take in the whole of your appearance.

Photos

Like mirrors, photographs can pose a real difficulty for people with body image problems. Many people will avoid having their photograph taken or tear photographs up. Alternatively, they might repeatedly take a picture using their phone.

Photographs can also fuel brooding – for example, when you look at a photograph of yourself at a time when you thought you looked acceptable, and repeatedly go over the thought 'if only I looked like that now'. As with mirrors, try to integrate photographs into your life as part of normal everyday life and allow your mind to become used to them again. This may form part of the 'exposure' programme described above. Alternatively, if you are using photos to check your appearance, then use the form above to monitor how often you are checking and carry out the same analysis you did for mirror checking.

Avoid avoidance

If you manage to resist your repetitive behaviour, do not compensate by increasing your avoidance. For example, you stop checking in mirrors but are now avoiding mirrors altogether. This is not recommended as it just creates another problem. You have to both resist checking and do exposure – in this case to using mirrors in a healthy way.

Develop an alternative behaviour to seeking (or giving yourself) reassurance

Seeking or giving reassurance is a type of repetitive behaviour. Just stopping giving reassurance can be fraught with problems for the loved one. Here are some common ones:

- The loved one knows it is unhelpful to give reassurance but feels stuck and unable to cope. A person with a body image problem may become distressed, frustrated, angry and resentful when their loved one just stops giving reassurance.
- If they just stop giving reassurance, then the body image questioning becomes more subtle or sneakier, and the loved one is still drawn into the cycle.
- It's often impossible to stick to, and so increases the blame and shame on both the person with the body image problem and the loved one.
- If the loved one manages to be consistent in not responding to your reassurance-seeking, the connection between you may become diminished. The

TAKING ACTION

person with a body image problem may then seek reassurance from someone else, or develop more self-reassurance (which is a mental compulsion), and so the problem has not gone away.

The solution to the person with a body image problem seeking reassurance and the loved one giving reassurance is to seek and give emotional support. So the person with a body image problem might seek compassion and care from their loved one when they are wanting reassurance. The loved one needs to respond naturally when the person with a body image problem is wanting reassurance. The definition of compassion is being sensitive to the person suffering and being deeply committed to relieving it. There are thus two sides to compassion: one is being empathic, sympathetic, caring and soothing; the other is turning towards the distress and not avoiding anxiety. It involves being non-judgemental and acting as if you had courage and wisdom. This may require a bit of planning and role-playing. It's important that the person with the body image problem and the family or people who give reassurance have an agreed joint plan of action; the help of a therapist may make it easier. What this means in practice is the person with a body image problem being sensitive to their own suffering and, instead of seeking reassurance, labelling the feeling and trying to express what they need (not what they want). They might say something like, 'I'm feeling really anxious right now.' If they can, it would help for them to say what might help – for example, 'Can I have a hug?', 'Can I have a cup of tea?' or 'Can we go for a walk?' Note that there's no request to discuss what they are anxious about – it's similar to an exposure task, where the person is identifying and labelling their emotion to themselves: 'OK Anna, these are the feelings of anxiety – this is tough, but let's try to just stick with it.' Now if the person with BDD can identify what they need (and it is realistic), the loved one can then try to help in a way that avoids reassurance or debate, and hence avoid fuelling preoccupation.

Equally, it is important for the person with a body image problem not to answer back with rational responses, and reassure themselves that others cannot see their nose being crooked or whatever, but they can talk to themselves in a caring and encouraging manner, in the same way as their relative or loved one.

Some examples of exposure

The nature of an exposure task will depend upon your particular form of body image problem and whether you're someone who is avoiding lots of situations or activities (where it's easier to come up with suitable exposure), or a person who is avoiding fewer things but has lots of checking (where you may need to be a little more creative).

> *Rusha's approach to change was to treat her problem as if she had an emotional and thinking problem rather than a problem with the appearance of her nose (even though she didn't believe it). After all, if by treating it as Theory B for several months didn't work then she could always go*

back to her previous way of treating it as Theory A. She also recognised that there may have been ghosts from the past, such as when she was bullied, that influenced the way she felt about her appearance. Furthermore, she recognised that some of her ways of coping were making her preoccupation worse and she was on an endless treadmill of further checking. Although she was very fearful of being humiliated and left alone in the world, she also knew that many of her solutions were now the problem, and causing much of her unhappiness and making her feel alone.

The first step was for Rusha to keep a record of how often she checked her nose with both her fingers and in the mirror, using a tally counter she bought online. This helped her to monitor her checking, make her more aware of just how much checking she was doing, and to steadily reduce and stop it.

She learned how to use mirrors in a healthy way, and to refocus her attention more on what she saw without making any judgement.

At the same time Rusha developed a hierarchy of situations she was anxious about or was avoiding:

Trigger (object, place, person, situation):	Estimated distress (0–100)
Asking an attractive man out on a date, without my hat and without checking beforehand	100
Going to an interview	90
Sitting and having a meal in a brightly lit fast-food restaurant	80
Asking for directions in the street on a brightly lit day	70
Going for a walk around the local park on a busy day without my hat	70
Going for a walk around the park on a quiet day without my hat	65
Sitting and having a meal in a dimly lit restaurant	60
Standing, profile on, in a long queue in shop	60
Having a friend to my home for coffee and deliberately allowing them to see me from the side	50

Rusha found using the hierarchy helpful in three main ways:

1. *It helped her see more clearly that recovery could be a series of gradual steps rather than her more 'all or nothing' view of 'stop being so silly' or 'of course I'm devastated, so would anyone else be'.*

2. *She used it as a guide for areas to conduct 'behavioural experiments' (see example below).*

3. *She used it as a guide to practise approaching situations without her safety behaviours and redirecting her attention into the surroundings, away from her felt impression of how she was coming across. This was particularly difficult, and the main strategy to refocus her attention was 'task-concentration training' (see Chapter 6). She rediscovered her love for nature, and found it especially helpful in the early stages to practise refocusing her attention onto trees and plants as she walked. This would help to 'anchor' her attention in the outside world, and then she found she could more readily move it around to other aspects of her task or environment.*

OVERCOMING BODY DYSMORPHIC DISORDER

Rusha's behavioural experiment sheet:

1. Task that I planned (e.g. when, where, how and with whom) (include a description of how you will act without safety behaviours)	Going into brightly lit restaurant without my hat, make-up or checking myself in the mirror.
2. How distressing I am predicting task will be at the peak (0–100%)	100%
3. How long I am predicting that the distress will take to halve (minutes or hours)	Never
4. What I am predicting will happen (for example, how others will behave towards me) or whether the result will best fit a particular theory, and how strongly I believe it (0–100%)	People in the restaurant will notice my nose. The waitress will be awkward and uncomfortable, other people will stare and make comments to each other, trying not to let me hear. I'll have to run into the bathroom to see what everyone else is noticing.
5. What I actually did during the task (including using any safety behaviours and degree of self-focused attention)	I tried really hard to keep my attention focused on the outside world. I resisted feeling my nose or checking in the bathroom. I remembered that thoughts that people were thinking negatively about me were 'mind-reading' and being driven by my own preoccupation.
6. How distressing the task was at the peak (0–100)	80%
7. How long it actually took for the distress to halve (minutes or hours)	45 mins

8. What actually happened? Does this differ from what I predicted in (4)? Do the results best fit my theory that I have a problem with my appearance, or the alternative that the problem is being excessively preoccupied by my appearance?	Nobody really paid much attention to me. I have no evidence that anyone said anything to each other about me, even though I did feel self-conscious, which was more down to my anxiety than anything anyone else did or said. The waitress was nice enough but was really too busy to pay me much attention. This does confirm the theory that I tend to worry far too much about how people will respond to my appearance. I need to practise this more until I feel much more comfortable.

Rusha learned to stop brooding about her nose, recognising that this just made her feel worse and more preoccupied. Her mind constantly generated more questions, more solutions that never ended.

After she had made some progress with changing her behaviour, Rusha learned to develop a different relationship with her intrusive thoughts and images about her appearance. She viewed her thoughts and images about her appearance as her internal 'BDD TV'. She considered that her thoughts could be like a 'history channel' (for when she brooded about the past), the 'BDD propaganda news flash' (for when an upsetting image or thoughts would suddenly enter her head), or 'adverts' (when her mind was telling her that she 'needed to know how exactly she looked' or how she could fix it and had a strong urge to check her appearance). Over time, the thoughts and images became less frequent and distressing. She was able to return to work in her office. She contacted some of her old friends and, about six months later, developed a new relationship.

Obstacles

A common obstacle is the belief that 'I can only stop avoiding situations or drop my safety behaviours when I feel comfortable or "right", or when I know for certain that the consequences I fear will not happen, or when I feel confident enough to test out my fears.' This applies to a wide range of avoidance and safety behaviours. There may be a high level of emotional intolerance and a struggle to stop controlling events. Progress will be based on the willingness to accept and embrace uncomfortable thoughts and feelings, and a willingness to drop the shovel with a 'leap of faith' (see Chapter 2). This means doing tasks uncomfortably, with uncertainty and unconfidently in the short term, in order to obtain the long-term gains. Some people may have a good intellectual understanding of the problem but are not yet ready to change to test out their predictions. In such situations, you may have to think of smaller steps, get professional help and really commit yourself to testing out an alternative, otherwise your suffering and the interference in your life is likely to persist.

The problem with 'normal' – treatment first, normal later

You might be concerned at some of the suggestions that we or a therapist might make for exposure at the top of your hierarchy, but they are a means towards an end. As soon as you have overcome your body image problem, you can bin them. People sometimes complain that what they are being encouraged to do during exposure is 'abnormal' and therefore unreasonable. Thus, someone preoccupied with their spots or redness on their skin may be encouraged to exaggerate their redness or spots by the use of make-up. Another person, who is encouraged to refrain from washing their hair or applying make-up for two weeks, might say something like, 'Even someone without a body image problem wouldn't do that!' as if the therapist is being entirely unreasonable. (We're not saying therapists are never unreasonable; it's just that this is more likely to be a problem of misunderstanding!) However, for someone with a body image problem who believes that others would reject them and they would be alone all their life, this is a powerful way of testing this out.

Thus, the ultimate tasks would involve not just the dropping of safety behaviours but highlighting or exaggerating the 'defect'. If you think about it, many treatments for human ailments involve doing the unusual. Consider the 'normality' of swallowing toxic chemicals every day, while 'chemotherapy' for cancer involves just that. Or perhaps the normality of wrapping a leg in plaster, while if you have a broken leg, this is very helpful! We accept these 'abnormal' activities as part of 'normal' treatment for physical problems. Part of the issue when tackling a psychological problem is that, because of the stigma and shame surrounding psychological and emotional problems, the normal processes of overcoming fears are not so readily discussed and understood.

So remember, if you are reading this book as part of your plan to overcome your body image problem, your exposure can be enhanced by testing out the predictions that you are making. However, it needs to be frequent enough, long enough and 'potent' enough, and without safety behaviours to reduce your feeling of threat. Would you expect a medication to be effective if you took less than the recommended dose and less often than prescribed?

> **PIT STOP**
>
> Let's stop and think about what you have just been reading. Can you summarise the key ideas you have taken on board? What is sticking in your mind? Maybe write it down. If you have any questions, jot those down too. You can return to them once you have had a chance to digest the information.
>
> What is sticking in my mind from my reading so far?
>
> 1.
>
> 2.
>
> 3.

8

Tackling depression and reclaiming your life

Low mood and body image problems

Because of the marked impact a body image problem has on a person's life, it's hardly surprising that many body image problem sufferers also experience some degree of depression. There are also several processes that are common to both body image problems and depression, in particular avoidance, social isolation and overthinking. A key feature of depression is emotional numbness and not being able to enjoy normal pleasures in life. It may interfere in your sleep, appetite and sexual interests. You may be tearful or irritable and find it difficult to concentrate. You may be excessively self-critical (and not just about your appearance). All this can lead to hopelessness and pessimism about the prospect of recovery and connecting with others, and this in turn can affect an individual's ability to engage with the tasks required to overcome their body image problem. In this way, the problem drags on for longer, seemingly confirming the view that the problem will never go away, and so the vicious circle is complete.

You may wish to clarify whether your depression is secondary to your body image problem so that you can decide which to focus on as a priority: did it develop after the onset of your body image problem? If we had a magic wand and your body image problem was sorted, would you still be seeking help for your mood? Most people report that depression comes after the onset of their body image problem and that, as this starts to improve, their depression also begins to lift. This makes particular sense when reclaiming your social life, for example, which for many people is not only a key step in recovering from a body image problem but also a powerful step in countering the avoidance that maintains low mood.

If you have fused your thoughts with reality and believe them to be true, it's not surprising that you want to escape from them. Thus, you may experience an emotional escape by feeling numb or uninterested. In order to escape unpleasant thoughts and feelings, you might start to:

- avoid activities and people that you have previously enjoyed, and become more focused on yourself
- withdraw from friends or family
- spend more time in bed
- use alcohol or drugs to numb your feelings
- brood about the past and try to work out reasons for the way you feel
- avoid calling friends because you think you may be humiliated or rejected
- try to distract yourself by browsing the internet or watching videos

- 'put your head in the sand' and pretend that the problems around you will go away if you ignore them
- ignore the doorbell or telephone.

Such behaviours become habitual, so you may not even be aware of why you are doing them. In many ways, escape is a natural response to try to avoid bad feelings. However, it merely digs you deeper into your hole.

When depression is the primary problem

For a small minority of individuals, their body image problem appears to be secondary to depression. Here the depressed mood comes first, and persistent feelings of ugliness follow, in the context of the depression. Examples may be found in people who have recurrent depression or bipolar depression. Determining whether you are suffering from depression and if it is primary or secondary is best done by a health professional experienced in body image conditions. You can however complete the screening test below to determine whether you are likely to be suffering from depression.

How bad is your depression?

The Hospital Anxiety and Depression (HAD) Scale is a screening tool for depression by Dr Snaith.

THE HOSPITAL AND ANXIETY DEPRESSION (HAD) SCALE

Please read each group of statements carefully, and then pick the one (by writing the number in the box) that comes closest to how you have been feeling in the past week and write that number in the box. Don't take too long over your replies: your immediate reaction to each item will probably be more accurate than a long-thought-out response.

	Anxiety	Depression
1. I feel tense or 'wound up': 3 Most of the time 2 A lot of the time 1 From time to time, occasionally 0 Not at all	☐	
2. I still enjoy the things I used to enjoy: 0 Definitely as much 1 Not quite so much 2 Only a little 3 Hardly at all		☐
3. I get a sort of frightened feeling as if something awful is about to happen: 3 Very definitely and quite badly 2 Yes, but not too badly 1 A little, but it doesn't worry me 0 Not at all	☐	
4. I can laugh and see the funny side of things: 0 As much as I always could 1 Not quite so much now 2 Definitely not so much now 3 Not at all		☐

	Anxiety	Depression

5. Worrying thoughts go through my mind:

   3 A great deal of the time
   2 A lot of the time
   1 From time to time but not too often
   0 Only occasionally

   ☐ (Anxiety)

6. I feel cheerful:

   3 Not at all
   2 Not often
   1 Sometimes
   0 Most of the time

   ☐ (Depression)

7. I can sit at ease and feel relaxed:

   0 Definitely
   1 Usually
   2 Not often
   3 Not at all

   ☐ (Anxiety)

8. I feel as if I am slowed down:

   3 Nearly all the time
   2 Very often
   1 Sometimes
   0 Not at all

   ☐ (Depression)

9. I get a sort of frightened feeling like 'butterflies' in the stomach:

   0 Not at all
   1 Occasionally
   2 Quite often
   3 Very often

   ☐ (Anxiety)

OVERCOMING BODY DYSMORPHIC DISORDER

	Anxiety	Depression
10. I have lost interest in my appearance: 3 Definitely 2 I don't take so much care as I should 1 I may not take quite as much care 0 I take just as much care as ever		☐
11. I feel restless as if I have to be on the move: 3 Very much indeed 2 Quite a lot 1 Not very much 0 Not at all	☐	
12. I look forward with enjoyment to things: 0 As much as I ever did 1 Rather less than I used to 2 Definitely less than I used to 3 Hardly at all		☐
13. I get sudden feelings of panic: 3 Very often indeed 2 Quite often 1 Not very often 0 Not at all	☐	
14. I can enjoy a good book or radio or TV programme: 0 Often 1 Sometimes 2 Not often 3 Very seldom		☐
TOTAL	Anxiety ☐	Depression ☐

> Add up your scores for anxiety (in the left-hand column) and depression (in the right-hand column).
>
> The scores can be summarised on a chart completed at regular intervals so that you can monitor progress.
>
> If you score 9 or more on the depression subscale, you are probably experiencing depression. Similarly, if you score 9 or more on the anxiety subscale, you are probably experiencing an anxiety disorder. Higher scores (15 or more on the depression subscale) could mean that a self-help book might not be suitable for you, and you might need to seek additional professional help.

Please read each group of statements carefully, and then pick the one statement (by writing the number in the box) that comes closest to describing how you have been feeling in the past week. Don't take too long over your replies: your immediate reaction will probably be more accurate than a long-thought-out response.

Answer each question and add up your scores.

What should I tackle first?

Our answer, for most people, is to tackle your body image problem and depression together. While psychiatric diagnosis is a system of different categories, and helpful for identifying the type of problem for the patient, for treatment and for research your emotional problems are not separate. They are part of your mental condition, which in turn is part of your overall health and wellbeing. It is sensible to make changes that are directed at improving your mood and behaviours related to your body image. The healthier your feelings about your appearance become, the more likely it is that your mood will lift as you are no longer living with such adversity. The better your mood becomes, the more able you will feel to tackle your fears head on and resist your safety-seeking behaviours. Being less depressed can improve a number of ways in which you see things, including your body.

So, in planning to overcome the avoidance driven by your appearance shame and anxiety it is helpful to include targets likely to improve your mood. Remember, targets for mood improvement are those that are likely to increase the amount of reward or reduce 'punishment' (adversity) and therefore make you more likely to act in the same way again. Here are some examples. Some of these might seem incredibly obvious, but the aim here is to be practical rather than groundbreaking:

- going out for a walk in the daytime and focusing on your surroundings
- allowing yourself to sit near other people in a restaurant
- spending time walking around a supermarket, giving yourself the time to choose foods you might really enjoy
- wearing the clothes you really like, rather than using clothing to cover up parts of your appearance.

Note below particular changes that might be worth prioritising because they are likely to also improve your mood:

_____

_____

_____

_____

Ultimately, improving your body image will reduce your suffering, increase your ability to live a rewarding life and thus help you lift your mood.

THOUGHTS ABOUT ENDING YOUR LIFE

If you are feeling hopeless about the future, and have developed a plan to end your life, please see a doctor or go to Accident & Emergency straight away. It is especially important to hold on to hope. Remember that feeling trapped and hopeless is a symptom of depression and does not reflect reality. So please suspend your judgement until you've improved your relationship with your appearance and mood. We know that recovery can be hard work, and that you will need to work at it consistently and regularly, even when it's difficult. We have seen so many people get better over the years; we are convinced that no

> situation is hopeless. There are many sources of help that you could phone. In the UK call the Samaritans' 24-hour helpline on 116 123 or email jo@samaritans.org. You can also call SANEline on 0845 767 8000 (6 pm–11 pm) or CALM on 0800 58 58 58 (every day from 5 pm until midnight).

Behavioural activation

One of the approaches in breaking free from depression involves changing your behaviour; it is called behavioural activation. This alone has been shown to be as effective as standard treatments such as antidepressant medication and cognitive behavioural therapy. You can read about behavioural activation in more detail in our book entitled *Manage Your Mood*. It is based on the observation that when you are depressed, everything becomes an effort and you tire easily. You avoid things that are uncomfortable. You might avoid conflict or making difficult decisions. You do less and become socially withdrawn and inactive. You might then blame yourself for this, perhaps telling yourself, 'You should be able to pick yourself up and get on with life.' You become more negative about yourself, overthink and believe you can do nothing; you become more depressed and a vicious circle is established.

You may stay at home or in bed during the day, distract yourself watching TV or playing computer games, and give up your normal activities. Your lifestyle changes, so you may eat little or just junk food and no longer exercise. Your tendency to avoid activities may be reinforced as it may stop unpleasant feelings in the short term. However, the solution has again become the problem: not engaging with the world and being inactive means a less rewarding life without any positive experiences. Being inactive makes you more likely to overthink about the things you feel are lost or missing in your life, and makes you even more depressed. You now have two closely related problems: your anxiety and shame related to your appearance, and a life that's not going particularly well, as well as a disconnect from the world, which is going to make you more depressed. Reversing such behaviours can significantly improve your mood and motivate you to tackle your problems.

The first step is to monitor your daily activity for at least a week on a chart that breaks the days of the week into one-hour blocks. Below is an example of a record of a patient with BDD and low mood.

Next, review your behaviour to find what you are avoiding and what you are no longer doing that is important in your life. Such responses maintain your depressed state. The next step is to gradually 'activate' yourself (usually in small steps to begin with), targeting specific changes in your behaviour that would help improve mood. This will include:

- scheduling activities to help you be less withdrawn, isolated or inactive
- reducing behaviours you do to excess (such as sleeping, eating, overthinking)

OVERCOMING BODY DYSMORPHIC DISORDER

Time	Monday	Tuesday	Wednesday	Thursday	Friday	Saturday	Sunday
7–9 am	Sleep	Lay in bed	Sleep	Lay in bed	Sleep	Lay in bed	Sleep
9–11 am	Doze in bed	Lay in bed Instagram	Lay in bed Instagram	Lay in bed Instagram	Lay in bed Instagram	Coursework	Sleep
11 am–1 pm	Lay in bed Instagram	Uni	TV	Uni	Listened to podcast	Went for walk	Lay in bed
1–3 pm	Watch TV Sandwich	Tried to sleep Biscuits	Lunch: instant noodles	Tried to sleep Pizza	Tried to sleep Pizza	Lunch: instant noodles	Lay in bed Instagram
3–5 pm	Tried to sleep	Lunch	Watched stuff on laptop in bed	Watched film	Uni	Watched TV	Coursework
5–7 pm	Messaged or called friends	Coursework	Chatted to brother on phone	Scrolled on phone	Uni – left early	Listened to podcast	Online shopping
7–9 pm	Gaming Pizza	Watched TV	Gaming	TV	Called Mum Watched YouTube.	Lay in bed	Researched dermatologist

TACKLING DEPRESSION AND RECLAIMING YOUR LIFE

9–11 pm	Gaming	TV	Gaming	TV	Lay in bed Instagram Burger	Chinese takeaway	TV/computer
11 pm–1 am	Gaming Instant noodles	TV Dinner: sandwich	Gaming	Gaming Messaged friends	Messaged or called friends	Gaming	Messaged friend
1 am–3 am	Watch TV until gone 3 am	Researched skin products	Gaming	Gaming Biscuits and crisps	Sleep	Gaming	Bed
3 am–7 am	Sleep	Sleep	Sleep	Sleep	Sleep	Gaming/sleep	Tried to sleep but didn't get much

OVERCOMING BODY DYSMORPHIC DISORDER

Time	Monday	Tuesday	Wednesday	Thursday	Friday	Saturday	Sunday
7–9 am	Up 8 am Breakfast Walk	Up 8 am Breakfast	Up 8 am Breakfast Walk	Up 8 am Breakfast Walk	Up 8 am Breakfast	Up 9 am	Up 9 am
9–11 am	Uni	Gym	Reading	Uni	Gym	Chill	Play football
11 am–1 pm	Uni	Uni	Shopping	Uni	Lunch	Coursework	
1–3 pm	Lunch	Uni	Lunch	Uni	Uni 2 pm	Lunch	Lunch
3–5 pm	Swim	Uni	Film society	Uni	Uni	Watch football at pub	Coursework
5–7 pm	TV	Coursework	Coursework	Play pool	Practise guitar	Chill	Batch cooking and dinner
7–9 pm	Dinner: Stir-fry Gaming	Dinner: Veg pasta TV	Dinner: Chicken and veg wrap	Dinner: Veg noodles Gaming	Dinner: Curry Coursework	Pizza with friend 8.30 pm	Practise guitar

TACKLING DEPRESSION AND RECLAIMING YOUR LIFE

9–11 pm	Gaming	Practise guitar	TV with friends	Football training	Watch film with flatmates	Club	TV
11 pm–1 am	Bed 11 pm	Bed 11 pm	Bed 11 pm	Bed 11 pm	Bed midnight	Club	Bed 11 pm
1 am–3 am	Sleep	Sleep	Sleep	Sleep	Sleep	Sleep	Sleep
3 am–7 am	Sleep	Sleep	Sleep	Sleep	Sleep	Sleep	Sleep

OVERCOMING BODY DYSMORPHIC DISORDER

Time	Monday	Tuesday	Wednesday	Thursday	Friday	Saturday	Sunday
7–9 am							
9–11 am							
11 am–1 pm							
1–3 pm							
3–5 pm							
5–7 pm							

TACKLING DEPRESSION AND RECLAIMING YOUR LIFE

7–9 pm	9–11 pm	11 pm–1 am	1 am–3 am	3 am–7 am

- planning activities you are avoiding or putting off – like household chores or admin – in small, manageable, steps.

Above is an example of a planned activity schedule.

When activating yourself, it is especially important to act according to a plan or goal, regardless of the way you feel. If you wait until you feel motivated or derive pleasure from an activity then nothing will change. However, the more you act towards your goals, the more likely you are to come into contact with more pleasant activities, so deriving more pleasure from life experiences and improving your mood. Start small, and be sympathetic to how difficult it can be to break free from the low motivation and lack of energy that comes with depression. But, with this in mind, try to follow the plan, not how you feel.

Christopher Martell, one of the clinicians who developed behavioural activation, has a way to remember what to do, using the word 'ACTION':

A – Assess to see if what I am doing is avoidance.
C – Choose either to continue to avoid and be depressed or to engage in a different activity.
T – Try the activity chosen.
I – Integrate my new behaviours into a routine. Once is not enough, as old behaviours are well-established patterns.
O – Observe the results.
N – Never give up: keep trying this as an experiment.

Depressive overthinking

We saw earlier in the book that overthinking is a core problem in BDD. It is also extremely common to go over and over problems or regrets in your mind when you feel depressed. This way of thinking involves dwelling on a problem over and over again without getting anywhere. To assess whether you do this, ask yourself the following questions:

- Do I spend a lot of time thinking about myself and how I feel?
- Do I worry a lot about the future or question myself a lot about the past?
- Am I constantly judging or rating myself?
- Do I rate and check on how badly I am doing against some ideal that I think I should follow?

Overthinking about the past tends to begin 'Why . . .?' or 'If only . . .'. For example:

- Why is it me that has developed these problems?
- Why am I even bothering to try to improve? I'm bound to be one of those people who don't recover, so what's the point?
- If only I had made different choices in life.

These 'Why . . .?' and 'If only . . .' questions generally can't be answered and are powerful in lowering mood.

Write down any such questions you ask yourself:

___

___

___

___

A pattern of shame and worry about the future usually takes the form of 'What if . . .?' For example:

- What if my appearance gets worse?
- What if people don't like me?
- I'm sure other people can overcome their BDD, but what if I can't overcome mine?

Often, worry questions have no answers or are non-existent problems. They work because they make you feel more in control in the short term but of course just feed your anxiety.

Write down any 'worry questions' you tend to ask yourself:

___

___

___

___

Key to understanding worry and depressive overthinking is that:

- they make you feel worse and more depressed, anxious or tired
- they rarely solve anything and generate more questions ('But what if. . .?' or 'If only' or 'Why . . .?') for you to think over
- they lead you to avoid making decisions, engaging in activities or solving your problems, and encourage you to procrastinate (losing time that could usefully be spent on exposure tasks).

If you have a real problem, then solving it will involve turning 'Why . . .?' type questions into 'How can I . . .?' type questions. An example might be a car breaking down just as you have to leave for an important appointment. You could overthink on:

- 'Why does it happen to me?'
- 'This is a disaster'
- 'I am so useless'

which will lead to procrastination, missing your appointment and further depression.

Or you could turn the question into:

- 'How am I going to get to my appointment?'

and then decide whether to call a taxi, ring a friend, telephone and postpone the appointment, or whatever.

> ### EXERCISE: TURNING 'WHY?' AND 'WHAT IF?' INTO 'HOW CAN I?'
>
> Look back at the 'Why . . .?' and 'What if . . .?' questions you noted down above and see if you can convert each of them into a 'How can I . . .?' question.
>
> Why _____?
>
> How can I _____?
>
> Why _____?
>
> How can I _____?
>
> What if _____?
>
> How can I _____?
>
> What if _____?
>
> How can I _____?

When you are feeling depressed about your body image problem, refocus your thinking on to:

- what you can do by your own actions, or
- who you can get help from in overcoming your body image problem.

If and when an actual problem arises, then you can use your

problem-solving skills. If, however, it is a problem that can't be solved (e.g. 'What will happen when I die?'), then don't even attempt to engage with the question or try to solve it.

Only if there is a significant risk of an event happening should you prepare for it, and then only if it involves action. For example:

- if you have an exam or interview, revising for it
- if you are being teased or bullied, then prepare for what you can say by doing a role play with a friend
- an annual check to make sure the smoke detectors in your home are functioning.

These are actions you can take, as opposed to overthinking that stops you getting on with life. For more ideas on tackling overthinking related to BDD, please review Chapter 6.

What if behavioural activation doesn't lift my mood?

Pessimistic thoughts are a very common effect of depression, including those about whether any strategy might help you. A powerful way of overcoming pessimism is to treat your thoughts as theories to be tested out. This means acting against the way you feel, and doing so consistently and regularly. If you're having trouble with pessimism and hopelessness about recovery, hang on to the fact that recovery *is* possible. Try out the principles outlined in this book, and make a date with yourself in eight weeks to review if they are helping.

Chronic low self-esteem and difficulties with personality are more difficult to tackle. Many people with a body image problem have had their life altered from a young age and have missed out on the sort of activities or friendships we normally have while growing up. They have developed a sense of being alone in the world, and regard themselves as worthless or unlovable. They may not be suffering from a clinical depression but have difficulties in social situations and are very sensitive to the slightest sense of criticism or rejection. They may overcompensate and demand impossibly high standards or be perfectionists. Such problems usually require longer therapy. Meanwhile, a good start would be to read *Reinventing Your Life*, by Jeffrey Young and Janet Klosko (see Appendix 2).

Medications that are used for the treatment of BDD can also be prescribed for moderate to severe depression. You can read more about these in Chapter 13.

Lifestyle changes

We mentioned above the lifestyles that often occur in depression. Here is a list of lifestyles that may aggravate depression and therefore your body image problem:

- a restricted or chaotic diet
- eating large amounts of junk food
- staying up late at night and getting up at irregular hours
- not exercising
- increasing alcohol or illegal drug use.

You probably know that these are unhelpful and contribute to a depressed mood. It is important to regulate your appetite and sleep. The best approach is to plan eating and rest into your activity schedule so that you sleep regularly, get up by 7.30 am and go for a short walk in the sunlight, and eat a diverse range of food at regular times. Drinking excessively and many recreational drugs (especially cocaine and speed, and possibly cannabis and ecstasy) can make depression and body image problems worse in the long term.

> **PIT STOP**
>
> Let's stop and think about what you have just been reading. Can you summarise the key ideas you have taken on board? What is sticking in your mind? Maybe write it down. If you have any questions, jot those down too. You can return to them once you have had a chance to digest the information.
>
> What is sticking in my mind from my reading so far?
>
> 1.
>
> 2.
>
> 3.

9

Helping someone with BDD

This chapter is written primarily for family members or friends of people with body dysmorphic disorder (BDD). One of the practical things a friend or relative can do is become an ally for the individual in overcoming their BDD. Offering warmth, support and encouragement on the road to recovery can be very helpful. This chapter aims to offer some useful ideas to consider along the way.

If you are a parent reading this book as a companion to professional therapy for a child who has BDD, you'll probably need to be significantly involved. However, like adults, teenagers should usually be given a choice as to whether or not their parent is involved.

If you live with someone with BDD, one of the biggest challenges can be managing the extent to which you allow your home or lifestyle to change to make them feel more comfortable. The dilemma, of course, is that short-term comfort actions (like checking, avoiding being seen and cosmetic 'solutions') are not usually compatible with long-term gains. In the psychological literature this is called 'accommodation', and is something from which partners and family members are strongly discouraged. However, dealing with (sometimes very desperate) requests for accommodation can be tricky: resisting adapting to the person's fears in the early days is one challenge; untangling months or years of changes to home life can be even more demanding for all involved. It might seem like a huge request, but staying patient, warm and helping the person with BDD to choose to change (rather than feeling forced to do so) can really make a difference.

In cognitive behavioural therapy (CBT), the 'ally' who teams up with the therapist to support recovery is called a 'co-therapist'. Such allies can be of enormous value and can help in numerous ways. If you decide to be an ally or co-therapist for a relative with BDD, it will make sense for both of you to work through this book and review it together as you progress. However, be aware that your relative may come to feel that you are over-involved with monitoring their homework or progress. If this happens, you will need to negotiate your degree of involvement.

If your relative is in therapy and you think they are not being honest with the therapist, it is usually possible to inform the therapist of your observations without the therapist breaching confidentiality. Ultimately, though, it's up to the person with BDD to do their homework and to be honest with their therapist about their difficulties. As their ally, you can gently remind them that having setbacks is part of overcoming BDD.

General guidelines for those supporting someone with BDD

Know your enemy!

If you are a relative or friend – or, especially, a partner – of someone with BDD, get to know as much as you can about the condition (for example, by reading books like this), the common behaviours and the treatment. It's worth emphasising three key points:

1. However much the behaviours may not make sense to you, they are just part of BDD. BDD is not a sign of madness – it's simply a disorder, of the kind that can affect many people at some stage in their life. BDD is not 'bad' behaviour done to annoy you.
2. If you have an adolescent with BDD, it's still important to set consistent boundaries with behaviours that are unrelated to BDD, and to problem-solve BDD behaviour where it impinges on your family life (e.g. the length of time the person spends in the bathroom when everyone is getting ready in the morning).
3. BDD is not something that can easily be stopped. It will take time, commitment and the right guidance to improve everyone's quality of life. Each person needs to overcome their problems at their own pace, and this may be a lengthy process. Avoid comparing your relative or friend with other individuals with (or, indeed, without) a mental health problem.

Avoid the blame game

No one should be blamed for BDD. It's not the fault of the person who has it, nor is it your fault as a relative or friend. Hence there is no need to feel guilty for 'causing' BDD, even if there is a possible genetic link. If you start blaming your genes then you can go all the way back to Adam and Eve!

Encourage your relative or friend to seek help

Encourage your relative or friend with BDD to try out the principles explained in this book, and to seek professional help with therapy or medication if they need it. Support them in either or both routes, and do everything you can to help them change. This means:

- helping them to understand and define their problems clearly
- if they want you to, being an ally as described above
- encouraging them to persist with their treatment
- praising improvement, however small.

Don't participate in BDD

Families should not try to adapt their ways of doing things to accommodate a relative's worries. Don't put family life on hold. Accept that BDD may complicate family life, but get on with it anyway, and encourage your relative to maintain as normal a lifestyle as possible:

- Don't take on their responsibilities (unless of course you are a parent of a child).
- Don't make excuses for them (e.g. about their being late for work or an appointment).
- Don't collaborate in trying to find 'cosmetic solutions', such as by researching on the internet or offering to pay for surgery or provide a loan.
- If necessary, compromise in the short term in the way we have described, but draw the line when new avoidance behaviours and safety behaviours start.

If you have been participating in your relative's BDD up to now, start to find ways of changing this:

- If the person is in therapy, ask if you can see the therapist with them and discuss a programme of reducing your involvement in your relative's BDD.
- If the person is not in therapy, try to negotiate a programme of gradual withdrawal from the person's safety and avoidance behaviour before you implement it.
- Make sure that you communicate that you are changing your involvement in order to help rather than punish.
- Practise saying 'I understand that this is tough', and offer to give them a hug when there is request for reassurance, verification or checking. The key is not to discuss the content of the worry but to still offer warmth and emotional support.
- Help them to see the downside of your participating

in avoidance and safety behaviours, and the effect on your relationship. Highlight how long the effect of the reassurance lasts for and what the effect is on their doubts.

Anticipate how you will deal with your relative or friend becoming stressed or irritated by your new way of responding, and have a plan that you can both agree upon if they become aggressive or angry. Where aggression is a problem, always ensure your own safety, if necessary by calling the police. You may have to be very persistent until requests for reassurance or rituals stop happening, because if you respond just once, it immediately becomes more likely that they will involve you again.

Remember:

- Individuals with BDD will not come to any harm as a result of anxiety, though they may be distressed in the short term.
- Accommodating rituals and avoidance means that you are helping to fuel BDD in the long term – and you are not taking care of yourself. It may feel as if you're protecting yourself from stress and helping someone with BDD, but the effect is the opposite.
- What is good for the family is usually good for the person with BDD, and this can only occur when no one else engages in the BDD. A family who are all pulling together can provide better support for their relative with BDD. Its members can also better support one another and solve problems more efficiently.

Be a coach and cheerleader

You and your relative or friend both need to see BDD, and not the individual experiencing it, as your shared enemy. Approach the problem as a team, working together. As they improve, see yourself as a coach shouting encouragement from the sidelines, or cheerleading, as you become less involved. Enthusiasm, understanding and general support are the best help you can provide.

Look after your own needs

Maintain your own interests and have your own sources of support. At times you may need time out (or respite care). When this happens, tell your relative that you need a break but have not given up on them, and try to get others to help.

- Feelings such as guilt, sadness or anger are normal in those caring for a relative with any long-term disability.
- Try not to engage in self-pitying thoughts such as 'Why me?' or 'Poor me, I don't deserve to have BDD in the family.' These will only make you feel worse and feed another vicious circle.
- Try to detach yourself emotionally from your relative's BDD and take it less personally.
- If you're not coping emotionally or it is affecting other areas of your life, seek help. There might be a local caregivers' group or, even better, a group for caregivers of individuals with BDD. Alternatively, see

your family doctor for a referral or go directly to a therapist. You might also find it helpful to read our book *Manage Your Mood*, also published by Robinson.

Decatastrophise anxiety and discomfort

We've met many family members who seem to believe that anxiety and discomfort should be avoided, and have even been critical of CBT because it requires the tolerance of discomfort. In some cases this is entirely understandable, given the profound distress that the individual with BDD, whom they care about, experiences as they wrestle with a doubt or intrusive thought.

Some families share 'rules' about emotions that can be unhelpful in overcoming BDD. For example:

- Emotions are a sign of weakness and should be controlled.
- If something upsets you, don't think about it.
- Being upset is terrible, and it's important to do something to make yourself feel better as soon as possible.
- If something bothers you, do something to take your mind off it.
- Be careful about showing other people that you feel upset; they might use it against you.
- If you get too upset it could make you ill, so it's best to avoid intense emotions.

These rules are unhelpful as they interfere in someone's ability to recover from BDD, since recovery will involve pushing through uncomfortable emotions. They are sometimes explicitly taught; at other times they are taught by the way a family or person within that family behaves.

If you think you or your family share any rules like these, which might make experiencing emotions even harder, try to communicate to the person with BDD the message that you are confident that feeling short-term distress is a sensible and helpful thing to do when overcoming BDD.

Be prepared for setbacks

It's likely that on some days your relative or friend will be better able to deal with symptoms than on others. It will be harder for both of you at certain times – for example, when either of you is feeling tired or stressed by other problems. Setbacks are to be expected, and to a certain extent can be planned for. Taking time out can be helpful at these points.

Each person with BDD will need to overcome their problems at their own pace, even though this may be a lengthy process. It's entirely normal to experience setbacks along the road to recovery. Don't lose heart. You can help by staying optimistic and encouraging them to keep trying. You probably won't see the hundred times that BDD doesn't get in the way, but you are bound to notice the time that it does!

Keep a sense of humour

People with BDD are often aware of the humorous aspects of their worries. BDD support groups are frequently filled with laughter, and many people are relieved at not having to take things too seriously. Such mirth can be used to help people with BDD distance themselves from the condition and their catastrophic thoughts. However, it is very important that friends and relatives resist any temptation to mock the person with BDD for their symptoms, as this may cause additional stress, shame and embarrassment.

Keep communicating

Make sure that you communicate, both with your relative who has BDD and with everyone else in your family.

- Remember that you may need help and support yourself.
- Make sure that you continue to do things you enjoy, and have people to talk to about your own feelings and concerns.
- Eventually, you may decide that, for the sake of your own mental health, you can't carry on caring for your relative or friend with BDD. In that case you'll need to communicate as a family and get help from the local services.

What if your relative has BDD but doesn't appear to want help from a mental health professional? This can be a very trying situation, as the following case study makes clear.

One of us had a telephone call from Sarah. She told us that she and her husband were desperate for help for their daughter, who was now aged twenty-three and still living with them. She was quite attractive but had suffered from BDD since the age of about twelve and it had become worse when she was at college. She had dropped out of her degree course and now rarely went out. She had refused any help from her family doctor or local mental health services. She spent several hours a day engaged in various checking rituals in the bathroom and skin-picking. She avoided going out unless it was late at night. She tended to neglect herself. Her sleep/wake cycle was reversed so that she would spend much of the night awake watching TV or using the internet/computer. She did not accept that she had BDD and did not believe that she had a mental health problem that needed help; she would get a job and get on with her life when she felt she looked right.

Sarah and her husband understandably felt helpless and desperate in the face of their daughter's plight. They found some benefit in attending a support group for people with BDD, which gave them a welcome opportunity to get some support and stop blaming themselves. They began to realise that they couldn't take responsibility for their daughter's behaviour. They also came to realise that their daughter's BDD was dominating their household and that they were talking about little else. They continued to encourage her to seek help and reduce her avoidance and rituals, but also began to try harder to talk to Sarah about things that weren't related to her BDD.

There is a significant minority of individuals with severe and chronic BDD who are hidden in the community. Many such people are cared for by ageing parents, who become increasingly concerned at the effect BDD is having on them. As professionals, we find this is one of the most difficult situations in which to help. We recognise the limited influence we have on someone with BDD. No one can make someone with BDD change.

We would normally recommend that Sarah tries to engage her daughter in therapy by asking for a home visit by a psychiatrist and subsequent visits by a qualified CBT therapist, who would focus on what Sarah's daughter really wants to do in life and her real values, which are being obscured by the BDD. If this were not possible, the therapist could try to engage her over the telephone. An exceptional mental health team, with therapists who are familiar with BDD, may provide this service. However, the success of any treatment will still depend on the cooperation of the person with BDD, and ultimately on their willingness to see a therapist and do the homework.

When you have an adult with chronic BDD in your home, it can be difficult to get them to accept help. The road ahead may be a long and hard one, and you'll need to look after yourself as well as them. Earlier in this chapter, in the section titled 'General guidelines for those supporting someone with BDD', we offered some suggestions on how to do this.

What if they play down the problem?

If your relative or friend insists that BDD is having hardly any effect on their life, there are various things you can do to encourage them to face up to the problem and seek help.

Try to find out:

- what their real feelings are about having such a problem (shame, for example, can make people very reluctant to acknowledge it; see Chapter 4 in this book)
- what they fear and/or
- what doubts they have about therapy or change.

Ensure that as a family, or if possible as a wider group, including friends, you take a consistent approach, and that nobody is accommodating the BDD. Agree upon your message, and if necessary talk to the individual both within the family (or wider) group and with a mental health professional.

One person in the group might draw up, along with the person with BDD, a list of costs (or disadvantages) and benefits (advantages) of:

1. staying the way they are, or
2. engaging in a programme of therapy.

A blank copy of the cost–benefit analysis form is included in Appendix 3, or you can print out a version from https://overcoming.co.uk/715/resources-to-download. Each of the costs and benefits may be divided into those for the 'self' and those for 'others'. Even if the person sees few disadvantages in staying the same, you can emphasise the costs of BDD to others in the family or group, and the benefits to the person with BDD in the long term. Do go on emphasising that you will still provide support and help during therapy. If your relative or friend finally agrees to seek help, discuss the time frame within which this can be done, and the process it will involve.

What if they refuse to seek help?

If your relative with BDD continues to refuse help and you decide that you cannot go on any longer with things the way they are, you will need to explore your own options, such as finding them independent living arrangements by getting help from your local mental health services.

Local mental health services do not always respond positively to requests for help for a relative with BDD who does not want help. The main priority for a psychiatrist in public health services is patients with 'severe mental illness', especially those who may be suicidal or a danger to the community. UK and US mental health law allows a patient to be detained in hospital against their will in certain circumstances; but in the absence of a risk to themselves or self-neglect, patients with BDD are unlikely to be admitted to hospital and would, in any case, be unlikely to benefit much from admission to the average acute psychiatric ward. Short-term inpatient care in a national specialist unit, where the staff are used to dealing with patients with BDD and regular CBT is available, is more likely to be helpful. Sometimes, a trial of medication can be given against a person's will, which might be helpful to some people.

It must be emphasised, though, that CBT is powerless without the cooperation of the person with BDD. It is both unethical and counterproductive to forcibly expose someone to feared situations or activities. Therapists will encourage and challenge a patient, but would never force exposure or spring something on their patient unannounced. Nor should you ever do this to a relative with BDD. A programme of CBT has to be followed voluntarily, and the motivation has to come from the patient, if it is to be ethical and effective.

Is anyone with BDD untreatable?

Many people who successfully overcome their BDD have made previous unsuccessful attempts, and some have even been diagnosed as 'untreatable'. This book is not the place to discuss the practical and ethical aspects of deciding under what circumstances a person should be considered unable to recover from BDD. What is clear, however, is that many people with BDD (and some less well-informed healthcare practitioners) arrive at the 'untreatable' conclusion much too quickly. On the whole, the best advice you can give to your relative with BDD is to keep fighting to change the BDD, rather than fight to change their appearance and hide from the world.

Very few people with BDD are beyond the skills of mental health professionals and the provisions of mental health law, and cannot be engaged in treatment. These individuals often have values that have become idealised and central to their identity. Such values are more likely to be seen in those who cannot bear anxiety and strenuously avoid situations that may provoke any distress.

They feel that they must have a high degree of control so that everything has to be done their way, and at a time and speed that suits them. In this case, as a relative, we would advise you to seek help for yourself from your family doctor. It's perfectly acceptable for your mental health, if you decide you can't carry on caring for your relative, to ask local services to find suitable independent living arrangements for them.

Remember: recovery from BDD is a process

When your relative is recovering, you might expect everything to go back to how it used to be. However, this may not be how it happens at all, and the family might need to go through various stages of adjustment. This is normal. Each person will adjust and recover at a different rate. You might want to see BDD as something that is 'over' or 'finished', but remember that setbacks are part of the process.

In summary, BDD can have a profound effect on the person with BDD and on the person or people who look after them. However, though the situation may sometimes be difficult, it is never hopeless, and there is a lot that you can do as a team to help each other.

PIT STOP

Let's stop and think about what you have just been reading. Can you summarise the key ideas you have taken on board? What is sticking in your mind? Maybe write it down. If you have any questions, jot those down too. You can return to them once you have had a chance to digest the information.

What is sticking in my mind from my reading so far?

1.

2.

3.

10

Compulsive skin-picking, hair-pulling and other habits

This chapter focuses on skin-picking, hair-pulling (trichotillomania) and other body-focused repetitive behaviours (BFRBs). We explain the strategies you can try out to break free from them. What's important to understand about BFRBs is that they are common, nothing to be ashamed of, and that most people can't 'just stop'. Tackling a BFRB takes deliberate planning and practice, and with this, many people have successfully overcome, or at least learned to manage, the problem.

BFRB is the official name, but it is a bit cumbersome. BFRBs are characterised by recurrent and habitual actions directed at your body, typically accompanied by unsuccessful attempts to decrease or stop the behaviour involved. They lead to unintended consequences (e.g. hair loss, skin lesions, lip abrasions). There are two main BFRBs: hair-pulling and skin-picking. Other BFRBs include nail-biting and lip- or cheek-biting.

Hair-pulling (trichotillomania)

This is characterised by recurrent pulling of one's own hair, leading to significant hair loss, accompanied by unsuccessful attempts to decrease or stop the behaviour. Hair-pulling may occur from any region of the body on which hair grows, but the most common sites are the scalp, eyebrows and eyelids (i.e. pulling out eyelashes). Less common areas are the armpits, facial and pubic regions. Hair-pulling may occur in brief episodes scattered throughout the day or in less frequent but more sustained periods. It can lead to noticeable hair loss. To qualify for a diagnosis it must lead to either significant distress or impairment in one's life. Occasional pulling of a grey or out-of-place hair is normal and done by most people at some time in their lives. However, having pulled the hair, the person with trichotillomania will often feel less tense and sometimes have a sense of gratification; they may then become ashamed of the consequences of hair-pulling and will strenuously try to cover any resulting patches of baldness. There are rituals surrounding hair, such as visually examining the hair with one's fingers or lips after it has been pulled. Some people may swallow or eat the hair that has been pulled (trichophagia). This can potentially lead to serious bowel problems if it collects in a ball and blocks the bowel.

Skin-picking (or excoriation disorder)

Skin-picking disorder is characterised by recurrent picking of one's own skin, leading to skin lesions and scars. It includes scratching, picking, gouging, lancing, digging, rubbing or squeezing of the skin. It is accompanied by unsuccessful attempts to decrease or stop the behaviour. Skin-picking may occur in brief episodes scattered throughout the day or in less frequent but more sustained periods. Occasional picking of the skin is normal and done by most people at some time in their lives. This does not qualify for a diagnosis of skin-picking disorder, which would involve recurrent picking and be associated with significant time, distress or impairment that is not present in normal skin-picking.

Because it is usually the most relevant to individuals with BDD, this chapter will focus on skin-picking. However, the principles described here will apply to other forms of BFRB. Research has shown that as many as one-third of people with BDD suffer from skin-picking. Additionally, people with skin-picking often have body image problems and feel ashamed about the damage they have caused. A minority of patients may pick skin only in response to sensations such as a feeling of itchiness or an underlying dermatological condition. When it's part of BDD, it can be an attempt to remove minor irregularities in the skin that are hardly noticeable to others. However, once the skin-picking has started, then it may develop into an automatic or impulsive behaviour and the original reason for picking may be forgotten.

The questionnaire below can help you to define whether skin-picking is a problem for you.

QUESTIONNAIRE: DO YOU HAVE A SKIN-PICKING PROBLEM?

1. Do you repeatedly scratch, pick, gouge, dig, rub or squeeze your skin, leading to significant skin damage?

   Yes/No

2. Have you had unsuccessful attempts to stop or decrease your skin-picking?

   Yes/No

   If you answered 'yes' to both of the above questions, then proceed to question 3. If you did not answer 'yes' to both questions then you do not need to complete this questionnaire.

3. Do the urges or behaviours associated with skin-picking cause you marked distress?

   Yes/No

4. Are the urges or behaviours associated with skin-picking significantly time-consuming or do they interfere with your relationships, social life or work?

   Yes/No

5. Do the behaviours result in medical problems (e.g. infections or significant scarring)?

   Yes/No

If you answered 'yes' to the first two questions and to one or more of questions 3 to 5 then you probably have a skin-picking problem. However, only a health professional can diagnose you as suffering from skin-picking disorder or tell you if there is an underlying problem such as BDD. Rarely, a medical condition can account better for your behaviour.

People who pick their skin usually have healthy skin or minimal acne. They target pimples, scabs, mosquito bites, 'large' pores, 'bumps', 'small black dots', 'white dots', 'ugly things', 'cysts' or apparent imperfections or dirt, pus or 'impurities' from under their skin. More often than not, individuals with skin-picking disorder have healthy skin, or at least they had healthy skin until they picked. If you have skin-picking disorder then you might be using your fingernails to pick, pinch or squeeze your skin. Most individuals pick with their fingernails, although some may use tweezers, needles, knives, pins, razor blades or other objects.

The face, arms and hands are the most frequent site for picking, but many individuals pick from multiple body sites. These include the back, neck, scalp, ears, chest and legs. This may lead to marked scarring, infections and visible disfigurement of the skin. There may be rituals such as preparing the skin to be picked, and inspecting the skin visually or by feeling it.

You are likely to avoid activities that involve letting others see damaged skin, such as intimacy, sexual activity or sports. You might be trying to camouflage yourself with cosmetics, clothing or bandages to cover the damage on your skin. We understand that most people are extremely ashamed of their picking and don't want to do it. Some people become housebound or suicidal because of their picking.

Skin-picking tends to occur in the evenings and, for women, either premenstrually or during menstruation. The most common trigger is standing in front of a mirror or touching your skin when you are alone at home. Other triggers include a feeling of itchiness under your skin, or a sensation of something underneath the surface of the skin.

The damage caused by skin-picking ranges from red patches, swelling, blisters, denuded areas and crusts to cuts and scars. Complications can include bleeding, infections, ulcers, permanent discolouration and scarring that is disfiguring. This in turn leads to further scabs or imperfections, which become a further target for skin-picking, creating a vicious circle. The complications can require dermatological treatment, for which you should seek advice. If inflammation is a problem, then dermatological treatment (e.g. hydrocortisone) or Eurax cream (hydrocortisone and crotamiton) can help and decrease the sensation of itching. Dry skin should be moisturised regularly (e.g. using Eucerin). Don't be ashamed to reveal you have a problem with picking – doctors are used to seeing such problems. If, for some reason, your doctor does not seem to understand, you should think about seeing a different one.

In addition to skin-picking, people often have other repetitive behaviours, such as nail-biting, hair-pulling, lip-biting, knuckle-cracking, cheek-chewing or body-rocking. These are all habit disorders that can be treated in a similar way to skin-picking. Research into skin-picking is limited, but the recommended treatment consists of a type of behaviour therapy called self-monitoring and habit reversal, which we describe below.

Completing the questionnaire below will help you to understand your skin-picking problem.

QUESTIONNAIRE: UNDERSTANDING YOUR SKIN-PICKING PROBLEM

The first step in overcoming skin-picking is to have a good understanding of the problem. This will also help the therapist that you see.

1. How old were you when you first started skin-picking?

___

2. How old were you when skin-picking first became a problem?

___

3. What was happening at the time your skin-picking started (e.g. acne or a stressful event)?

___

4. Which areas of your body do you tend to pick? Has this varied over time?

___

5. What do you target for picking (e.g. pimples, scabs, mosquito bites, scars, healthy skin)? Has this varied over time?

___

6. What methods do you currently use to pick (e.g. fingers or fingernails, scratching, squeezing, razors, picking, digging or lancing with pins, tweezers)? Has this varied over time?

___

7. What are the typical times of day when you pick, and how long does each episode last for?

_____

8. Why do you want to stop picking now? Are you ready to stop?

_____

If you are ambivalent about stopping, you might find it helpful to do a cost–benefit analysis. What are the costs and benefits of stopping? What are the costs and benefits of continuing to pick?

A blank version of the cost–benefit analysis form can be found in Appendix 3, or you can print out a version from https://overcoming.co.uk/715/resources-to-download, for further cost–benefit analyses.

The shame of skin-picking

Like many other sufferers, you might feel ashamed of your excessive skin-picking, thinking that you are a freak or should be able to just stop it, which is likely to make you quite secretive about it. Perhaps you even have a parent, friend or partner who has already been quite critical of your skin-picking, and this further increases your desire to not get caught. This can lead to a destructive cycle in which more of your attention gets focused on hiding your skin-picking than on overcoming it. To help combat your shame, you need to begin by taking an accepting and compassionate attitude towards yourself for having the problem. No matter how alarmed someone else might be about your picking, remember that you are in good company and that it is a recognised problem. With calm determination, you can overcome skin-picking, especially if you can detach from unkind and critical thinking about having the problem.

Analysing your skin-picking problem

Triggers (or 'antecedents')

This section asks you to describe in as much detail as possible the chain or sequence of events that leads up to picking. There are two types of trigger: the events immediately before you start picking, and the events that make the picking easier or harder to do.

Triggers before the picking

Two types of trigger usually occur before picking: those that are external (i.e. generated outside of you) or those that are internal (i.e. generated inside you).

Examples of external triggers include different:

- settings (e.g. being alone in front of your bathroom mirror, putting on make-up, driving, planning to go out socially and coming out of the shower, being up late at night on the computer)
- implements (e.g. the presence of a mirror or a pair of tweezers)

- visual triggers (e.g. 'looking in a mirror and seeing a scab').

Examples of internal triggers include:

- emotional states – any emotional state can be a trigger for picking or pulling, but the most common are being bored, lonely, empty, hurt or anxious
- tactile sensations (e.g. 'feeling a bump on your skin with your fingers', 'feeling a tingling sensation on your skin')
- physical sensations at the site (e.g. an itch, irritation, burning under your skin, feeling greasy)
- thoughts – a specific intrusive thought, rumination or image (e.g. 'my skin is dirty and disgusting and has pus under it, I have to get it out. Maybe the pus has been pushed inwards, or maybe it is just swelling up in preparation for a spot appearing but hasn't formed yet').

We want you to describe in as much detail as possible the chain or sequence of events that leads up to your picking – for example, 'I come home feeling tired, I start to think about my skin, I then feel for bumps with my fingers, I go to the bathroom and look for imperfections in the mirror. I see a mark' or 'I start doing my homework in my bedroom, I'm feeling a bit bored and I get a tingling sensation on my skin, I have a thought – that sensation means there is something that shouldn't be there and my hand goes up to my face.'

In the space provided below, describe in as much detail as possible your particular chain of events. There may be several different scenarios you need to describe. If so, continue on another sheet.

_____

_____

_____

_____

_____

_____

How aware are you of the triggers before you start picking, or during your actual picking? Is the picking done 'on autopilot' (where you have little awareness of what you are doing)? Or is it planned? Or is it a mixture of the two?

_____

_____

_____

_____

_____

_____

Triggers that make it easier or harder to pick

The next step is to identify the things that make it easier or harder for you to pick. Examples of external triggers are being with someone or not having a pair of tweezers. Both of these make it harder to pick. However, having a drink might make it easier to pick. Examples of internal triggers that make it easier include certain postures, such as 'holding my hand near my face'. Thoughts that make picking easier include 'I deserve this pick.'

What makes your picking easier to do? Make a note in the space provided below.

_____

_____

_____

_____

What makes your picking harder to do? Again, make a note in the space provided below.

_____

_____

_____

_____

Picking behaviour

Next, write down a detailed description of your actual picking, in sequence. There are usually three different stages:

1. In the preparatory stage, you might go to a specific place, find your implements, choose a site on the body, and inspect or clean the skin excessively.
2. In the second stage, you might pick the skin, squeeze it, gouge it, remove and examine it.
3. The final stage usually involves getting rid of the skin and perhaps camouflaging it with cover-up sticks or using make-up.

In the space below, describe the sequence of what you do in as much detail as possible.

_____

_____

_____

_____

_____

_____

Consequences: the effects of picking

What are the immediate consequences of your picking that provide a pay-off? For example, you might get a positive feeling of satisfaction from removing a scab; or it might be escape from bad feelings such as feeling lonely or bored, or a physical sensation.

_____

_____

_____

_____

What are the unintended consequences of your picking? Examples might include the physical damage, such as ulcers or scarring, or a deep sense of shame, or criticism from others.

_____

_____

_____

_____

What leads you to finish picking?

Examples might include feeling ashamed (which could also act as a trigger for further picking), or because you become aware of the damage you are causing or you are feeling pain. Alternatively, you might finish because someone interrupts or you have to leave for an appointment.

_____

_____

Taking steps to overcome your picking

Having done your analysis, you will now be able to choose the most appropriate steps to take and when to use them. We'll assume that you are 'ready' to change and you want to stop (or at least reduce how often you pick), rather than just wanting to stop feeling ashamed about your picking.

If you are not ready to change, then it won't work and you may need to talk through some of the benefits and costs of picking with a therapist first. It may not be the right time because there are stresses in your life (unrelated to skin-picking).

You may need to test out your motivation to pick. For example, if you believe 'I must have smooth skin or I will be rejected', you can test this belief by seeing whether others do indeed respond to you differently on a day when you feel worse about your skin. You may find that they don't react to you any differently, or that you can cope with this belief differently.

Step 1: Self-monitoring

The first step towards overcoming compulsive skin-picking is self-monitoring. The rationale for self-monitoring is that:

- you increase your awareness of your picking, so you are better able to resist the urge
- you can build on the analysis you have already done and identify different chains of events so it is possible to predict when and where future episodes of picking will occur; being more aware of the chain of events allows you to anticipate high-risk situations, and therefore to resist the urge to pick
- you can monitor whether or not what you do to help yourself works by a change in how often you pick.

We have provided a skin-picking self-monitoring form here. Try to complete it while you are picking or immediately after picking, so it will be as accurate as possible. Do this for at least one or two weeks and keep a record of the number of times you picked each day. When this is frequent you might find it easier to count how often you pick by using a tally counter, which you can order online.

COMPULSIVE SKIN-PICKING AND OTHER HABITS

SKIN-PICKING SELF-MONITORING FORM

Date/time	Duration: How long did you pick for?	Location: Where were you?	Activity: What were you doing before picking?	Strength of urge to pick on a scale of 0 to 10, where 0 is no urge	Degree of awareness of picking on a scale of 0 to 10, where 0 is no awareness	Notable feelings before you picked (0–100%)	Notable thoughts or images before you picked	Notable sensations before you picked (e.g. itching or burning)
1.								
2.								

Step 2: Using habit reversal

You can train your mind to stop picking by using a method called habit reversal. First, you need to identify a 'competing response' that is incompatible with picking (for example, clenching your hand into a fist, clasping your hands together tightly, sitting on your hands by moving them under your thighs while you are seated, or squeezing a ball in your hands).

Whatever you choose:

- it should be incompatible with the habit
- it should be possible to maintain for a minute or more
- if you are with others, you should be able to do it without behaving oddly
- it should not interfere with normal activities
- it should heighten your awareness that the picking is not occurring.

Practise the competing response at times of the day when you are not picking so that it becomes a habit. It should be held for at least one or two minutes until the urge to pick has subsided. You should also practise the competing response in your imagination and ten times in a row at least three times a day when there is no urge to pick. In this way it will eventually become automatic and a part of your routine. It may be helpful to practise relaxing and breathing with your diaphragm when the picking urge occurs, before applying the competing response.

Now introduce the competing response as soon as you are aware of your urge to pick. If you start to pick, use the competing response to interrupt the picking, or use it as soon as you have finished picking. If the urge persists, then the competing response should be repeated. When you get the urge, just notice the urge and any intrusive thoughts and feelings, without buying into them. When you have been successful, encourage yourself immediately after successfully resisting an urge to pick. The more often you use the competing response, the easier it will then become.

An alternative to a competing response is described by Dr Steffen Moritz in Germany, who calls his method 'decoupling'. It makes sense to us and there is some evidence for its benefit in BFRBs. Decoupling consists of two steps during which the unwanted behaviour, such as skin-picking, is slowly replaced and unlearned. It works by mimicking and redirecting the old movements so that they lead to a dead end. For example, imagine moving your hand and fingers towards your face as if you are about to pick, but do not allow your fingers to touch your skin where you would pick. Instead, quickly flick your hand and deflect it towards your ear just before contact. The fingers still make contact, but not with the skin on your face. In this case, contact is made with the earlobe instead. Thus, the urge is satisfied but in a way that doesn't result in a skin damage. *The new movement should be performed with some tension and acceleration* to ensure that you are fully conscious of the old behavioural routine of skin-picking being diverted. A key issue for decoupling is that the alternative, replacement behaviour is similar to the old behaviour. This makes it easier to unlearn or redirect the old behaviour.

You'll need to practise the new 'decoupled' behaviour several times a day with full awareness. Practise it ten times in a row each time you do it, and do it at least three times a day. You may find it helpful to set an alarm on your smartphone for when you tend to do the skin-picking.

Keep a record of your practice, and the number of times you use the competing response or decoupling, on the habit reversal form provided below. Note whether you used the competing response before, during or after an episode of picking. You can also use the form to keep a record of the number of times you practised the competing response when there was no urge to pick.

You should have identified a typical chain of events in your analysis. Although the goal is to use the competing response before the chain begins, you may have to start by introducing the competing response near the end of the chain. With practice, you will be able to add the competing response earlier and earlier in the chain so that it eventually replaces the picking.

It is worth emphasising that the success of the technique cannot at first be measured in terms of reducing how often you pick but by whether you are using the competing response at all (even if you use it after you pick). This is important, as many people will otherwise give up too early.

COMPULSIVE SKIN-PICKING AND OTHER HABITS

HABIT REVERSAL FORM

Site: Where did you pick?	What effect did picking have on your feelings?	What effect did picking have on your thoughts?	What effect did picking have on your sensations?	How strong was your effort to resist picking on a scale of 0 to 10, where 0 is no effort at all?	What did you do to try to resist picking?
1.					
2.					

Step 3: Making it less likely that you will pick

There are various things you can do to help you relax in the high-risk situations that you identified in your self-monitoring chart. You could use meditation or exercise, take a warm bath, do some relaxation exercises or diaphragmatic breathing. Have an action plan ready with a list of the activities you can do when you get the urge (e.g. do some exercise, make a phone call, bake a cake). Try to distract yourself when the urge occurs (e.g. have a bath or shower – possibly a cold shower; apply an ice pack, especially if you have an itching or burning sensation on your skin; or put on a facial mask).

Some people have found that it is easier to resist the urge to pick by wearing gloves, using artificial (acrylic) nails over their real nails or cutting their fingernails short. These strategies may also enhance awareness training as they alter the sensations on the skin. Try sticking 'High-risk area' signs on the door of the bathroom and other areas associated with picking.

Various strategies can help block the habit by decreasing the opportunity to pick – for example, agreeing not to touch your skin unless it is for an agreed activity; wearing bandages on the fingers you use for picking; wearing white cotton dermatological gloves in bed or other high-risk areas; keeping your nails trimmed and smooth. Some people have enlarged a photo of the area of picking, taken at its worst, and kept it by the most common locations for picking. Others have used a reminder of all the unintended consequences of picking, which you can easily read in locations where you are likely to pick.

Step 4: Disrupt your triggers to pick

Try to disrupt the chain of events in your daily routines that lead to picking. This might mean altering the settings in which you pick to disrupt your opportunity to pick, and reducing the time spent in high-risk areas. For example, you could:

- remove or temporarily cover mirrors (especially magnifying mirrors) or bright lights
- wear dark or tinted glasses when around mirrors
- remove any glasses or contact lenses before looking in a mirror
- give the equipment you use for picking to a significant other, or throw it away
- switch grooming and applying make-up to times of the day when they are less risky
- stay out of certain high-risk area rooms or find an alternative
- tell a significant other(s) about your picking and allow them to point it out when you pick
- reduce time spent alone and adopt a different routine
- use plasters and petroleum jelly or antibiotic ointment on scabs and skin to aid healing.

Step 5: Stimulate or distract yourself

It may also be necessary to replace or increase stimulation in your fingers in high-risk situations. This could include activities such as knitting, crocheting, embroidery or sewing; playing a musical instrument (or taking lessons); stroking or massaging a pet; playing with Silly Putty or squeezy balls; popping the bubbles on bubble wrap; playing with worry beads; playing a video game that requires the use of both hands on a controller; nibbling food (e.g. sunflower seeds); or taking a facial steam bath (to provide a feeling that impurities are being removed from your face).

Step 6: Cue exposure

When you are ready, and have managed to stop picking for a few months, try re-exposing yourself to those situations that are associated with picking. You should begin with low-risk situations for short periods of time (e.g. up to five minutes). You can then gradually increase the time and location, eventually reaching high-risk situations. Continue to resist the urge to pick, and try to visualise your desired outcome instead of picking.

Below is a description of Sharon's experience of overcoming skin-picking.

Sharon is twenty-nine years old. She usually picks her skin in the bathroom mirror at night when her boyfriend is asleep and she has privacy, or when she has just come home and checks her skin when she feels dirty and tired. This is more likely to occur if she feels anxious, bored, brooding, hurt or frustrated. When she sees or feels a spot or blemish, immediately she will squeeze it and it will lead her to check and squeeze the rest of her face. Sometimes she will feel a scab in the morning in bed and mindlessly pick it, even if it has not healed. Touching and looking at scabs often will lead her to pick them off before they have healed (which then leaves a scar and leads to a further bout of squeezing and scabs). Physical sensations such as feeling greasy or throbbing will also make her more likely to pick. Her picking might also start while feeling her face for small imperfections, which is done automatically with no intention of picking. The problem becomes more voluntary if she happens to find a blemish. She then becomes like a shark smelling blood, something else takes over and she feels she cannot stop.

She will not squeeze in front of others (apart from very superficial squeezing in front of a family member). The absence of tweezers will probably help for the rare occasions that she might use them. The absence of mirrors, a hand compact or bright lighting helps her not to pick. If it is hot and humid and she feels sweaty, then she feels her skin gets spottier and so her urge to squeeze increases. She then thinks her skin is greasy and pus is gathering under the skin and her skin is getting out of control. If she aimlessly puts her fingers over her skin, this encourages picking. If she has scars forming, then she tells herself that she will allow herself to pick at just one spot, as if to appease her craving. Unfortunately, this always triggers further picking. Very occasionally if she has resisted the urge to pick then she thinks she can reward herself, and releases the tension and allows herself to squeeze. Initially it feels like a relief, but this is short-lived as it prompts further picking, and she then feels deflated and angry with herself.

When she does pick she just squeezes the spot with her fingernails. Usually she will squeeze it a bit more than necessary to ensure everything is out. If it is deep down, sometimes she will scratch off the first layer of skin with her nails and then squeeze it, so it has a way of being expelled rather than sinking deeper. If the pus will not come out, sometimes she makes it worse when she really scratches at her skin until it bleeds and presses the flesh together to squeeze it in a very violent way. Sometimes she will use tweezers to pluck the flesh and hairs away. The amount of stuff becomes insignificant and laughable when she sees how little it is, but she feels satisfied as it no longer feels under her skin. If it has been an insignificant picking session that hasn't caused much damage, she will usually just splash her face with cold water, cover up the spots with make-up and go to sleep (so that her boyfriend will not be able to see her spots in the darkness). But if she has caused a lot of damage to her face, usually she will have to wash her face, and apply make-up for hours, in between holding a tissue or cloth to her wounds to soak up the fluid. She has to stop the fluid flowing so that she can apply the make-up powder in a way that it sticks.

The immediate pay-off is a sense of satisfaction if she has squeezed a lot of pus out, especially if it is a 'problem spot', which means one she has been trying to expel the pus from for a while but been unable to. Very occasionally, if the squeezing is straightforward and not messy, and hasn't left any significant damage or red marks, she feels extremely proud of herself that she has managed to clean up her face without losing control and hurting herself.

However, the long-term consequence is shame and anger against herself. This just triggers her to pick more. Ultimately what usually stops her is when she is feeling out of control in her picking and there is nothing more to squeeze, making her face an absolute mess. In these cases it is not shame or realisation of damage that stops her. It is simply impossible to squeeze anything else out.

Sharon found the functional analysis helpful in making sense of her skin-picking. The act of self-monitoring started to make her more aware of her picking and times of vulnerability, and how her picking became a self-perpetuating cycle. She found it particularly helpful to identify frequent chains of events that inevitably resulted in skin-picking. Having identified the chain of events, she found it important to talk to her boyfriend and get his support in encouraging her to go to bed earlier. She would also talk to a friend on the telephone or have a cold shower, in order to disrupt the chain of events when she came home and felt vulnerable. She found it helpful to have a Turkish bath at the gym, so she felt that impurities were being removed. Of course it was not all plain sailing and there were frequent setbacks. However, she practised habit reversal as soon as she was aware that the chain had begun. At first she practised a competing response (clenching her fist) after she had picked and in situations that did not lead to picking. She then gradually managed to increase awareness of her actions. She had some success with the competing response but then decided to use decoupling at an earlier stage. This meant practising by moving her hand towards her face and then, before she touched her skin, she tensed her hand and fingers and quickly flicked it towards her earlobe. She practised several times a day, so that eventually she was able to use the decoupling before she picked. Her skin improved and she had help to reduce her self-consciousness, learning not to engage with the skin-picking.

PIT STOP

Let's stop and think about what you have just been reading. Can you summarise the key ideas you have taken on board? What is sticking in your mind? Maybe write it down. If you have any questions, jot those down too. You can return to them once you have had a chance to digest the information.

What is sticking in my mind from my reading so far?

1.

2.

3.

11

Special problems of disfiguring conditions

This chapter is written for people with disfiguring conditions. If you have body dysmorphic disorder (BDD) or an eating disorder and are preoccupied by a defect in your appearance that others cannot really notice, you might be intrigued by the way in which people with disfiguring conditions cope with an unusual appearance. This is something that health professionals have found interesting too. It can seem self-evident that someone with very severe burns scarring is going to find life more problematic than someone with, say, minor scaring from acne, but in fact there is no evidence for this. One of the ways that the principles outlined below can be helpful for someone with BDD would be for them to assume temporarily that the flaw in their appearance *is* as bad as they think it is, and then follow the advice outlined in this chapter.

> *Geraldine has very severe burns scarring resulting from a house fire. The scarring is visible all over her body. One of the practical problems she has is keeping cool*

in the summer, since she cannot lose heat through her skin via sweating. The easiest thing for her is to swim. She does so several times a day when it is very hot. She knows that people notice her scarring and sometimes ask about it. She has therefore developed some good answers to questions, which give a minimum of information but satisfy other people's curiosity: 'I know I'm unusual, and I understand that people are curious, but I don't intend to tell them my life story.' Geraldine is confident, successful and good fun to be with. She has a partner and her appearance is not a barrier to living a full life.

Louise has very minor scarring on her face following a car accident. She is very aware of it, but it is hardly noticeable to other people. She manages this by wearing a baseball cap pulled down low so that no one can see her face, and she avoids eye contact or speaking to other people. She has stopped working and any kind of social activity, and does not go out. Her life has changed dramatically and her mood is low. She is very pessimistic and feels that her chances of a happy life are now over. She is not unusual in feeling devastated by a relatively minor change, and what makes this worse for her is the well-meaning family and friends who tell her that she is making a fuss about nothing and that, compared with other people, there is nothing really wrong with her.

Even though Geraldine rates her condition as far more noticeable than Louise's, she is less preoccupied by it. The target of treatment for Louise will be to reduce her level of preoccupation and worry. Geraldine, of course, does not need any treatment!

Many people with very obvious disfigurements live totally normal lives – so what is it that makes concerns about appearance such a problem for some people and not for others? Why is Geraldine able to manage, while Louise is finding life so hard?

The answer has a lot to do with the value placed on appearance. In the following diagram, a circle has been divided up to represent the importance of appearance to different aspects of Geraldine's identity.

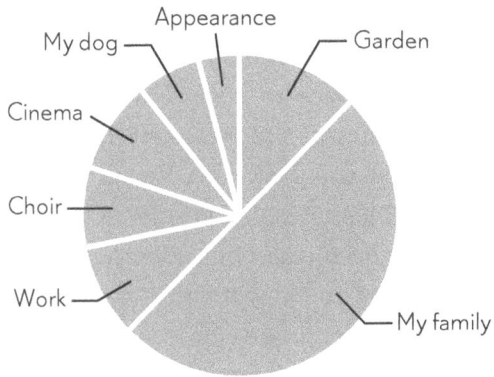

You can see that 'appearance' occupies one 'slice' of the pie. Most people are concerned that they fit in to their peer group and do not stand out in a negative way. For teenagers, this slice might be larger. But there are lots of other slices too. Much more important here are 'my family' and 'my dog'. 'Work' is a slice, 'cinema' and 'choir' are additional slices, and so on.

For some people, the 'appearance slice' can take over the whole circle. The preoccupation with a particular feature, and the search for a means of changing it, becomes more important than many of the other things in their life. Before treatment, that's what Louise's pie chart looked like. She felt very self-conscious, unable to cope with the idea that people would notice her face, and her self-esteem had sunk low. After treatment, her preoccupation with appearance was far less, she was able to go out and her social life started to take up much more space in the circle again.

Psychological treatments aim to help people manage their concerns about appearance and gradually restore the appearance slice back to a small or moderate level of importance. Self-esteem and self-confidence depend on far more than what you look like. We all like to feel that other people think about us in a positive way. Although we may believe (and the media encourage us to believe) that appearance has a lot to do with this, our behaviour and personality are far more important in how we are regarded by other people. One of the most attractive things about other people, and something that makes you feel good about yourself, is being comfortable in social situations and able to demonstrate an interest in other people rather than yourself. People who we know cope well with visible difference or disfigurement tend to be those who have very good social skills.

SPECIAL PROBLEMS OF DISFIGURING CONDITIONS

In this chapter, we look at the particular challenges faced by someone who has an obvious facial difference, together with the practical ways of meeting these challenges. Even if you do not consider yourself to have a facial difference, it is worthwhile reading this chapter and using some of these skills and strategies yourself. They will help you to 'focus out' on what is happening in social situations rather than 'focusing in' and becoming preoccupied with what people are thinking about you; this is the key to becoming more comfortable with other people and gradually building your self-esteem.

Causes of visible difference

Visible difference is more common than we think. Severe burn injuries, accidents and trauma such as dog bites, account for some changes in the way people look. Skin conditions, cancer and other diseases account for more. Thyroid gland problems can have an impact on the appearance of your eyes, and rheumatic diseases can change the appearance of your joints, particularly in the fingers. Steroid medication can alter the shape of your face and body; chemotherapy can cause hair loss. Surgery to remove cancer can leave scars. There are therefore many people who experience visible changes in their appearance related to accident or illness. A second group of people are those who are born with a visible difference. This includes conditions such as cleft lip and palate, birthmarks such as port wine stains, and other craniofacial syndromes that affect the way in which the bones of the skull are fused together and therefore the appearance of the face. Research has demonstrated many similarities between all these groups in terms of the kinds of challenges that are faced in day-to-day life, and therefore we treat any problems that arise in the same way.

The problems of visible difference

Staring by others is commonly reported. The human brain is hardwired to take note of anything that is unusual or outside our experience. You can see that babies and children are constantly gazing at objects and people as they build up a picture of the world. This curiosity never leaves us – we may learn some social skills that prevent us from staring at others, but most of us will notice, or do a 'double take', when we see someone who looks unusual. It is important to note that this is a response stimulated by curiosity. It can feel like a problem, though, if it is accompanied by comments, questions or a whispered aside to a companion. However, some people feel as if they are being stared at when the problem is more to do with being excessively self-conscious and worrying about what others are thinking. You may only be sure that people are staring, for example, if it is confirmed by someone else who is with you or the person staring is asking questions or pointing at you.

Questions are common. Curiosity is often followed by the impulse to ask more: 'I hope you don't mind me asking, but what happened to you?' There are not many people with a visible difference who are not familiar with this response from other people. Choosing how to answer this question is important in determining whether the encounter is going to be a positive one.

Comments — either directly to you or about you to others — are often infuriating, even if kindly meant. 'I think you are so brave, dear' is designed to be reassuring but can feel patronising and unhelpful. 'People like you should stay at home' tells you far more about the ignorance of the person who makes the comment than the person it is made about but can still be experienced as hurtful and aggressive.

Loss of anonymity is a way of summing up this experience. Many of us underestimate the luxury of being able to walk down a crowded street and know that no one is taking any notice of us. The sense that we stand out, that others notice us or pay us special attention can be uncomfortable. Note that people whose faces are well known, who have become celebrities, often complain about this kind of intrusion. Attention does not have to be negative to impact in a negative way — it simply needs to be unsolicited, or outside your control. The fear of standing out, of people looking at us, is extremely common in all kinds of body image disorder and can lead to unhelpful choices in how we respond. The easiest thing is avoidance. If you stay at home or avoid crowded places, then this apparently solves the problem — except, as we have seen elsewhere in this book, it is important to confront fears by learning the skills that allow us to stay in situations we find difficult. In doing so, we become able to do everything that anyone else can, without constant worry about whether people are looking at us or what they think.

Note that for many people with body image concerns, it is the fear of standing out, of looking unusual or 'ugly', that preoccupies them and prevents them participating fully in social activities. For someone with a visible disfigurement, the fear that someone will notice is often a reality. People do notice, they are curious and they do ask questions. But this is manageable. In treating people with a visible difference, we work on the basis that intrusions will definitely happen so we are going to learn how to manage them – from dealing with staring to answering questions in different ways. Mastering these skills is not difficult – in fact, they are useful life skills for anyone to develop. For people with body image problems generally, working out how you would deal with the thing you fear most is far better than simply dreading it happening and avoiding other people in case it does. This might mean practising a role play with a friend so you will know how to cope with questions or other people making comments.

Interpreting the world around you

Before we go on to think about managing an unusual appearance, it is worth considering some key pieces of research that tell us more about how the way you think, and your beliefs or expectations, colour the way in which you interpret what happens around you.

In the 1980s, psychologists interested in social research used make-up to mimic different kinds of visible difference, including port wine stains (a purple mark) on the

SPECIAL PROBLEMS OF DISFIGURING CONDITIONS

face and facial scarring. They were interested in measuring the experience that people who had these conditions were reporting. The participants in these experiments were asked to report back on how it felt to stand out in a crowd – and they reported many experiences of discomfort, staring by others and generally feeling conspicuous. So this seemed to support the things that people with a visible difference were telling us. However, half this experimental group did not in fact appear disfigured at all. Before sending them out to gather data, the researchers had removed the make-up with a solvent while pretending that they were 'fixing it' or setting it so that it would not rub off. These groups reported just the same experience of intrusion and staring from others as the group who really did look different.

How can we make sense of this? The best way is by acknowledging that we tend to see what we expect to see. So if we go into a situation with a preconceived idea of what is going to happen, it is very easy to interpret what happens in line with this. There is another explanation. It may be that when we expect a hostile or intrusive response from others, we change our behaviour, and it is this change that attracts people's attention. For example, we may avoid eye contact, walk with our head down, pull a baseball cap low over our face – all patterns of behaviour that are very understandable when we feel conspicuous, but that have the opposite effect from that intended: they attract rather than reduce attention. While both of these accounts explain what the researchers discovered, they are not mutually exclusive – in other words, the findings may be due to a little of both.

The psychologist Professor Nichola Rumsey was very interested in the second explanation: the idea that people may change their behaviour when they have visible differences. She continued to carry out research into this 'behavioural' explanation for the problem of facial difference. She was intrigued, partly because she had observed 'avoidant' behaviour in people who had problems managing facial difference, but also because she believed that social skills training, or learning to behave differently in social situations, might be a way of teaching people skills that they could use to cope more positively. By chance, she met James Partridge, who had set up a charity, Changing Faces, to help people with facial disfigurements, following his experience in managing his own burn injury. They discovered that they had come to the same conclusions from their completely different backgrounds in the subject. Good social skills could profoundly alter and improve the experience of facial difference. Changing Faces then developed this social skills idea further, while Professor Rumsey evaluated their findings and demonstrated that their ideas really worked.

Managing facial difference using a CBT approach

Cognitive behavioural therapy (CBT), as you have seen throughout this book, is a means of changing the way in which you think about a problem and how you actually behave. Psychologists working in this field have developed the CBT approach to include social skills training, and have

SPECIAL PROBLEMS OF DISFIGURING CONDITIONS

shown that this is the most effective way to help people who do not cope very confidently with a visible difference. The aim is to teach people to manage as effectively as those for whom having a visible difference is not a barrier to achieving all that they want to. In the UK, the charity Changing Faces has made a huge contribution to the development, evaluation and publicising of these approaches, and this section draws on its work.

Identifying and challenging unhelpful beliefs

We have seen that certain kinds of 'thinking styles', or unhelpful patterns of thinking, can become automatic (see Chapter 5). Many people – particularly if their appearance changes suddenly – can 'write themselves off' and convince themselves that they no longer have the opportunities the rest of us may have. 'All-or-nothing' thinking often lies behind this.

Examples include:

- 'No one is going to employ someone who looks like this'
- 'I am never going to get a girlfriend looking the way I do'
- 'None of my friends will want to know me any more'
- 'How can I take the children to school when I look like this?'

These are all real examples, and they are all examples of all-or-nothing thinking, which can lead to people writing themselves off. One way of reducing the harm that these negative thoughts can cause is by keeping a record of them on paper. You can then distance yourself from such thoughts and not engage with them (see Chapter 6). You can also examine the evidence for each belief and see if there is an alternative. For example, for the belief 'No one is going to employ someone who looks like this', is it true to say that no one would employ someone with a visible difference? Clearly not. Many people with an unusual appearance have jobs just like anyone else. So an alternative belief might be:

- Most employers are looking for someone with good skills and experience, who is prepared to work hard and who is reliable.

Similarly, the belief 'I am never going to get a girlfriend looking the way I do' is about partnerships. Many people with a visible difference are married or in happy long-term relationships with others. So a more realistic belief might be:

- Happy relationships are based on who you are, not what you look like.

The belief 'None of my friends will want to know me any more' can be challenged:

- Good friends enjoy being with me because they have a good time – not because of how I look.

Finally, 'How can I take the children to school when I look like this?' Children are far less interested in appearances than adults are. Given a good explanation, and provided they see that you are coping well with your altered appearance, they will cope well too.

Note that the alternatives given above avoid the all-or-nothing patterns typical of the unhelpful beliefs. We are not challenging the idea that finding a girlfriend or a job may sometimes be harder – we live in a very appearance-conscious society where some people may make judgements that are overly dependent on appearance. But it is not true that all, or even most, people think in this way.

Remember the example we gave above about the make-up experiments, of how anticipating a problem can become a self-fulfilling prophecy? This is very true when it comes to finding a job or developing a relationship. If you write yourself off before you get there, this will come across in the interview. If you appear confident and self-assured, this will act in your favour. It is very tempting to label lack of success in terms of appearance. The reason you do not get a job is equally likely to be because there was a better candidate with more experience. The reason someone does not want to go out with you may equally be because you do not share the same interests or think very differently about important issues.

Another very common example of all-or-nothing thinking is the belief that 'Everybody's staring at me!' Again, a cognitive behavioural therapist would examine the evidence for holding this belief. One way of doing this is by designing a 'behavioural experiment'.

George, who was anxious about being stared at, conducted the following behavioural experiment. He decided to count how many people he passed on the way to his office from the train station. He also kept a note of how many people stared hard in his direction.

How many people I expect to stare	Most of them, 90%
How many people did I pass?	About 100
How many people stared?	One, therefore 1%

George noted that he had passed about a hundred people and only one had stared at him. So he was easily able to challenge his all-or-nothing thinking. In fact, 99 per cent of people took no notice of him. (There was a nice bonus to this experiment; the person who had been staring hard at him finally came up and asked him directions; far from being identified in a negative way, George had been identified in a positive way as someone who looked friendly and helpful.)

Personalisation

Another common type of thinking error that characterises people with appearance-related concerns is personalisation. This is the tendency to think that every mention of appearance is somehow stimulated by seeing you. So if someone comments that someone else is looking fatter, has let themselves go, should get a haircut, or similar, you may think:

- They are really thinking that I should do something about my appearance.
- It is really my nose that is making them think about another person's appearance.

Again, challenging these thoughts is done by looking for evidence to support them, and then finding an alternative explanation that is equally likely to account for what was said. We have provided a form that can be used to consider an alternative explanation, which can then be tested out in an experiment.

Alternative explanations form

Date/time	What happened?	What did you think?	How could you challenge this?	How could you test it out?

Here is an example of someone using this form, who had a very large and distinctive nose characteristic of his racial group.

Date, time	What happened?	What did you think?	How could you challenge this?	How could you test it out?
Saturday, 8 pm	I was sitting with friends in the pub and they started talking about a programme they had seen on TV about plastic surgery	It is because they have noticed my nose – it has reminded them …	Lots of people are interested in plastic surgery. They may be thinking about surgery themselves	I could say: 'I thought it was interesting too. Would you ever think about surgery?'

When he asked the question noted in the right-hand column, his friend responded by telling him about his sister who had recently had a breast-reduction operation. He was then able to reduce the strength of his belief that it was his appearance that had triggered the conversation.

Are you making the most of your appearance?

Before considering behaviour and how to change it, it is worth making a particular point about appearance. We have already talked about write-off thinking. One common mistake people can make is to think that because they have a visible difference, it is not worth bothering with other aspects of appearance. This could not be more wrong! If you give other people a strong message that you have given up on yourself, why would they be interested in you?

So – you *do* need to have your hair cut or styled regularly. You *do* need to dress in a way that is appropriate for your lifestyle. Wearing appropriate clothes, looking tidy and ensuring that you do not have food spilt all down you is important. Your personal hygiene should be good. Making an effort to fit into your peer group will help people to see you for who you are and not as an outsider. In this context, it is important to note that, sometimes, clothes or make-up designed to be helpful or to disguise a feature can have the opposite effect. Baseball caps are particularly unhelpful and we work hard with our patients to get rid of them. UK society associates them with aggressive behaviour, and you can easily make yourself look threatening, especially if wearing a cap is associated with poor eye contact. It usually is – reducing eye contact is why people wear them! (See also the discussion of the role of safety-seeking behaviours in Chapter 7.) Similarly, wearing very large jackets in the summer draws attention to people rather than disguising problems, and unskilled use of camouflage creams can make a facial disfigurement more rather than less obvious.

Catastrophising

This is a common pattern that people with a visible disfigurement fall into. Having noticed someone glance your way, the negative automatic thoughts follow this sort of course: 'Oh no, I hope she doesn't notice my face. She is thinking how awful I look and wondering how she can get away from me. She is just like everyone else. What's the use of coming to places like this – it always ends up being the same. I shall never fit in; I shall never have any friends or be able to enjoy my life. What's the point of living like this?'

You can see that the first automatic thought has triggered a whole spiral of further negatives so that just the thought of being noticed has led to feeling life is not worth living, which may then lead you to start brooding, as described in Chapter 5. This catastrophic outcome has evolved in six steps from the simple question of whether or not someone has looked your way! This is also an example of writing negative scripts for other people based on no evidence. In fact, when we do some behavioural experiments, we often find that people have not noticed anything unusual. They may find it hard to describe the person who believes their appearance to be so distinctive. Or they may express surprise that the person is so worried by it because it makes no difference to the judgements they make about them. It is therefore really important to stop yourself and challenge the automatic thought at the start, and before you allow these unhelpful beliefs to depress your mood and change your behaviour.

Developing a positive approach to visible difference

Social skills are a good place to start. We talked above about

SPECIAL PROBLEMS OF DISFIGURING CONDITIONS

making the most of your appearance. Go through your wardrobe and check for anything that needs either washing or mending. You do not have to always wear black. One of the things we encourage people to do as they become more confident is to wear clothes that are more colourful and help to challenge the idea that you are trying to hide. How do you style your hair? It can be tempting to wear a long fringe or to try to drape your hair over your face to cover a facial condition, but keeping this in place means walking with your head down. Like hats, this is less helpful than it might seem. If you have a disfiguring condition elsewhere on your body, then wearing long sleeves and high-necked tops can be automatic, but you can become dependent on them.

> *Veronica, who had a skin condition called vitiligo, developed patches on her skin that lacked pigment. She always used make-up to camouflage her skin. Veronica was worried that she would get constant questions from other people. As her skin condition progressed, she got fed up with the time it was taking to put on the make-up. She decided to try going out with her face bare. To her surprise, although people glanced her way, they really took very little notice of her. She decided that she would wear her make-up some, but not all, of the time. Now, if she is going to work or if she is dressing up to go somewhere special, she wears it. But if she is home with her family or with friends that she knows well, she does not bother.*

This example illustrates the kind of cognitive errors that we described earlier. The beliefs that 'everyone will notice and ask me questions', 'everyone will think my scars are ugly' were successfully overcome by Veronica putting them to the test.

Posture

How you stand is important. If you tend to look down and away from people, your behaviour is not open and inviting. Try to make a conscious effort to stand upright and look straight ahead.

Smiling

You will be amazed at the difference it makes when you look at other people and smile. This gives a positive message instantly! Sometimes when people have a facial condition that means their face either moves asymmetrically (more on one side than the other) or, for some people without a facial nerve, not at all, they are unable to smile, or try to avoid it. Using other forms of communication – commenting on the situation or using touch – can be ways of signalling pleasure. For those of us who can smile, responding to others in this way, on the bus, in a queue, in the street, gives a very different message from hurrying past, head down.

Eye contact

Eye contact is the basis of communication with one another

(think how difficult it is to communicate with someone who wears dark glasses). We use it to signal interest, that we are listening and whose turn it is to speak in a conversation. Trying to avoid the gaze of others will always come across as negative. You are giving a clear signal that you do not want to engage in any kind of contact with them. It is very easy to misinterpret other people's gaze as intrusive – staring at a feature you dislike – when in fact people are simply trying to talk to you. There are lots of good books and information about improving social skills. The charity Changing Faces publishes information directly relevant to the issues that may concern you.

Developing verbal skills: learning to have a conversation

People often describe the fear of going blank in social settings – being unable to think of what to say. It is more likely to happen when you are focused 'in' on your own appearance and how people are responding to you, rather than listening and being involved in what people are saying. Anxiety tends to heighten the temptation to 'self-monitor', so it can be doubly hard to relax and really focus on what is going on around you rather than other people's reactions to you. (See Chapter 6 for some strategies to help you overcome problems with inattention.)

It can also be hard to get going again if you have been avoiding social situations because of concerns about staring or questions. (This is another reason to avoid withdrawing from others – it is much harder to pick up again than to keep your social life going, even if at a slower pace.)

Developing verbal skills is a matter of practice, but there are some simple things that will help. First, it is helpful to listen. What do other people talk about in different settings? The easiest place to start is at work or in a situation where you have lots in common with the other people there, or are with a group of people that you know well. You might have friends in common and can ask how they are. You might have a job in common and can ask about that. Asking people about themselves is a very productive way to get a conversation started. So asking if people live nearby, what they do for living, whether their children go to the local school, and similar questions, are all ways of initiating a conversation. Similarly, topical subjects are things that other people will have a view about, so the result of the latest big football match or recent election, the price of petrol or prominent news stories are all good places to start.

It can be a good idea to identify something about the other person that you can use as a question if there is a pause in the conversation. For instance, you might notice someone is wearing a particular piece of jewellery or an interesting tie. T-shirts often have slogans or flags, or something you can comment about. If someone looks tanned, you can ask if they have been on holiday. (Note that, in this context, it is not surprising that people ask about your appearance if it is something that stands out – it is something about you that is unusual and therefore an ideal way of getting you to talk about yourself. Other people are simply using the same tactic as you are using yourself.)

Practising with a friend is a good way to build your skills and confidence. Try the following role-playing exercises.

ROLE-PLAYING EXERCISES

1. You arrive at a crowded party. You can't see anyone you know. Another person is standing on their own looking as if they do not recognise anyone. They are wearing an Arsenal football shirt. Ask your friend to play this role. Now you go over and start a conversation with them.

2. Imagine that your car has broken down miles from anywhere. You phone the AA, but when the mechanic arrives they can't mend your car. They call for assistance and decide to wait with you. What can you talk to them about? (There is a good chance that they are interested in cars!) Ask your friend to role-play the mechanic, and see how long you can sustain the conversation.

Answering questions about your appearance

We have already seen that questions from others are likely, but are related to curiosity and not a negative judgement about you. However, it is important that you do not feel trapped into giving away more information than feels comfortable. You do not have to tell 'your story' to other people unless you want to. We would advise you to develop three different ways of answering questions about your appearance.

Think about answering the question 'What happened to your face?' Here we suggest some alternative ways you could respond to it.

Q: *'What happened to your face?'*
A: *'I was in a house fire. It started at two in the morning and the first thing I remember is waking up and all the heat and the noise. My mother ran into the room . . . [etc., etc.]'*

This kind of answer is full, detailed and often lengthy. It is best reserved for the medical team who have been involved in your care and those very close to you, when relevant. However, interestingly, for people who worry about answering questions about their appearance, it is often the only one they ever use – with the result that they feel conspicuous and as if their private life is an open book to anyone who wants to know. Not surprisingly, they dread that opening line 'I hope you don't mind me asking, but . . .'.

The second answer is the complete opposite. It is a simple response that closes down the questioning firmly, while giving very little or no detail.

Q: *'What happened to your face?'*
A: *'It's a long story. I'll tell you about it some time'* or *'It was years ago – you don't want to hear all about that.'*

SPECIAL PROBLEMS OF DISFIGURING CONDITIONS

Together with firm eye contact and a smile, both these answers work superbly at turning off the questioning. They are particularly effective if you then switch the attention to the questioner. For example:

Q: *'What happened to your face?'*
A: *'It's a long story. I'll tell you about it some time. I hear you've just come back from America. How long were you there?'*

The third way of answering the question is to give a more general response, about your condition rather than about you. For example:

Q: *'What happened to your face?'*
A: *'I was injured in a fire. Luckily, now that smoke alarms are available, injuries like mine are far less common.'*

It is a really useful exercise to write down some of these alternatives and personalise them so that they apply to you. Then practise, and see how much more in control of the situation you feel. There are no right or wrong answers, although some answers tend to invite more questioning. For example, look at these answers to the question:

Q: *'Why are you wearing that scarf on your head?'*
A: *'I have my reasons!'* or *'I've had a small operation and I am keeping the stitches covered.'*

The first answer invites all kinds of speculation about what is under the scarf. The second answer gives a very simple explanation. Any further questioning can be managed with the 'turn off the questions' approach above.

Answering children's questions is very straightforward. They say exactly what they think but are equally happy with a simple explanation.

Q: *'Why have you got a funny arm?'*
A: *'It's because I was burned in a fire. So don't play with matches, will you?'*

Sometimes humour can be helpful. Tom, who is in his early twenties, was recently asked how he had lost a finger, to which he responded: 'It wouldn't fit up my nose so I cut it off!'

This is a great reply! It made the questioner laugh, gave nothing away, and made Tom feel comfortable and in control. You will find, as you develop your own answers, that there will be certain favourites you use again and again, and then some new ideas that you add in. The aim is to have them on the tip of your tongue so you are never caught out. Sometimes you can be ambushed by a question that comes in the middle of a conversation about something else, but provided you have an answer ready you won't be caught unawares.

Try using the chart below to plan some good replies to keep in mind. Think about some questions that people have asked you. What did you say? What could you have said

SPECIAL PROBLEMS OF DISFIGURING CONDITIONS

instead? Try to develop three different ways of answering each question – one with lots of detail, one that closes down the question and one that distances you from the subject – as described above.

Questions I have been asked	What did I say?	What could I say instead?
		To give lots of detail: To close down the questioning: To distance myself from the conversation:
		To give lots of detail: To close down the questioning: To distance myself from the conversation:

		To give lots of detail:
		To close down the questioning:
		To distance myself from the conversation:

Managing staring

Sometimes it is easier to answer questions than to be in a setting where you can see someone is staring at you but does not ask anything. Often when they get into conversation with you, the curiosity will pass. People often become firm friends with others without ever discussing why one of them has a visible difference, and over time it simply becomes insignificant. However, sometimes the staring can be very intrusive. Sitting on a bus or the tube with a pair of eyes that keep drifting back to your face is annoying. A firm stare back is often very effective. Or a question: 'Have we met before? You seem to be trying to remember who I am.' An aggressive response, though sometimes tempting, is not usually helpful.

Distraction is another very easy way to focus away from the situation. A newspaper or book to read, particularly if you can hold it up and interrupt the staring, is helpful. A 'shoe review', where you estimate who has the most expensive trainers or exotic sandals, is a simple distraction. You can also use visualisation methods to imagine shrinking down the person into a tiny little figure or putting them into a different context (in their pyjamas). All of these strategies will allow you to feel more in control of the situation and, as you feel able to manage more situations so going out becomes less of an ordeal.

The charity mentioned earlier, Changing Faces (see Appendix 1 for details), is a very good source of more ideas about managing staring, comments and questions. In addition to written information, it has a website and video materials, and is developing online interactive programmes that will help you practise different social situations before you start doing them for real.

Putting it all into practice

The key to being successful in managing a visible difference is to take a positive approach to social situations, work on developing your social skills and then practise them in a graded way. By this we mean tackling some of the things you find easiest before you tackle something harder. For example, Fran had been bitten by a dog and had a very visible 'v'-shaped scar on her cheek. She was a very stylish woman in her thirties who liked clothes and make-up and was devastated by this change in her appearance. She stopped work, stayed at home and became increasingly depressed.

Her greatest fear was that if she went out someone would notice her face and ask about it.

We started treatment by developing some answers to questions. Fran settled on a very simple answer:

Q: *'What happened to your face?'*
A: *'I was bitten by that Alsatian at number 32.'*

We then designed a 'hierarchy' of exposure tasks (see Chapter 7), which was in the form of a simple ladder with easier items at the bottom and harder items as you climb each rung. Fran's ladder looked like the one opposite.

Fran then carried out each step and repeated it until she felt comfortable doing it. She very quickly managed the first one. She then spent a week going up to the corner shop and back every day but without going in. Gradually, her anxiety about going in to the shop got less. She then went in and picked up a paper and came home. She repeated this twice more and then went up to number three. Fran successfully completed this treatment and went back to work. There is an interesting aspect to Fran's programme. When she got to number six, she waited patiently in the queue, rehearsing her answer to the question she was expecting – and nothing happened. In the end, she got so tired of waiting that she pointed out her dog bite herself. 'What do you think of this, then? I was bitten by the dog at number 32!' The shopkeeper had noticed, but had politely refrained from asking. Fran laughed as she told us about this. You do not necessarily have to do the same thing, but it does illustrate,

SPECIAL PROBLEMS OF DISFIGURING CONDITIONS

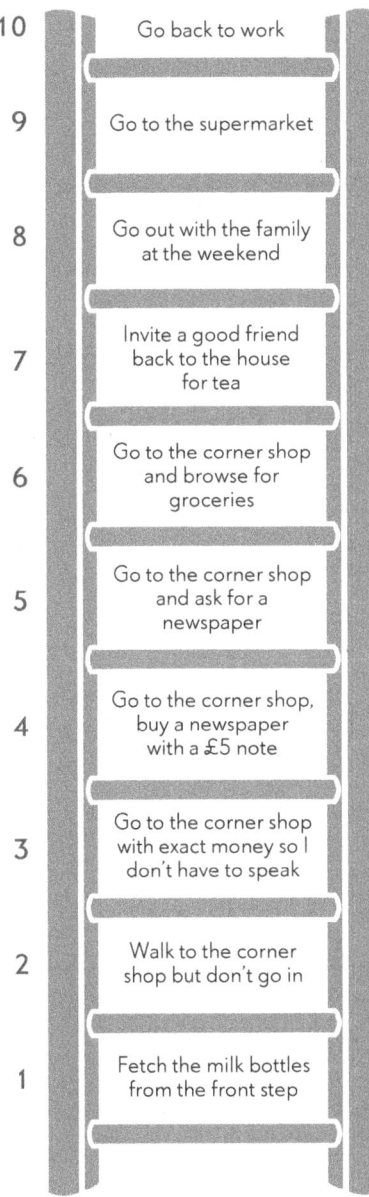

once again, how taking control of the situation had so lessened her anxiety that she felt able to introduce the topic of her face to a stranger. This was very different from how she imagined herself to be at the start of her treatment.

If you find certain situations very daunting, it is worth trying to work out your own hierarchy like the one above. Take it steadily, with not too big a jump between each step. Then make sure you only progress to the next rung of the ladder when you are completely happy on the rung below. It does not matter how long this takes you. Regular practice is more helpful. Doing an activity every day means that you will progress much faster than if you do it once a week. Be ready for a bad day, but don't let this put you off. You can often have an experience that does not go so well just before a real breakthrough in behaviour change. Go back to the rung below to build your confidence, and then try again.

Ending the search for surgical solutions

All the examples given in this chapter are real ones drawn from clinical experience. They all have something else in common: all these people went on to successfully change their behaviour and live normal lives without surgical removal of their disfiguring conditions. They all had surgery at some point in their lives, and some were able to improve their appearance a small amount, but all of them learned to live with a visible difference for which no further surgical treatment was possible.

Plastic surgery achieves an enormous amount for people who have disfiguring conditions. However, the media can sometimes portray surgery as offering 'magic' solutions. The reality is that all surgery has its limitations. All surgery leaves a scar, but some scars can be concealed better than others – for example, in the natural contours of the skin. It is impossible to completely modify a disfiguring condition so that the person looks exactly as they did before an accident. Even cleft lip and palate repairs, which produce very good results for children born with this craniofacial condition, will leave a fine scar.

At some point, a decision must be made about whether or not the benefits of further surgery are outweighed by the costs. Going on and on with endless surgical procedures is not necessarily a guarantee of being able to restore appearance. The real goal, after all, is to be able to live a normal life. So drawing a line under surgery when your surgeon suggests it, or when you yourself feel that the results are 'good enough', is a very important day. Addressing any challenges that you still face using a psychological approach, as the people in the examples we have given have done, is a very healthy way forward.

Summary

This chapter has considered the special case of disfiguring conditions, within the context of body image concerns. We have seen that objectively minor conditions can cause considerable distress, while other people cope with a very significant difference without any distress.

Positive coping strategies, taking the initiative, good social skills and social support are helpful. Avoiding difficult situations, increased social withdrawal, or coping using non-prescription drugs and alcohol is not helpful.

Cognitive behavioural therapy (CBT), in which you challenge unhelpful beliefs, develop social skills and then practise positive coping behaviour, can enable you to manage your condition even when surgery has no more to offer. This is achieved in a gradual way by tackling difficult situations step by step. Staring, comments and questions are intrusive, but everyone can learn to manage them.

Acceptance and commitment therapy (ACT) is an alternative therapeutic approach related to CBT. Essentially, ACT invites the individual to identify and accept thoughts and feelings as rational reactions to the challenges they experience. Researchers at the Centre for Appearance Research are evaluating this approach to managing visible difference using new resources, including online tools such as apps.

For people whose concerns are less to do with objective difference and more to do with an internal dissatisfaction with appearance, these approaches are still very helpful. The preoccupation with appearance, which is typical in BDD, can be a real barrier in social situations. If you believe that other people are as distracted by, for example, your nose as you are, then it becomes very difficult to focus on the situation rather than on other people's response to you. Anxiety about how to interact in this situation means that it can be hard to concentrate on what is really happening and not to write an agenda based on what you think or fear might be happening. For this reason, the section on social skills (page 319) will be helpful for you too. It is also useful to note that there are answers to appearance-related anxiety that do not involve surgery, and that people with a very obvious visible difference can live just as happily and successfully as anyone else.

> **PIT STOP**
>
> Let's stop and think about what you have just been reading. Can you summarise the key ideas you have taken on board? What is sticking in your mind? Maybe write it down. If you have any questions, jot those down too. You can return to them once you have had a chance to digest the information.
>
> What is sticking in my mind from my reading so far?
>
> 1.
>
> 2.
>
> 3.

12

Psychological aspects of cosmetic procedures

'If I looked better, then I would feel better.'

Cosmetic surgery is often thought of as 'body image surgery', and most people who request cosmetic procedures agree with the statement above. It seems self-evident that if you dislike your appearance, a procedure that can change that appearance must be a good thing. However, understanding the impact of surgery, whether it works, who will benefit and for whom surgery is a bad idea, is much more complicated. In this chapter, we will attempt to untangle some of these issues and help you to decide whether surgery is really a good option for you.

What is cosmetic surgery?

Plastic surgery has a reconstructive and cosmetic component. The reconstructive aspect of the work involves repair or modification of the body to restore function and appearance after injury or disease. The term 'cosmetic' is usually used to describe surgery that alters appearance, in the absence of any objective abnormality.

In fact, many surgical procedures have both a reconstructive and cosmetic element, as described in the examples below.

> *Jessie was on a safari holiday when she was involved in a car accident and thrown from the vehicle she was travelling in. She received severe facial injuries and needed many procedures to reconstruct her face. Her insurers were happy to pay for the initial surgery, which they regarded as reconstruction, but challenged later procedures of scar revision because they described these as 'cosmetic'.*

In the example above, Jessie's insurers are defining all surgery that is modifying appearance only (not treating disability or disease) as cosmetic, regardless of the cause of the problem or whether there is an objective disfigurement.

> *Pauline had breast cancer and had a mastectomy [removal of the breast], which successfully treated the disease. She then underwent a breast reconstruction operation in which skin and muscle from her abdomen was used to recreate the breast.*

Pauline's operation is classified as a reconstructive procedure because it is addressing a problem caused by disease and its treatment. However, it is also true to say that it is entirely aimed at recreating the appearance rather than the function of the breast. So there is a cosmetic aspect to the procedure.

Tanya is a beautician. She places a high value on her own appearance and feels that this is important in her career. She is dissatisfied with the size of her breasts. Although she has well-shaped breasts, she feels that she would prefer more fullness and would like to be two cup sizes bigger.

Tanya has normal breasts for her build and no history of disease. There is no reconstructive element in this surgery; her surgery would be classified as entirely cosmetic.

These examples are relatively straightforward, but in practice, deciding whether a procedure is cosmetic or not can be very difficult. This is important because there is an increasing demand on the NHS in the UK to provide procedures traditionally defined as cosmetic. Guidelines for when and for whom these can be provided vary from place to place, and usually depend on whether an individual's need is exceptional and whether there is good evidence that surgery will have clear, measurable benefits. For example, a breast-reduction operation, which we know to be an operation that can reduce pain in women with very large, heavy breasts, is available in some parts of the UK provided the individual case meets local guidelines. In reality, and given the increase in popularity of cosmetic surgery and the competing financial pressures in the NHS, it is increasingly unlikely that any cosmetic procedures will be available in the future, except in the private sector. This is not of course an issue in most other countries, where all cosmetic procedures are done privately.

Cosmetic procedures also include a whole range of non-surgical procedures such as dermabrasion, laser treatment and modification of wrinkles using botulinum toxin. Even less is known about the psychological effects of such procedures compared to surgery.

Why do people request cosmetic procedures?

The most common reason for requesting cosmetic surgery is because someone feels 'abnormal' or substandard in some way. They compare their own feature with their idea of what a 'normal' feature should look like, and decide that there is room for improvement. Often people worry that this will be seen by others as vanity. Sometimes there is a sense of wanting to improve appearance to be better than others, but more usually there is a much stronger sense that people want to fit in; they do not want be different or not as good as others.

There are various reasons why people feel abnormal or unusual, and these are tremendously important. Sometimes these reasons are based on 'ghosts from the past' or incorrect information.

The impact of media images

> *'This isn't about other people. I'm not thinking about surgery because of what other people think of me – I'm doing this for myself.'*

Although it is really important not to bow to pressure from other people, the fact that you may undergo cosmetic surgery for yourself is far from being a safe reason to go ahead with a procedure. You may well have become dissatisfied with your appearance by comparing yourself with an ideal, and that is derived from what you see around you – whether or not you want surgery for yourself, to improve your career prospects or for other reasons.

Fifty years ago it would be unheard of for magazines, TV shows and other media to blatantly display pictures of semi-clad models and celebrities with 'ideal' bodies. People were generally more reserved in how they dressed and how much of their own body they displayed. Nowadays the media bombard us with images of ideal bodies in our day-to-day lives. This can substantially raise expectations of the image you develop for your 'ideal' self, and may mean that you are more ready to compare your appearance unfavourably with others.

> *Deborah was very unhappy about the shape of her breasts. Compared with the pictures that she saw in magazines, she felt that her breasts were excessively lax. She described them as 'droopy'. In fact, when she was examined, her breasts were completely normal. When Deborah produced*

> the pictures that she was using for comparison, it was clear that she had selected pictures of women with artificially high or prominent breasts following breast augmentation. For Deborah, these images seemed normal.
>
> Jane presented with a similar belief that her breasts were abnormal. But for her, this was based on comparison with her own breasts before she had children. Breast shape changes for most women following pregnancy regardless of whether they breastfeed. Breasts also fall under their own weight over time. So, although Jane no longer looks as she used to look, her breasts are not abnormal.

These examples show that there may be a difference between having a normal feature and an ideal feature, but that this does not necessarily mean you are unusual.

Not only do people value appearance to a greater or lesser extent, but the amount by which body image impacts their own life also varies. For example, body image issues tend to be more prevalent in the summer when we need to wear fewer clothes. Body image issues may also be more important at different ages – for example, at the point of leaving home and meeting a lot of new people at work or college.

It is also worth noting in this context that many of the images we are exposed to are not necessarily 'real' people at all. Digital images are usually enhanced to produce an ideal image (some celebrities have complained about this!). Imperfections are airbrushed out, or images of different people combined to create an idea of perfection. The supermodel Kate Moss has referred to glamorous pictures of herself as 'an image – not pictures of me'.

Some people are very vulnerable to these ideal images – and fail to recognise their artificiality. It is also true to say that as more and more people have cosmetic procedures, the range of variation in society becomes smaller. Over time, there may well be fewer women with either very small or very large breasts – and so those at the extremes may begin to feel more unusual. It's very important that you recognise media images as art and entertainment, not reflections of reality, otherwise cosmetic surgery and digital enhancement may begin to define what you understand as 'normal'.

Seeking an objective opinion

Sometimes it can be helpful to consider other people's opinions about your appearance, but a constant seeking of reassurance from others about your looks is very unhelpful and may suggest you have BDD.

Jake was very worried about his nose. He felt that it did not look normal, and spent considerable time looking at it with a hand mirror, trying to see how it looked in profile. He chose where he sat very carefully when in company so that no one could see him from the side. Objectively, there was nothing remarkable or unusual about Jake's nose. When asked if people commented or asked him about it, he said that people did not do so 'because they were too polite'. However, he was convinced that they were looking at him.

Paul was becoming increasingly preoccupied with his nose since breaking it in a football match two years previously. He felt that it looked different from how it had done before, and that there was a clear twist that was visible when you looked at him straight on. He tried ignoring his nose, but was getting increasingly fed up with people asking him what he had done to it.

The fact that you have a visible difference should never be the sole reason for surgery – many people, as we saw in Chapter 11, do not place as great an importance on their appearance as they do on other aspects of their sense of self. They cope positively and are perfectly happy as they are. No one 'should' have cosmetic surgery just to comply with an external ideal. Nor should the opinion of other people be the prime motivation for having surgery. The fact that someone else thinks you 'ought' to do something is not a good a reason for surgery if you are happy the way you are.

However, the fact that other people can identify what it is that bothers you is helpful. For a start, it means that you and the surgeon can agree on exactly what it is that you dislike and want to change. For Paul in the example above, there is a clear twist to his nose. Both he, his friends and his surgeon can agree they see it, and they can start to talk about how likely it is that surgery can provide a solution. This is often a very important reason to avoid cosmetic surgery if you suffer from body dysmorphic disorder, in which people often do not regard your 'flaw' as anywhere near as noticeable or abnormal as you do.

The second reason it is helpful if others can see the problem is that it helps you to focus on the results of surgery, the outcomes or what you hope is going to change. Paul will easily be able to tell if his surgery is successful because people will stop asking him what he has done to his nose. The intrusive comments will stop and that is one very clear reason that he wants to have surgery. (Remember, though, he does not have to address this problem through the surgical route – the strategies outlined in Chapter 11 are a very good way of dealing with other people's curiosity.)

Jake is more complicated. He knows that he is dissatisfied with his nose but he is not absolutely sure he knows why. He wants his surgeon to provide him with a 'nicer' nose, but it is very difficult to pin down exactly what he means by this. He tends to explain his position by saying 'Anything is better than this' or 'The surgeon is the one with the experience so I am going to leave it up to them.' However, without a clearer idea of what it is that Jake wants to change, the surgeon is left guessing what kind of surgery will help and, for Jake, this increases the chances of post-operative dissatisfaction.

Equally worrying is the fact that no one else can see a problem. Jake believes his friends are too polite to comment. He is wrong about this. People who have a visible difference can always give examples of specific comments and questions from others. Not everyone intrudes like this, but the absence of any evidence of comments from other people is a really helpful indication that Jake needs to take his time before proceeding to surgery. His ideas of what he wants to change are too vague, and he therefore has no clear idea how he will know if the operation has been a success. Some surgeons use computer modelling to illustrate potential changes and to make a clear surgical plan. But working with human tissue is not the same as working with a clay model, and part of any assessment will include determining if expectations are realistic. In Jake's case, he should think about seeing a specialist psychologist who works in this area to help him to clarify his ideas, and to think about whether surgery is really the answer for his concerns.

> *'I just want it to be subtle: I don't want anyone else to notice that I've had anything done.'*

If you really think about the above statement, which is a very common request, you can see that this is a very difficult challenge for a surgeon. On the one hand, you are concerned enough about a particular feature to feel that this warrants surgery with all the associated risks (and financial costs); in other words, you are asking for a significant change. But, on the other hand, because you are hoping no one will notice, you are also asking for a very small change. One way or another, you are very likely to be disappointed. Either the change will be too subtle – 'I'm really pleased with the results, but I just wish the surgeon had taken a little more off' – or 'I think I look really great, but I wish that it wasn't so obvious to other people. Everyone keeps asking who my surgeon is.'

If this is how you are thinking, then you need to examine your motivation for surgery. If you are really keen to achieve a change then that is your priority. If you feel so embarrassed about cosmetic surgery that you don't want other people to know, then should you really be having it? Decisions that are not consistent with your values and beliefs can lead to psychological problems in the long run. When this happens, people tend to be preoccupied by feelings of shame and regret, and can even become anxious about going out. In this context, it is also advisable to give your surgeon permission to liaise with your GP. Keeping surgery a secret means that any complications, such as infection, will be more difficult to diagnose and manage, and lack of information about your past medical history may put you at unnecessary risk. Indeed, some plastic surgeons refuse to operate unless they have your GP's details.

Can surgery make you happier?

The examples throughout this chapter are all based on real people. You can see that there are some common themes in their motivation for change. They vary according to the feature that they dislike, and they also vary in the degree to which their feature can be seen by others – the objective difference from the norm. What they have in common is a real sense that they will be happier if they can change the way that they look. Unfortunately, there is still not very good evidence of a direct link between surgery and psychological wellbeing.

PSYCHOLOGICAL ASPECTS OF COSMETIC PROCEDURES

Most of the people that come to a cosmetic clinic talk in terms of improving their self-confidence and self-esteem. Although their immediate goal is to have surgery, they hope that this will enable them to achieve something that is currently missing in their lives. This is sometimes something very simple, such as the ability to wear a swimsuit. But the impact may be more far-reaching.

Moira had a complication of pregnancy that meant she retained a lot of water and put on a great deal of weight. Although her weight fell with sensible eating and exercise, she was unable to do anything about a large fold of extra skin. This caused sweating underneath it and rashes, particularly in the summer. Moira was very embarrassed about her husband seeing her and started to make excuses to avoid sex. She also felt very conspicuous in a swimsuit, felt she could not take the children swimming and would not go on holiday. Gradually she began to buy baggy clothing, large sweatshirts and jackets, and would not take these off even when it was very hot.

Moira decided to have an abdominoplasty (tummy tuck). Although she knew that this could not make her look exactly as she had done before she had the children, and that she would have very significant scarring, she felt that the removal of the abdominal fold would allow her to do lots of activities that she felt unable to do.

Her goals for surgery were very clear:

Goals for surgery	Chances of achieving goal (0–10)
Remove some skin excess	10
Reduce sweating and rash	9–10
Wear normal clothes	9–10
Wear swimming costume	8–9
Take children swimming	8–9
Go on holiday	7–8
Less self-conscious about sex	4–5

She had a very high chance of achieving some of these. Some goals were ranked lower because they depended on how she felt rather than on her behaviour. An impact on feelings often takes longer and depends in part on the other things on the list: how her husband felt about the surgery, and so on. In general, the more Moira was able to identify and work towards significant changes in her behaviour, the more likely she would feel good about herself in the longer term.

Moira's surgery left her with a large scar from hip to hip. It could not remove her stretch marks and she had some unevenness at the end of the scar. However, she achieved all the goals on her list and was very satisfied with the impact of cosmetic surgery in changing her behaviour and improving her self-esteem.

We have seen elsewhere in this book that the way you think and act can change the extent to which you are preoccupied by your appearance. One way of thinking about Moira's surgery is that it enabled her to change how she behaved; this then lessened her preoccupation with her abdomen and allowed her to relax with her husband. She might describe this as increasing her self-confidence, but it was the change in behaviour that came first. People often get this relationship the wrong way round. They talk about making changes in their life in the future, when they feel more confident in themselves. But this self-confidence is far more likely to grow from making the changes, altering your behaviour in a gradual way and building self-esteem though gradually succeeding at the things you find difficult. You will find examples of this graded approach to changing behaviour throughout this book. Look back at Chapter 11, for example, at the hierarchy Fran used to begin going out again after her dog bite (page 327). Building on the small steps allowed her to achieve all her goals and go back to work, without relying on surgery to do this for her.

Research evidence on the psychological benefits of cosmetic surgery

Most people who suffer from body dysmorphic disorder are not satisfied with the outcome of cosmetic surgery. Alternatively, if they are satisfied with the procedure then the preoccupation quite commonly moves to another area of their body. In other words, the procedure does not alter the symptoms of BDD in terms of the preoccupation, distress and disability. Since CBT has far better evidence for positive outcomes in BDD, this is the approach recommended in current National Institute for Health and Care Excellence (NICE) guidelines.

> *Jose is aged twenty-four and has body dysmorphic disorder. He has had four operations to his nose. About ten years ago he was bullied and he thought that it was because of his appearance. Despite the surgery, he remained very distressed and preoccupied by the shape of his nose. His parents were finding it difficult to make ends meet after paying for the surgery. They thought that they were giving him the best even though they did not think that he needed it doing. He was virtually housebound and would only come out in the dark. He felt that previous surgeons were incompetent and had made his nose look worse in some respects. He frequently brooded on why he had chosen the first surgeon and wished he had seen someone else. He continued to spend time searching on the internet for a surgeon who could help him. He felt he could not do anything in life until he felt comfortable with his nose.*

The evidence for the psychological benefits of cosmetic surgery in people without BDD is poor. It is generally based on small samples, measures different psychological factors and deals with short-term outcomes. Scientists have not yet been able to carry out studies that are rigorous enough for us to fully interpret the findings. This means we are able to explain the findings in too many different ways to allow us to be clear about whether surgery has psychological benefits or not. Being satisfied with surgery is not the same as showing a clear psychological benefit, and unfortunately satisfaction is what most research studies have measured. Before and after studies are not good enough on their own. They do not tell us enough without a comparison group who are having another kind of treatment. It might be that any kind of treatment is equally effective, or that the attention people get from the surgical team accounts for some of the explanation when they end up feeling good about themselves.

We also do not know whether a cosmetic procedure works in the long term. We know that most people without BDD are usually satisfied immediately after surgery, but that could be due to the fact that they have so much invested in it, or to other psychological reasons. Although the examples given in the media or the people who undergo surgery on TV report very positive changes, we simply do not know whether the changes they expect in the long term happen or not. Many people come back for repeat procedures, but this could be because they are really pleased with the outcome of the first – or because the initial effect was good but wore off very quickly, or because it didn't work but there is a desperate hope that it might work the next time. So we have much more research to do before we can be certain. However, we do know enough to be able to give some broad guidelines.

Where cosmetic surgery appears to be most effective is where it works, as with Moira in the example above. This is summarised in the box below.

Predictors of good outcome after surgery

- There is a measurable problem (feature is too big/small/asymmetric).
- The problem is clearly identifiable by others: friends/family/surgeon.
- The impact (the way that behaviour is affected) can be described.
- There are clear goals for surgery.
- The surgeon and patient agree on surgical goals and the likelihood of achieving them.
- There are clear, achievable and realistic targets for behaviour change after surgery.
- Goals are expressed as 'what I can do' not 'how I will feel'.

Predictors of poor outcome after surgery

All the following have been linked to poor outcome and need specialist assessment before a procedure is considered:

- The motivation for surgery comes from someone other than yourself.
- You cannot describe the problem clearly, or have lots of different features you dislike.
- Other people are unable to see what is wrong.
- You are suffering from body dysmorphic disorder (e.g. you have excessive preoccupation and

> distress with a feature that others say is not particularly noticeable or abnormal).
> - You are unclear about how the problem impacts on your life.
> - There are vague goals for surgery ('I want it to look more attractive').
> - The surgeon and you have not agreed specific surgical goals.
> - Outcomes are expressed as feelings rather than behaviour ('I want to feel more confident').
> - Outcomes are unrealistic ('I want my life to be completely different').
> - The behaviour to be changed is someone else's ('I want my husband to stop seeing other women').
> - There have been repeated cosmetic procedures that have had poor outcomes in the past.

We can illustrate this with another example:

Sally was referred after having undergone a rhinoplasty and being very unhappy about the results. She had asked her surgeon to give her a nicer nose. The surgeon suggested they make her nose narrower and reduce the size of her nostrils. After surgery, Sally said that she still disliked her nose. She had the procedure done again but remained unhappy and even more preoccupied with her nose.

When we planned out her goals as they might have been when she first considered surgery, they looked like this:

Goals for surgery	(Therapist-rated) Chances of achieving goal (0–10)
Make my nose look nicer	1–2
Reduce my preoccupation with my nose	1–2
Make me more confident	0–1
Make me feel better about myself	0–1
Help me get a boyfriend	0–1

You can see from this list that Sally was far more characteristic of someone for whom the outcomes are unsatisfactory. She was vague about what she wanted the surgeon to do, and none of the things she hoped to achieve were within her control. She needed to identify specific examples of behaviour that she hoped to change:

Goals for surgery	(Therapist-rated) Chances of achieving goal (0–10)
Make my nose narrower at the base	9–10
Reduce the size of the nostrils	9–10
Reduce the time I spend looking in the mirror	7–8
Help me to socialise with friends	4–5
Help me get a boyfriend	4–5

You can see that Sally can clearly measure the first three things on the list. She can then begin to work on socialising with her friends – in fact, she can enlist their support with this. If she is going out with friends, she is far more likely to find a boyfriend, so we have raised the probability of this too.

Unfortunately, when surgery is not successful, when it does not meet expectations, many people respond by having more surgery. You might tell yourself that it is nearly right, but a little more is needed. Or think that a surgeon elsewhere might be better, or that a hospital overseas might be a good option. Sometimes we see people having a procedure repeated over and over again. Unfortunately, this has the effect of increasing rather than reducing their preoccupation with the feature in question. It can be very difficult to treat this problem successfully. There is also the risk that repeated surgery and scarring will result in the feature being less satisfactory than it was in the first place. This is clearly a very bad outcome, so it is always a good idea to talk through the reasons for your disappointment with a psychologist, as well as your surgeon, before rushing back for more surgery. Some of the most depressed and suicidal individuals with BDD are those who blame themselves for having cosmetic procedures that they feel have made their appearance worse.

Timing of cosmetic surgery

What is the trigger for thinking about surgery? Even if you are someone who has thought about surgery for years as an option for you in the future, it is important to work out why now is a good time. It can be very tempting to think about a change in appearance as a response to other significant changes in your life. Psychologists talk about 'life events', or the significant challenges we all face at some point in our lives. These include changes in relationships, jobs, bereavement, children leaving home, moving house, and so on. Rushing to make an irreversible change when you are unhappy is something that people often regret. It is better to leave a reasonable gap – a few months – before planning surgery after any of these significant changes in your life. This is particularly important if lots of changes have occurred together.

Cosmetic surgery for children

Cosmetic procedures such as correction of ears that stick out (pinnaplasty) are regularly carried out for children. Indeed, the NHS will only carry out these procedures for children and not adults. The rationale is to prevent teasing and bullying. Other procedures are not ideal in young people, for the very practical reason that they are still growing. It is therefore unusual to offer cosmetic procedures to those under the age of eighteen. However, breast reduction or augmentation and rhinoplasty are increasingly requested at milestones such as leaving school. People are choosing to 'correct' a feature that they feel to be abnormal before meeting a new group of friends. It is important that people are made aware of any particular contraindications associated with different procedures. For example, there is a considerably reduced likelihood of being able to breastfeed after bilateral breast reduction (BBR), and many surgeons prefer to offer this procedure to older women who have already completed their families.

Pressure from others

There is a growing fashion for giving people gift vouchers for private cosmetic surgery. If surgery is not something you have considered, do not be influenced by the idea of doing it cheaply. Similarly, reputable clinics should not encourage you to have further procedures. Offering a cut-price procedure if you sign up to more than one is an indication that you should choose a different provider. People sometimes choose to go for cosmetic surgery in pairs or with a group of friends. This is not a good idea. You need to be able to stand back and make a decision without group pressure. This is not the same as taking a friend with you to a consultation to listen and help you to ask relevant questions. The pressure comes when you are all planning to have the same procedure together. Someone in the group will be the least certain that they want this, and it can be very hard to withdraw when everyone else is going ahead.

Regulation of cosmetic surgery and finding a surgeon

The regulation of cosmetic surgery has received considerable criticism, with various reports and calls for tighter guidelines. For example, there have been recommendations that advertising should not make unrealistic promises, that surgery should not be offered to those under the age of eighteen, that care should be taken to assess the psychological issues associated with the request for surgery, and that all surgeons should be properly trained. Unfortunately, you cannot assume that because you are in a clinic, the doctor you see has training in plastic surgery.

To ensure that a surgeon has the proper experience, make sure that they are included on the list produced by the British Association of Aesthetic Plastic Surgeons (see Appendix 1 for contact details).

As an additional guide, most reputable aesthetic (cosmetic) surgeons are, or have been, consultant surgeons in the NHS. It can be tempting to look for the cheapest source of surgery, but many people end up spending more in the end. Reputable surgeons recognise that there are potential complications in all surgery. Infection, or the need to revise a scar, are examples. As a rough guide, 10 per cent of patients may need further revision or treatments that are additional to the initial treatment. To cover this potential cost, reputable surgeons spread the risk across their whole practice and therefore charge slightly more for all patients, so that no further payment for treatment is required should anyone encounter a problem post-operatively. Less reputable surgeons cut costs but do not provide any safety net if you are not happy with the outcome of surgery. It is very important to identify in advance the arrangements for care should you have a problem, and paying a little more for high-quality practice is well worth doing.

You can also expect that surgeons will ask about your psychological motivation for surgery alongside your expectations for physical change. It is also increasingly common for them to recommend an assessment from a psychological practitioner who specialises in this area.

Seeking surgery abroad (cosmetic tourism), while cheaper, is a very high-risk strategy. If you incur a complication such as an infection, which is not uncommon, you will be a long way from advice. In this circumstance you will need to rely on the NHS. While they will treat an emergency (indeed, cosmetic tourism costs the NHS a large sum every year), they will not offer remedial surgery (e.g. replace an infected breast implant).

An experienced surgeon is a source not only of top-quality surgery but also top-quality advice. If the advice to you is that surgery can offer only very modest change or that you are at high risk of a poor outcome, then it is safer to change the way you manage your concerns rather than look for another surgical provider.

Are there people who should never have cosmetic surgery?

There are some medical conditions that make any kind of surgery more dangerous (e.g. heart conditions), and undergoing any elective (non-essential) surgery is unwise in this situation.

Other risk factors for surgery include smoking and obesity. Smoking increases the risk associated with anaesthetic and also makes the healing process less efficient by reducing the amount of oxygen available in the blood. Obesity also increases anaesthetic risk and the likelihood of complications such as infection. Cosmetic surgery is not a weight reduction technique. It is sometimes used to reduce surplus skin after weight loss, but procedures such as abdominoplasty are not designed to make people slimmer.

It may seem surprising that surgery is often considered inappropriate for some people with body image concerns. Body dysmorphic disorder is better treated using the CBT and/or medication that is outlined in this book. This is because the central problem in BDD is the preoccupation with a feature rather than the feature itself. Although surgery may change the appearance of the feature, it usually does not alter the extent to which people are worried or preoccupied, or continue to check their appearance in the mirror. In this sense, then, it fails to change the problem behaviour, or alter beliefs or mood. In fact it can make the problem worse if someone becomes trapped in a cycle of repeated surgery. It is wise to get advice from a psychologist or psychiatrist before seeking cosmetic surgery if your problems with appearance fit the pattern described in Chapter 2.

There are some other psychiatric conditions in which a cosmetic procedure may not be a good idea. An eating disorder or any body image problem that involves excessive preoccupation with appearance (like BDD) is unlikely to be successfully treated through surgery alone. Indeed, in BDD, repeated surgery usually leads to increasing dissatisfaction. Conditions such as depression are not necessarily a barrier to surgery, but timing is important. Generally, it is not a good idea to undertake surgery without further assessment if you are currently receiving psychological therapy or psychiatric medication, or are under any kind of stress or pressure in your life.

Should I be considering surgery?

Having read this chapter, you should be clearer about whether surgery is going to be appropriate for you, and if now is a good time. Take some time to think about the following questions and complete the exercise.

EXERCISE: SHOULD I BE CONSIDERING SURGERY?

Do your body image problems affect one area of your body or one feature?

_____

_____

Is your condition noticeable to other people? Do others currently comment or tease you on your appearance?

_____

_____

Have you tried to manage your condition by using the psychological methods outlined in this book?

_____

_____

Have you had cosmetic surgery in the past? If yes, were you satisfied with the outcome?

_____

_____

Do you have a condition such as body dysmorphic disorder, depression or an eating disorder?

_____

_____

Have you had any major changes or additional stress in your life recently? Or has a relationship recently ended?

_____

_____

Are you under pressure from others to consider surgery?

_____

_____

Are you able to tell people exactly what you dislike about your feature?

_____

_____

Are you able to pinpoint exactly how you would like that feature to change? Write down exactly how you would like to change your appearance. Use very objective language (e.g. 'longer', 'shorter', 'bigger', 'rounder') rather than value judgements (e.g. 'nicer', 'more attractive', 'normal').

_____

_____

_____

_____

_____

_____

What are the chances that surgery can achieve this change? (You may not know this without talking to a surgeon.)

_____

_____

How do you expect your life to be different after surgery? Write this down as specifically as you can. After surgery I will be able to . . .

_____

_____

If I am able to do the things I have listed above, I hope to achieve some longer-term goals, such as . . .

(Have a look at the example of Moira on page 345, to give you the idea.)

Have you been able to identify very clear target behaviours that you hope to achieve?

Can you achieve them without cosmetic surgery?

If you find this exercise difficult, it would be a good idea to get some advice. Appendix 1 will give you some suggestions for where to find someone who specialises in body image concerns who can help you. If you are in the least bit uncertain, this suggests that cosmetic surgery is not a good option for you at this particular point in your life.

> **PIT STOP**
>
> Let's stop and think about what you have just been reading. Can you summarise the key ideas you have taken on board? What is sticking in your mind? Maybe write it down. If you have any questions, jot those down too. You can return to them once you have had a chance to digest the information.
>
> What is sticking in my mind from my reading so far?
>
> 1.
>
> 2.
>
> 3.

13

A guide to medication for BDD

This chapter aims to help you make an informed choice about whether you wish to take medication for body dysmorphic disorder by discussing the potential benefits and disadvantages. The discussion may also be relevant for someone who is significantly depressed (e.g. as a result of a disfigurement). However, if after reading this chapter you have doubts and questions about medication, discuss these with your doctor, rather than just ignoring a prescription or stopping your medication.

If you have been recommended medication and decide to take it, it is also important that you take it in the correct dose and frequency. The possible side effects and what you can do to minimise them are also discussed in this chapter. In addition, we provide advice on how to come off antidepressant medication. Being well informed is vital, as some people prescribed medication will not get it dispensed at the pharmacy, while others may take it inappropriately (e.g. at a lower dose than recommended or not daily) or not at all.

Medication may be suggested:

- if you have moderate to severe symptoms of BDD, as an alternative to cognitive behavioural therapy (CBT) or in addition to CBT
- if you have BDD that has persisted despite CBT being delivered competently
- if you have BDD and are also significantly depressed or suicidal.

You may find it difficult to be offered CBT because of long waiting lists or other restrictions in public medicine or insurance cover. As a result, you may be offered medication before you receive CBT. More research is needed on how best to optimise medication to get the most out of combining treatments in BDD. CBT and medication are probably as effective as each other for most people with BDD (although we don't yet have published research evidence to support this). However, it is very important that individuals have a choice; unfortunately, CBT may be more costly to provide than drug therapy *in the short term*. However, in the long term, psychological treatments are usually more cost-effective, as the cost of the drug continues for several months and there is usually a higher risk of relapse with medication alone if it is stopped, compared with an effective psychological therapy.

Some individuals may do better on a combination of CBT and medication than either treatment alone. This is usually recommended when you fail to respond adequately to CBT or if your BDD is more severe. The problem is that no one can predict with any certainty who will respond best to what treatment.

Frequently asked questions about medication

Isn't taking medication a sign of weakness?

Taking medication is not a sign of weakness or failure. You probably wouldn't think that taking medication was a weakness if you had heart disease or cancer. Your relatives and friends are more likely to think of your behaviour as weak if you don't take medication, and find it difficult to understand why you don't do everything you can to get better. If some of them do criticise you for taking medication, they probably don't understand what you are experiencing, and their opinion is not worth considering. Mental disorder is no different from any other problem in this respect, and taking medication is a practical approach.

How quickly does medication work?

Even if medication is of benefit, it will not work right away. Most people notice some improvement in their symptoms after about four to six weeks, while maximum benefit should occur within four to six months. It is important to continue to take your medication at the highest dose you can tolerate for this period before judging how effective it has been.

How long will I need to take medication for?

Never stop taking medication without discussing it with your doctor first, and always ensure that you have another prescription ready before you run out of drugs. This is because if you do not take medication regularly, or stop it suddenly (e.g. you forget to take it with you on holiday), you may be at risk of experiencing withdrawal symptoms. This is discussed in detail at the end of this chapter.

Once you have recovered from BDD or depression and stop taking medication, you may find you relapse if you have had no other therapy. The risk of relapse will partly depend on the natural pattern of your BDD without treatment. For example, for a first episode of BDD the chance of recurrence is less if you continue to take an antidepressant for up to a year after you have recovered. If you have a second episode of BDD, then your chances of relapse are lower if you keep taking an antidepressant for a couple of years after you have got better. If you are someone whose BDD keeps recurring, then the risk of relapse is much higher, and you may be advised to remain on the medication for at least five years. A few people may need to be on medication for many years to reduce the risk of relapse.

For many people, the risk of relapse is minimised by combining the medication with CBT. If you are planning to stop medication, ensure you do it after discussion with your doctor and within an agreed time frame. Be aware that your depressive symptoms may start to return within a few weeks or months, so don't plan to stop before predictable major stresses and life events.

SSRIs

The first choice of medication for most people with BDD is a class of antidepressants called selective serotonergic reuptake inhibitors (or SSRIs for short) (see table). 'Serotonergic' means that the drugs act on serotonin nerve endings in the brain. 'Selective' refers to the fact that they act on serotonin nerve endings rather than others such as noradrenaline or histamine nerve endings. 'Reuptake inhibitor' refers to the way the drug acts: it helps to increase the concentration of serotonin in the nerve cells. This in turn helps to increase the messages passing along certain pathways in the brain and to reduce anxiety.

SSRI antidepressants

Chemical name	Common trade names	Usual starting dose	Target dose	Liquid preparation
Citalopram	Cipramil, Celexa	20 mg	50 mg	Yes (20 mg=5 ml)
Escitalopram	Cipralex, Lexapro	10 mg	20 mg	Yes (5 mg=5 ml)
Fluoxetine	Prozac	20 mg	60 mg	Yes (20 mg=5 ml)
Fluvoxamine	Faverin, Luvox	50 mg	200 mg	No
Paroxetine	Seroxat, Paxil	20 mg	60 mg	Yes (10 mg=5 ml)
Sertraline	Lustral, Zoloft	50 mg	200 mg	Yes (100 mg=5 ml)

For BDD, an SSRI may reduce your preoccupation and distress with your feature. In BDD, a part of your nervous system may have an excessive load on it as your mind tries to make things better. SSRIs *enhance* this normal activity of the brain, and improve its ability to dampen anxiety and reduce your preoccupation. SSRIs are also used for panic attacks, obsessive-compulsive disorder (OCD) and depression, so they are not used specifically for BDD. A family doctor may prescribe the drug or may refer you to a psychiatrist who can discuss your issues in more detail.

Which SSRI might be prescribed?

In general, all SSRIs are likely to be equally effective for BDD or depression, but people respond differently to different drugs. The most evidence for BDD is based on trials conducted with fluoxetine; however, your doctor will help you choose the most appropriate SSRI for you given your circumstances and history. For example, citalopram or escitalopram are usually a good choice if you are on other drugs at the same time, and are usually well tolerated. Citalopram is a mixture of two molecules, which are identical except that they are mirror images of each other. Escitalopram is the molecule that has the serotonin action and is available without a redundant molecule, which has no serotonin action. The result is the same, but escitalopram may have slightly fewer side effects.

Fluoxetine takes longer to be metabolised by the body, so if you forget a dose one day, you can get away with it because it does not vanish from the blood when you stop taking it. It is also the easiest to come off. However, some people find fluoxetine slightly more likely to increase anxiety when they first start taking the drug. Some SSRIs, such as paroxetine, may be more difficult to withdraw from (see 'Stopping or reducing antidepressant medication', page 385).

If you or someone in your family did well or poorly with a medication in the past, this may influence the choice. If you have medical problems (e.g. problems sleeping) or are taking another medication, these factors may influence your doctor's choice so that side effects and possible drug interactions are minimised. Make sure you tell your doctor if you:

- are pregnant or plan to get pregnant, or are breastfeeding
- have any other medical conditions
- are taking any other medication, or herbal drugs like St John's wort.

Can I drink alcohol with an SSRI?

In general, you can drink alcohol as long as you do so in moderation and do not binge-drink. However, people's reactions to alcohol do vary when taking medication and some people can become more aggressive or sedated. See how you respond to one drink initially. Fluvoxamine and sertraline may not mix very well with alcohol, so be aware that this mix may impair your judgement; also, when you are on one of these, you should not drive or operate machinery, for example. Excessive alcohol can also be a factor in depression and will interfere in your recovery. Compared with the older antidepressants, SSRIs are generally safe. An overdose will not generally harm you.

What dose of an SSRI should I be prescribed?

The normal starting dose and suitable target doses of different SSRIs are listed in the table on page 369. When progress is slow, there is some evidence that you may need to increase the dose. If you experience significant side effects, you can always start on a lower dose after discussion with your doctor. You can then build the dose up slowly. Tablets should be swallowed with some water while sitting or standing. This is to make sure that they do not stick in your throat. If you miss a dose, take it as soon as you remember it. However, if it is almost time for the next dose, skip the missed dose and continue your regular dose. Do not take a double dose to make up for a missed one.

Can vegans have SSRIs?

Citalopram elixir, fluoxetine elixir, clomipramine elixir, sertraline tablets and paroxetine tablets or liquid do not contain any animal products.

What about reports of SSRIs causing suicide?

There is some evidence that a few antidepressants can cause a slight increase in suicidal ideas (not acts) in young people with depression. For young adults, the increased risk of suicidal ideas is extremely small. So long as you monitor such feelings, talk about them openly with your doctor and relatives, and are seen regularly, this is something that can be managed. The thoughts of suicide will then decrease as your depression lifts.

Antidepressant medication for children and adolescents

Antidepressant medication for children with BDD or depression is not so well studied, and CBT is recommended as the first line of treatment. This is because scientists don't yet know the long-term effects of antidepressants on the immature brain of a child, and also because antidepressants are often ineffective in young people or may be associated with a slight increase in suicidal ideas (see above). Equally this needs to be judged against the risk of a young person with severe BDD or depression not using medication or not responding to CBT (or refusing it). If they are continuing to experience severe BDD, this may have a major adverse impact on both development and education. In such cases, an antidepressant is recommended. Only fluoxetine and sertraline have been shown in controlled trials to have a favourable balance of risks and benefits for the treatment of depression in the under-eighteens and these are the SSRIs usually recommended for BDD. The dose usually starts at half the adult dose (sertraline 25 mg or fluoxetine 10 mg) and may be increased gradually. Therefore, a psychiatrist should supervise the use of an antidepressant for a child or adolescent, and monitor his or her mental state closely (e.g. weekly for the first four weeks). An SSRI should be offered in combination with an evidence-based psychological treatment. If treatment with fluoxetine is unsuccessful or is not tolerated because of side effects, consideration should be given to the use of another antidepressant. In this case, sertraline or citalopram might be second-line treatments. Guidelines recommend that venlafaxine (Efexor) and paroxetine (Seroxat, Paxil) and clomipramine antidepressants should not be used for the treatment of depression in children and young people. The side effects listed below occur in children as they do in adults. In addition, children may become overexcited, irritable or 'silly'; if this is severe it may be a reason to stop the medication.

What side effects occur with SSRIs?

Some people experience side effects with SSRIs. Those who do normally find them to be minor irritations, which usually decrease after a few weeks. The main side effects are described in this section. Most people find that they are not usually a problem in the long term. They will not alter your personality or turn you into a zombie, and will cease when you stop taking the drug. The worst side effects usually occur in the first few days or weeks after commencing the drug. This is the time when you are most likely to stop taking the drug because you have not experienced any improvement in symptoms of your depression. (This is because it takes four to six weeks for the full benefits of the medication to become clear.) There is one side effect, though, that does not tend to improve over time: sexual difficulties. However, side effects that persist, including those of a sexual nature, will decrease when you stop taking the medication.

You are more likely to experience side effects if you are on a large dose or if your dose has been rapidly increased. If you are unable to tolerate the medication, you can try reducing the dose and then increasing it to the previous level more slowly. For example, if you find that you are feeling nauseous after a few days of taking fluoxetine 20 mg, you can reduce the dose to 10 mg for a week or two and then increase it to 20 mg again when your body has become more accustomed to the drug. This can also be done if it is a liquid, and increased very slowly. Another alternative is to switch to a different SSRI altogether. Again, discuss this with your doctor beforehand.

The possible side effects of SSRIs, and how to deal with them, are discussed below. The list looks rather daunting, but remember that the symptoms occur in a minority of people. They will stop if you discontinue the drug under guidance from your doctor. Alternatively, your doctor may discuss with you how to manage them better. Monitoring of your mood and possible side effects is the key to all treatments – keep track of how you feel with a standard measure, such as the Hospital and Anxiety Depression (HAD) Scale (see Chapter 4), and use it like a temperature chart, on a weekly basis. If your mood is not improving, and especially if you are becoming more suicidal, discuss the issue with your therapist or psychiatrist to see whether you need to change tack.

Nausea

Nausea (feeling sick) is the most common, but temporary, side effect of an SSRI. It affects about 25 per cent of patients taking an SSRI, compared with about 10 per cent of those on a placebo (dummy pill). Citalopram and fluvoxamine are slightly more likely than the other SSRIs to cause nausea. The feeling can be minimised by taking the drug after food. Alternatively, halve the dose for a couple of weeks and then increase it slowly back to the normal dose. If the nausea persists, an anti-nausea drug (e.g. metoclobemide) may help.

Diarrhoea or constipation

SSRIs can cause diarrhoea in up to 15 per cent of patients, compared with about 5 per cent who take a placebo. Diarrhoea can be minimised by drinking plenty of apple juice (which contains pectin) or the use of a drug called bismuth subsalicylate (Kaopectate). Constipation occurs in 5 per cent of patients taking an SSRI. Diarrhoea or constipation may be improved by taking bulking agents such as Fybogel or psyllium seed husk and eating plenty of bran and roughage. To help with both diarrhoea and constipation, you should drink at least two litres of water a day.

Headache

Up to 20 per cent of patients taking an SSRI find that they develop headaches. Headache is a common symptom of tension and occurs in about 15 per cent of patients taking a placebo. Symptoms of headache can usually be helped by simple painkillers such as paracetamol and should decrease after a few weeks of taking an SSRI.

Excessive sweating

Excessive sweating occurs in about 10 per cent of patients taking an SSRI, compared with 5 per cent of those taking a placebo. There is no easy solution to this problem, although it should decrease over time.

Dry mouth

Dry mouth affects about 10 per cent of patients taking an SSRI, compared with 5 per cent of those taking a placebo. Sucking on sugarless gum or sugar-free boiled sweets may stimulate the production of saliva, or you could try a spray that can be bought over the counter that provides artificial saliva. Again, the symptoms usually decrease over time.

Tremor

Shakiness, or tremor, occurs in about 10 per cent of patients taking an SSRI and 3 per cent of those on a placebo. A beta blocker (e.g. propranolol) may be prescribed to help reduce tremor if it is severe.

Sedation or insomnia

Between 10 and 20 per cent of patients on SSRIs feel sedated, and between 5 and 15 per cent cannot sleep. For some SSRIs, the problem can sometimes be resolved by changing the time of day you take your medication (take it at night, for example, if it makes you drowsy), temporarily reducing the dose, or taking a different SSRI altogether. Fluoxetine may be activating and should normally be taken in the mornings. Sertraline is less likely to cause sedation. Fluvoxamine and trazodone are more likely to cause sedation and are best prescribed at night. If sedation is a problem, do not drive or use machinery.

Sexual problems

Sexual side effects of SSRIs can take the form of delayed ejaculation in men and an inability to reach orgasm in women. They can also occasionally cause both men and women to lose libido, although this is complicated to assess in the presence of depression. (However, there is one case report of an SSRI causing orgasms with yawning!)

Some atypical serotonergic antidepressants do not cause delayed ejaculation. However, their benefit in BDD is not known. Trazodone is one example, which very rarely in men can cause 'priapism', which is a persistent and painful erection, and should be treated as an emergency at a casualty department. Other antidepressants to consider if sexual dysfunction is a problem are reboxetine or lofepramine, as they act on the noradrenergic nervous system. However, they are likely to be less effective for BDD.

In the case of SSRIs generally, if you are on a relatively high dose, the problem of sexual side effects can sometimes be solved by lowering the dose, or taking a 'drug holiday' and missing a dose on the day of planned sexual activity. However, this needs to be done with caution as you may experience some withdrawal symptoms (see below). Taking a drug holiday is usually safe with fluoxetine, which remains in the body for up to five weeks after you stop taking it. However, you should speak to your doctor before doing this.

There are also reports concerning the use of Viagra or Cialis for people taking SSRIs. Viagra has been reported as successful in reversing the sexual side effects of SSRIs. Again, this needs to be researched carefully. If you wish to take Viagra, try a dose of 50 mg one hour before sexual activity, having first discussed it with your doctor. If this does not improve things, or gives only a partial response, you could try increasing it to 100 mg. Some patients with heart conditions will not be able to take it. Cialis has a possible advantage of a longer-lasting effect. The possible side effects of Viagra or Cialis include headache, flushing and dizziness. Do not buy such drugs online as you have no guarantee of quality, and they could just be dummy pills.

Loss of appetite

Symptoms of loss of appetite and weight loss occur in between 5 and 10 per cent of patients taking SSRIs (especially fluoxetine). Reducing the dose can halt this effect, though the symptoms usually fade away over time anyway.

Some SSRIs can sometimes cause slight weight gain in the long term, and you may need to adjust your diet and exercise programme. Depression and inactivity will also contribute to weight gain.

Nervousness or agitation

Some people feel more anxious or 'wired' or more impulsive when starting an SSRI. This may be more common with fluoxetine, which may then cause agitation or insomnia if taken too late in the day. Sertraline may be less likely to cause anxiety. It is always difficult to tell whether anxiety is associated with the depression or might be caused by the drug. If it is caused by the drug, the problem may be solved by (a) trying a lower dose, (b) switching to a different SSRI or (c) adding a different drug that may reduce anxiety. The feeling of increased anxiety is usually temporary and will subside over time. Feelings of increased agitation in some SSRIs may rarely be associated with an increase in violence or suicidal ideas. This is more likely to occur in a young person. If this happens, seek urgent medical advice. The feelings will subside on gradual withdrawal of the medication, and you may need a different therapy or type of antidepressant.

Rashes

Rashes are rare, but if you do get one, you should immediately speak to your doctor. This is more likely to occur with fluoxetine.

Mania

Antidepressants can very occasionally induce mania, especially in someone prone to bipolar disorder. You may be overactive, disinhibited, full of energy, irritable and able to go without any sleep. This condition can involve dangerous or risky behaviours. You should seek medical attention quickly. You may be advised to discontinue the medication.

Summary

Whenever side effects are a problem, always discuss them with your doctor. They are likely to advise you to either:

- reduce the dose, or
- try a different SSRI, or
- add another medication to counteract side effects such as insomnia or sexual problems, or
- perhaps wait and see, as many of the side effects tend to improve over time.

All SSRIs are equally effective overall, but one person may get a better response from one than another, or your doctor may wish to try you on another or a different class of antidepressant according to how well your mood improves or how troublesome your side effects are.

Tricyclics

Tricyclics are an older class of antidepressants. They were first developed for the treatment of depression and obsessive-compulsive disorder in the 1960s. The name 'tricyclic' is used to describe the structure of the chemical that was first synthesised.

Tricyclics fell out of favour compared to the SSRIs because the former have more side effects. Clomipramine (trade name Anafranil) is a tricyclic that is used for treating BDD because, compared to other tricyclics, it is a potent serotonin reuptake inhibitor. It can also be used for depression. It is normally started with a low dosage (for example, 75 mg at night) and gradually increased to a maximum that you can tolerate. The minimum dose required for an effect is usually 125 mg. Higher doses, up to 300 mg a day, are sometimes used, although the usual dose is up to 225 mg. Higher doses tend to increase the frequency of side effects. Most of the side effects are related to the dose and tend to reduce over time, but some may persist. They will cease if the drug is discontinued. Clomipramine is more often prescribed at night so that the sedative side effects have worn off by the morning. Some people metabolise a tricyclic very quickly and so even when they are taking a high dose they may have a relatively low level of the drug in the bloodstream. If necessary, the level of a tricyclic and its metabolite can be checked by a blood test to determine if it is safe to increase the dose to a higher level. Alternatively, you may be given a genetic test to see if you are someone who metabolises such drugs faster than others.

Common side effects of clomipramine

- Dry mouth: At least two-thirds of patients taking clomipramine experience a dry mouth. You get a dry mouth when you produce less saliva than normal. Sucking on sugarless gum may stimulate production of saliva, or you could try a spray that can be bought over the counter that provides artificial saliva. Good mouth hygiene is important, as are regular visits to your dentist.
- Dizziness: Dizziness on standing is a common side effect for about 25 per cent of patients taking clomipramine. You can minimise dizziness by rising slowly or sitting on the side of the bed first and squeezing the muscles in your calves as you stand up.
- Tremor: About 15 per cent of patients taking clomipramine develop shakiness or tremor in their arms. There are no simple remedies for tremor, although another drug (a beta blocker, such as propranolol) may reduce tremor if it is severe.
- Weight gain: Weight gain can be a problem with clomipramine, and you should therefore be especially careful to eat healthily.
- Constipation: You have a one in four chance of becoming constipated if you take clomipramine. A diet full of roughage from vegetables or bran, and prunes or a bulking agent such as Fybogel or psyllium husks will help. Always remember to drink plenty of water. Laxatives that stimulate the bowel should not be used except occasionally.

- Drowsiness or fatigue: Clomipramine can cause drowsiness, which can be minimised by taking the dosage at night. Some people may still experience a 'hangover' in the morning; if that happens with you, spread the dose over the day.
- Blurred vision, headache: Clomipramine can also cause blurring of vision or a headache. There is no good solution to this apart from switching to a different antidepressant.
- Sexual problems: Clomipramine can be a reason for delayed ejaculation or, less commonly, impotence in men. It can also cause women difficulties in reaching orgasm. For suggested solutions see under side effects of SSRIs, above.
- Increased sweating: People taking clomipramine may complain that they sweat more or that their hot flushes have increased. There is no easy solution to this, but it should improve over time.
- Epileptic fit: There is a small risk (for about 0.5 per cent of individuals taking clomipramine) of having an epileptic fit. In this case, the drug will need to be discontinued or the dose significantly reduced. The majority of fits, however, occur in patients taking above 250 mg of clomipramine.
- Urinary problems: Occasionally, clomipramine can cause urinary retention or hesitancy in the elderly, in which case the drug will need to be discontinued.
- Heart problems: Individuals with pre-existing heart disease treated with a clomipramine should have an ECG

(electrocardiogram) before beginning treatment and at regular intervals during treatment, as it could cause some individuals to develop an irregular heartbeat.

Stopping or reducing antidepressant medication

If you are already taking antidepressant medication, then don't stop or change the dose on your own. The reason is that you may experience withdrawal symptoms from the antidepressant and it's best to reduce such medication slowly. Whether you experience withdrawal symptoms or not is unpredictable – many people do not have any or only minor ones; a small minority have marked or severe symptoms that require careful reduction of their medication. Note that some doctors may refer to withdrawal symptoms as 'discontinuation', which is partly a euphemism to avoid the association with an addiction or dependence. However, it is now generally recognised that, for a few people, it is a type of addiction as the stopping of the drug causes withdrawal symptoms and craving. The body finds it difficult to adapt if a drug is removed suddenly and it is sensible therefore to taper the dose gradually over several weeks. Withdrawal symptoms can be minimised or prevented if you are pre-warned and manage the situation. Always discuss your wishes with your doctor and plan things together. Do not be afraid to ask for a second opinion where necessary.

In most people these withdrawal effects are mild. For a small number of people – and no one can predict who they might be – the effects can be unpleasant if the medication is stopped suddenly. Being knowledgeable about potential withdrawal symptoms allows one to be forewarned and to manage any symptoms that emerge by reducing the dose more slowly. The speed at which the discontinuation of a drug causes withdrawal symptoms is related to how fast the drug is metabolised and gets out of your system. Fluoxetine is the least likely of all SSRIs to cause withdrawal symptoms. This is because it breaks down very slowly and is in your body for up to five weeks after your last dose. If it does cause withdrawal symptoms, they tend to come on within two or three weeks of stopping it. The 'worst' drugs linked to withdrawal symptoms are venlafaxine (Efexor) and paroxetine (Seroxat, Paxil), which can cause symptoms on the same day you miss a dose. Sertraline (Zoloft) commonly causes withdrawal symptoms within two to three days. Possible physical withdrawal symptoms can include the following:

- flu-like symptoms (aches, fever, sweats, chills, muscle cramps)
- gastroenteritis-like symptoms (nausea, vomiting, diarrhoea, abdominal pain or cramps)
- dizziness, spinning, feeling hungover, feeling unsteady
- headache, tremor
- sensory abnormalities (numbness, sensations that feel like electric shocks, abnormal visual sensations or smells, tinnitus).

The second group of symptoms that can occur are mainly psychological:

- depression (crying, deteriorating mood, fatigue, poor concentration, loss of appetite, suicidal thoughts/attempts)
- anxiety-like symptoms (anxious, nervous, panicky)
- preoccupation with and distress about your appearance
- irritability (agitation, impulsivity, aggression)
- confusion, memory problems
- mood swings (elation, mania)
- hallucinations (auditory, visual)
- feelings of dissociation (detachment, unreality, nightmares).

Are symptoms those of withdrawal or a relapse?

Another problem is deciding whether symptoms that emerge on stopping medication are those of withdrawal or whether they are a relapse of depression. The following differences may help you and your doctor to tell.

- **Do your symptoms come on suddenly over days or within a week after stopping?** Withdrawal symptoms come on relatively suddenly, within days to weeks of lowering or stopping an antidepressant. Symptoms of relapse of depression usually occur within one or more months of stopping.
- **Are your symptoms physical?** Physical symptoms, such as feeling dizzy or light-headed, having flu-like

aches, sweating, nausea, numbness, headaches or sensations that feel like electric shocks, are usually part of the withdrawal state. While some of these physical symptoms can occasionally occur in relapse of depression, they would have been part of the original symptoms you had, and you might recognise them as such.

- **How quickly do your symptoms improve when you stop medication?** Withdrawal symptoms peak within seven to ten days or so, and are usually gone within three weeks. By contrast, symptoms of a relapse of depression will persist and may get worse.
- **How quickly do your symptoms improve if you restart the medication?** Withdrawal symptoms immediately improve when you restart the drug. Symptoms of relapse may continue or get worse, and take several weeks to improve when you recommence an antidepressant.

How do my doctor and I reduce the drug slowly enough?

The first step is to decide when to reduce the dose. This normally depends on whether you have been well for long enough and whether you are still vulnerable to relapse. Have you had an effective psychological therapy that can now protect you? The optimum rate of reduction of an antidepressant to a standard dose is related to the type of drug. In general, each reduction should take place over a month.

The rate at which you reduce the drug depends on the nature of the drug, the dose you are taking and the severity of any withdrawal symptoms you experience. For example, paroxetine (Seroxat or Paxil) being prescribed at 20 mg daily might be reduced to 10 mg for two months. Each reduction would then guide the speed at which the medication is further reduced. If withdrawal symptoms emerge, you may have to slow down. For example:

- if you experience mild or no symptoms, then you need not change the rate of reduction (e.g. paroxetine from 10 mg to nothing)
- if you experience moderate withdrawal symptoms, the next reduction would be smaller (e.g. paroxetine from 10 mg to 5 mg)
- if you have severe withdrawal symptoms your doctor may restore the original dose and then start smaller dose reductions (e.g. paroxetine 20 mg to 15 mg for two months); if this results in no or mild symptoms, it could then be reduced to 12.5 mg.

Most withdrawal symptoms can be minimised by reducing the drugs slowly, and this should be done under the guidance of your doctor. Some patients have been advised to take the drug on alternate days, but this does not make sense unless it is long acting like fluoxetine. It is nearly always better to reduce the dose of an antidepressant by a small amount on a daily basis. Further discussion on withdrawing from antidepressants can be found in the very helpful book *Coming Off Antidepressants* (see Appendix 2 for details).

Liquid preparations

To obtain smaller doses for a withdrawal programme, or to start at a lower dose, you can either cut the tablets into smaller pieces or measure out a liquid, which is usually easier. If you are simply unable to tolerate a tablet, you may find it easier to have your medication in the form of a liquid (elixir). The drugs available as a liquid are listed in the table on page 369.

Use of medication in pregnancy and breastfeeding

Most of the SSRIs and clomipramine are generally considered to be safe for pregnant women. However, as no manufacturer wants to be sued, they all recommend 'caution' and say that their product should not be used in pregnancy or breastfeeding. No mother wants to cause harm to her baby, but in general there are no significant problems. Fluoxetine, paroxetine, sertraline and clomipramine are the most studied in pregnancy or breastfeeding, so these are the most widely prescribed drugs for pregnant women. Animal and human studies suggest a very low risk, but they are not fully conclusive. The risk of 'spontaneous abortion' may be very slightly higher than normal, but the figures are difficult to interpret. Most doctors prefer to be cautious and treat BDD or depression with a psychological treatment where pregnancy is possible or planned. However, if you and your doctor believe that medications are necessary (and depression commonly gets worse during pregnancy), or if you find a psychological approach difficult, it is nearly always better for you to be functioning as a mother than suffering from depression, whatever the precise risks involved, but discuss this fully with your doctor as there may be new evidence.

What if an SSRI or clomipramine fails?

There are other options if you do not get better with two or more SSRIs or clomipramine. This is best discussed with a psychiatrist. For example, there is some evidence for the benefit of combining different antidepressant drugs (e.g. an SSRI such as citalopram with clomipramine). Sometimes a very high dose of an SSRI may be used. Alternatively, your doctor might recommend a different class of antidepressant (e.g. venlafaxine) or combining an SSRI with buspirone in BDD. Buspirone is an anti-anxiety drug.

Antipsychotic drugs

Some doctors prescribe drugs for BDD that block dopamine receptors, either alone or as an additional treatment to an SSRI. These are also known as antipsychotic drugs and include olanzapine (Zyprexa), ziprasidone (Geodon), risperidone (Risperidal), aripiprazole (Abilify), haloperidol (Haldol), quetiapine (Seroquel), sulpiride, trifluoperazine, pimozide and chlorpromazine. Some antipsychotics (especially olanzapine and, to a lesser extent, risperidone) are more likely to cause weight gain and sedation.

Dopamine-blocking drugs are normally used for treating psychosis and paranoia. There is no evidence for the benefit of dopamine-blocking drugs, either alone or in combination with another drug in BDD. One study suggests that adding pimozide to people who have failed an SSRI medication did not make any difference compared to a dummy pill (placebo) in BDD. Antipsychotics may still be prescribed in the short term if you are very agitated, or for example have tics or more complex problems with paranoia.

What are the side effects of dopamine-blocking drugs?

In low doses, dopamine-blocking drugs may help to reduce anxiety and do not usually cause problems. The main side effect may be tiredness. Some anti-dopamine drugs cause weight gain and loss of libido. When dopamine blockers are prescribed in higher doses, they can have side effects such as stiffness in the limbs or slurred speech that can be countered by medication such as procyclidine. A small minority of women may experience hormonal changes, such as stimulation of prolactin, which stops the periods.

With a very high dose, or if you are especially sensitive, such drugs may cause abnormal movements such as tremor, and you may need other tablets to counteract these. They may also reduce libido. In general, an antipsychotic drug is not recommended in the long term for unipolar depression. In a higher dose it can emotionally numb you and prevent you from experiencing pleasure. If your main diagnosis is of unipolar depression and you are taking an antipsychotic drug, you may want to ask your doctor to review it.

If you are already taking such medication, then please don't stop or change the dose on your own. Always discuss your wishes with your doctor and plan things together. Do not be afraid to ask for a second opinion where necessary. Travelling to a specialised centre may be the most effective solution.

Tranquillisers

Tranquillisers are drugs that aim to reduce anxiety or are sedative. The most common are a group of drugs called benzodiazepines (diazepam or Valium, nitrazepam, lorazepam, clonazepam). Others are prescribed for sleep. There is no evidence for their benefit in treating BDD.

Tranquillisers used to be prescribed very commonly in the past but are less used now because of the risks of addiction. They are used for managing severe agitation in depression for the short term. The main side effects are slower reaction times, so they should not be used when operating machinery or driving. The main problem is of dependence, so that a sudden withdrawal can lead to a short-term increase in anxiety, insomnia, irritability, headaches and many other possible symptoms. Withdrawing from such drugs therefore needs to be managed carefully.

Psychedelics

Psilocybin (derived from magic mushrooms) and other psychedelics (e.g. LSD) are illegal in many countries. Research suggests they may be helpful in safely controlled conditions with psychological support. More research is required to determine safety and effectiveness before they can be prescribed in clinical practice. It is not known, for example, how often they need to be taken to maintain any improvements. The landscape is moving rapidly, and they can now be prescribed in Australia and some US states.

What about electroconvulsive therapy (ECT) for BDD?

There is no evidence that ECT helps in BDD. It might very occasionally be recommended where the person with BDD has very severe depression that has not responded to medication or a psychological treatment.

What about brain surgery for BDD?

There is no evidence for the benefit of neurosurgery in BDD. There are a few cases with mixed reports in BDD, but there are no controlled trials comparing surgery against a sham treatment. Neurosurgery is generally safe, but it can be followed by some rare complications such as epilepsy, haemorrhage, persistent headaches or infections.

Other medical techniques are being researched for BDD, but at the time of writing are still experimental. One, known as deep brain stimulation, passes an electric current to electrodes implanted in the brain. It is also experimental, but because the stimulator can be switched on and off, the effects are reversible.

PIT STOP

Let's stop and think about what you have just been reading. Can you summarise the key ideas you have taken on board? What is sticking in your mind? Maybe write it down. If you have any questions, jot those down too. You can return to them once you have had a chance to digest the information.

What is sticking in my mind from my reading so far?

1.

2.

3.

14

Finding help

When to consider professional help

A self-help book like this one could be all that is required for some people to overcome a body image problem. After all, even with professional help, it is likely to be your own efforts between sessions that make the biggest difference. You might consider using this book with the aid of a professional; this is called 'guided self-help'. In this case, the book can offer a shared way of understanding your problems and the strategies to improve the way you feel.

Professional help, with an appropriately trained practitioner, is often the most effective approach. This involves working with a psychologist, psychiatrist, therapist, counsellor or nurse therapist. Cognitive behavioural therapy (CBT) can help most people and will rarely make symptoms worse. We suggest that you seek professional help if your body image problem is in the moderate to severe range, and especially if your attempts at self-help are not bearing fruit after a month or so.

> **THOUGHTS ABOUT ENDING YOUR LIFE**
>
> If you are feeling hopeless about the future and are having thoughts about ending your life, please seek professional help immediately.

Getting the right kind of help

If you are prescribed medication like Prozac, you can virtually guarantee that any pharmacy you go to will give you the right dosage and that the Prozac will always be of the same quality. Unfortunately, this is not always true of psychological therapy. Of all the different forms of psychotherapy, only CBT has been shown to work effectively for a body image problem and it is therefore likely to be the treatment of choice. When choosing a suitable therapist, the alarm bells should ring when you encounter therapists who:

- do not tell you what type of therapy you are receiving
- just keep asking 'How does that make you feel?'
- spend most of the time wanting you to discuss your childhood and the cause of your body image problem
- do not share their understanding of what maintains your problem
- do not problem-solve with you
- do not negotiate relevant homework between sessions
- do not monitor your progress in overcoming your symptoms.

If you are not sure, ask what type of therapy or counselling you are receiving. There is no evidence that general counselling, psychodynamic therapy, psychoanalytical therapy, hypnotherapy or transactional analysis are of any benefit for moderate to severe body image problems. People can find such approaches supportive or helpful for some issues, but they are rarely helpful by themselves in overcoming a body image problem. Supportive psychological therapy might also, to a degree, help people with mild problems.

Similarly, beware of a doctor who offers only medication without also recommending a psychological treatment. There might also be problems with obtaining psychological therapies on the NHS because of the lack of funding, but this is not the fault of the doctor – it is a problem that requires political action and takes a long time to solve. In the meantime, seek support, use the principles outlined in this book (or other CBT-based self-help material), and consider asking your doctor for medication or opting for private therapy.

Fears about seeking help

You might have a number of worries about seeking help, such as:

- 'What if it doesn't help?'
- 'It will be too embarrassing to tell them about my problem.'
- 'They'll think I'm mad and want to keep me in hospital.'

- 'What if they pass the information on to social services or my employer?'

If you find it difficult to talk about some of your worries, it's usually helpful to say you are embarrassed or ashamed. Remember that worrying is normal and any health professional who has the slightest experience with body image problems will be sensitive to your difficulties. They will not consider you mad or want to keep you in hospital against your will. Individuals are assessed for detention only in extreme circumstances, such as if they are a danger to themselves or others (e.g. actively suicidal, neglecting themselves badly or very underweight). Such information is kept confidential and cannot be shared with other agencies or your employer without your permission. It does not go on any employment records or to social services. Only in extreme circumstances would a therapist ask someone to assess the impact of a person's body image problem on his/her family and children. Treatment may not help initially, as it can take a few weeks to take effect, but if nothing is risked, nothing is gained and your problem is likely to persist for some time. Furthermore, CBT or medication very rarely makes your problem worse.

In teaching centres, you may be asked if a student or trainee may sit in. It is important to continue training others in psychological treatment, but you are entitled to refuse without it affecting your treatment.

Remember, as with all other thoughts, try to treat your thoughts about seeking help as 'just thoughts', which are likely to be quite common under the circumstances. Rather than trying to ignore them or debating them in your mind, take your thoughts with a pinch of salt and act consistently towards pursuing your goal of overcoming your body image problem.

Getting the most from a psychological therapy

You will get the most from a psychological therapy if you:

- keep your appointments
- are honest and open with your therapist
- tell your therapist if you do feel very embarrassed or ashamed about your symptoms
- attempt the homework agreed between you and your therapist during therapy sessions (having a good relationship with your therapist is important, but adherence to daily testing out of alternatives is the biggest predictor of success in therapy)
- challenge your usual way of responding to your problem (e.g. the way you check, compare, brood, avoid) and act as if you don't have an emotional problem (even if you don't believe it)
- act against the way you feel, and do it 'unconfidently' and 'uncomfortably' even if you are not sure it will work
- have clear goals that you want to achieve and you can agree on with your therapist
- regularly monitor your progress with your therapist, using progress charts or scales

- record the sessions so you can listen to them again
- give the therapist feedback.

You might find that you are not ready for CBT, and it might be better to return when you feel more committed to change and able to do the homework regularly. Don't believe you are a 'hopeless case' – change is nearly always possible. Even a small change is worth making, and then you can build on it. Don't be afraid to seek a second opinion or a referral to a specialist centre.

Types of professionals offering help

There is a range of mental health professionals who will offer help for a body image problem. Most mental health teams are multidisciplinary, which means that they include people from different professional backgrounds.

- **Psychiatrists** are medical doctors who specialise in mental disorder. They can prescribe medication for BDD or bulimia, and will probably be more knowledgeable about dosage and other issues required for BDD and bulimia than your family doctor. Only a few psychiatrists are trained in CBT.
- **Clinical psychologists** have a basic training in psychology, and have then trained in the clinical application of psychological assessment and therapies. They do not prescribe medication. Many will offer CBT but might not have had the specialist training and supervision required.

- **Counselling psychologists** have a basic training in psychology, and are then trained in counselling and therapy. They do not prescribe medication. Some offer CBT but might not have had the specialist training required.
- **Nurse therapists** are originally trained in psychiatric nursing, and in the UK most have specialised in CBT.
- **Psychotherapists** and **counsellors** come from a broad range of therapy backgrounds. Most will listen to you and help you to work through issues in your life. They do not prescribe medication. They are not usually trained in CBT.

All of the above may be suitably trained and supervised in CBT but will not have a lot of experience with body image problems!

It is important to realise that, at the time of writing, there is nothing to stop anyone calling themselves a counsellor or psychotherapist, whether or not they are properly trained. No therapist with a recognised professional qualification is going to mind you asking about their relevant training and qualifications. It is very important to satisfy yourself about these things, as well as the type of therapy used. Here are some questions you may want to ask:

- What experience have they got of treating body image problems (e.g. how many patients or clients have they treated)?
- What therapy do they use?

- If providing CBT, are they accredited or accreditable as having a minimum training in CBT?
- What are their expectations for change at the end of therapy, and do these match your goals?
- Do you get on with the therapist?

Of course you will want someone who is experienced with body image problems, but if they are not, try to judge whether they are willing to learn more. Details of finding an accredited therapist are given below.

If you have problems with your therapist

If you want to complain about any professional, think clearly about the nature of the problem – for example, is it the type of treatment, the therapist, the location or something else?

Are there contributing factors (e.g. the personality of your therapist or you feeling more depressed)? Can you sort it out with the therapist or another member of the team? Can you think of possible solutions to discuss with the professional? If the professional is refusing further therapy, listen to their reasons and write them down. If the reasons are financial (e.g. it costs too much), don't give up, as you may have to persist to get another opinion.

Finding professional help in the UK

If you would like professional treatment in the UK, your family doctor or general practitioner is the best place to start. They will usually be aware of what services are available locally. If you are worried about seeing your GP, take a relative or friend with you. If you find it difficult to talk to your GP, write a letter and give it to them. At your consultation, write down the key points that you want answered. You can always change your GP if you think you might be better understood or treated by another.

The information that you tell your GP is confidential and cannot be shared without your permission. If your local mental health service is unable to assist, they might refer you to a national service. Unfortunately, getting referred to a specialist service is not always easy (due to funding shortages) and will usually depend upon the support of your local mental health team. Make it clear that you will need cognitive behavioural therapy from a trained practitioner. For therapy services in the NHS, you can usually be referred only to a department and not to a particular individual. Despite this, you could find it helpful to do your own research and find out the names of recommended therapists from a support group or national charity (see the list in Appendix 1).

In its treatment guidelines for OCD and BDD, the National Institute for Health and Care Excellence (NICE) recommends that patients should have access to an OCD/BDD multidisciplinary healthcare team, which will focus on the more severe cases and decide who should be referred onwards to a national service. One of the authors of this book (David Veale) runs a national service in the UK for BDD at the South London and Maudsley Trust. This is for outpatient treatment or for a more intensive treatment programme on a residential unit. There is also a separate stream of funding from the Department of Health and Social Care for a treatment refractory service; further details can be found on the website www.iop.kcl.ac.uk/ncg.

In the UK, it is usually quicker to obtain help privately, but this does not necessarily mean that the treatment will be any better. Good and bad treatment can occur both in the public and the private sector. It is best to ask for recommendations from your local support group or a national charity, which may keep a directory of practitioners. In the UK, you can also try searching for a private accredited therapist on the website of the British Association for Behavioural and Cognitive Psychotherapies (www.babcp.com) in the 'Find a Therapist' section. Not all cognitive behavioural therapists bother to become accredited, and there are many from psychiatry, psychology or nursing backgrounds who are excellent cognitive behavioural therapists.

Finding help in the USA

In the USA, finding a cognitive behavioural therapist may be difficult depending on where you live. You could ask for a referral from your family doctor, or a recommendation from an academic psychiatry or psychology department. The best recommendation could come from your local support group or charity. It is likely to be a member of the Association for Behavioral and Cognitive Therapies, which maintains a directory of therapists who can be contacted (www.abct.org). As in the UK, it is usually quicker to obtain help privately, but this does not mean you will necessarily get any better treatment. Good and bad treatment can occur both in the public and the private sector.

Finding help in the rest of the world

The European Association for Behavioural Cognitive Therapies lists member associations on its website at www.eabct.com. Details of the Australian Association for Cognitive and Behavioural Therapy can be found on its website at www.aacbt.org.au.

Charities and support groups

In addition to professional help, national charities and local support groups can be invaluable. If you are in the UK and have BDD, we recommend the BDD Foundation or OCD Action. If you have a disfigurement, support Changing Faces. For an eating disorder, support BEAT (formerly known as the Eating Disorders Association). In the USA, if you have BDD, you can support the Neysa Jane BDD fund and the OCD Foundation.

These charities will offer you information on local resources and support groups, which provide a forum for mutual acceptance, understanding and setting of goals. They will also be able to recommend local therapists or psychiatrists. People new to the area can talk to others who have learned successful ways of coping. Reading books and internet articles about body image problems are useful ways of getting further information or support. The more you know about the problem and the more you can become your own therapist, the better equipped you will be to overcome it. And when you recover from your body image problem, you can help raise funds for research into better treatments, and campaign for better services and for training for more cognitive behavioural therapists in public medicine. Unfortunately, many of these charities are too small to be able to focus enough energy on raising funds for research, especially compared with the big charities dealing with cancer or heart disease.

PIT STOP

Let's stop and think about what you have just been reading. Can you summarise the key ideas you have taken on board? What is sticking in your mind? Maybe write it down. If you have any questions, jot those down too. You can return to them once you have had a chance to digest the information.

What is sticking in my mind from my reading so far?

1.

2.

3.

APPENDIX 1

Useful contacts and information

AUSTRALIA
Anxiety Recovery Centre Victoria (ARCVic)
Website: www.arcvic.com.au
ARCVic is an organisation for people living with anxiety disorders.

Eating Disorders Association Inc.
Website: www.eda.org.au
The Eating Disorders Association provides support and information for people with an eating disorder.

CANADA
About Face
Website: aboutface.ca
About Face provides information and emotional support to individuals with facial differences.

GERMANY
UKE Hamburg
Website: ag-neuropsychologie.de/Technique_for_reducing_nail_biting_and_hair_pulling_trichotillomania
Professor Moritz's research pages for decoupling.

NEW ZEALAND
OCD NZ
Website: www.OCD.org.nz
The website provides a place for people with OCD and their families to share common ground, information and support.

UNITED KINGDOM
Acne Support Group
Website: acnesupport.org.uk
The Acne Support Group gives support and help for people with acne and rosacea.

BDD Foundation
Website: bddfoundation.org
The BDD Foundation aims to increase awareness and understanding of body dysmorphic disorder.

Beat (previously known as the Eating Disorders Association)
Website: www.beateatingdisorders.org.uk
Beat is a national charity based in the UK providing information, help and support for people affected by eating disorders.

BFRB UK & Ireland
Website: www.bfrbukireland.com
Charitable organisation focused on body-focused repetitive behaviours (BFRBs).

British Association of Aesthetic Plastic Surgeons
Website: baaps.org.uk/_userfiles/pages/files/thinking_about_having_cosmetic_surgery_1.pdf
This page of the BAAPS website gives advice if you are thinking about having cosmetic surgery.

Centre for Anxiety Disorders and Trauma (CADAT), The Maudsley Hospital, London
Website: slam.nhs.uk/search/service/centre-for-anxiety-disorders-and-trauma-112
A specialist NHS centre for BDD.

Changing Faces
Website: www.changingfaces.org.uk
Changing Faces provides support to people with disfigurements by publishing information and running workshops to help them improve their social skills and develop their self-confidence and self-esteem.

National Institute for Health and Care Excellence (NICE)
Website: www.nice.org.uk/Guidance/CG31
Best practice guidelines for OCD and BDD.

OCD Action
Website: www.ocdaction.org.uk
OCD Action is a user-led charity for individuals with OCD and BDD.

OCD Youth
Website: ocdyouth.org
OCD Youth is an organisation especially designed to help children and adolescents with OCD and other spectrum disorders.

Royal College of Psychiatrists (stopping antidepressants)
Website: www.rcpsych.ac.uk/mental-health/treatments-and-wellbeing/stopping-antidepressants
Useful information on coming off antidepressants.

Samaritans
Website: www.samaritans.org
Samaritans is a registered charity that offers confidential support to anyone experiencing a crisis or thinking of taking their own life.

SANE and SANEline
Website: www.sane.org.uk
SANEline is a national mental health helpline providing information and support, with a database of local and national services.

UNITED STATES OF AMERICA
International OCD Foundation
Website: iocdf.org
The International OCD Foundation is a non-profit organisation for people with OCD and spectrum disorders like BDD.

National Alliance for Eating Disorders
Website: www.allianceforeatingdisorders.com
This website seeks to offer accessible programmes across the nation that allow children and young adults to be educated about eating disorders.

The TLC Foundation
Website: bfrb.org
The TLC Foundation is dedicated to breaking down myths and misperceptions about people experiencing body-focused repetitive behaviours (BFRBs), such as compulsive skin-picking and hair-pulling. It provides lots of resources on overcoming BFRBs.

APPENDIX 2

Further reading

All titles listed below are user-friendly self-help books

Body dysmorphic disorder

Claiborn, J. and Pedrick, C., *The BDD Workbook* (New Harbinger Publications).

Phillips, K., *The Broken Mirror: Understanding and Treating Body Dysmorphic Disorder* (Oxford University Press).

Pope, H., Phillips, K. and Olivardia, R., *The Adonis Complex: How to Identify, Treat, and Prevent Body Obsession in Men and Boys* (Simon & Schuster).

Wilhelm, S., *Feeling Good About the Way You Look* (Guilford Publications).

Body image

Cash, T., *The Body Image Workbook* (New Harbinger Publications).

Cognitive behavioural therapy

Willson, R. and Branch, R., *Cognitive Behavioural Therapy for Dummies* (Wiley).

Depression

Addis, M. and Martell, C., *Overcoming Depression One Step at a Time* (New Harbinger Publications).

Burns, D., *Feeling Good* (Avon Books).

Dryden, W., *How to Accept Yourself* (Sheldon Press).

Fennell, M., *Overcoming Low Self-Esteem* (Robinson).

Gilbert, P., Overcoming Depression (Robinson).

Glenmullen, J., *Coming Off Antidepressants* (Robinson).

Veale, D. and Willson, R., *Manage Your Mood* (Robinson).

Young, J.E. and Klosko, J.S., *Reinventing Your Life: The Breakthrough Program to End Negative Behaviour and Feel Great Again* (Penguin).

Disfigurement

Partridge, J., Changing Faces: *The Challenge of Facial Disfigurement* (Penguin).

Eating disorders

Cooper, P. and Graham, P., *Overcoming Bulimia Nervosa* (Robinson).

Fairburn, C., *Overcoming Binge-Eating* (Guilford Publications).

Graham, P. and Freeman, C., *Overcoming Anorexia Nervosa* (Robinson).

Obsessive-compulsive disorder

Veale, D. and Willson, R., *Overcoming Obsessive Compulsive Disorder* (Robinson).

Social phobia
Butler, G., *Overcoming Social Anxiety and Shyness* (Robinson).

Trichotillomania and skin-picking
Claiborn, J. and Pedrick, C., *The Habit Change Workbook* (New Harbinger Publications).

Penzel, F., *The Hair Pulling Problem: A Complete Guide to Trichotillomania* (Oxford University Press).

APPENDIX 3

Assessment forms and progress charts

Chapter 2

Body image questionnaire

Please answer the following for how you have felt about your appearance over the past week.

1. How often do you **deliberately** check your feature(s) (not accidentally catch sight of it/them)? Please include looking at your feature(s) in a mirror or other reflective surfaces like a shop window, or looking at it directly or feeling it with your fingers.

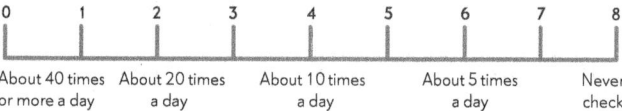

| 0 | 1 | 2 | 3 | 4 | 5 | 6 | 7 | 8 |
| About 40 times or more a day | | About 20 times a day | | About 10 times a day | | About 5 times a day | | Never check |

2. To what extent do you feel your feature(s) are **currently** ugly, unattractive or 'not right'?

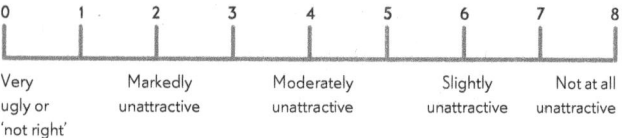

| 0 | 1 | 2 | 3 | 4 | 5 | 6 | 7 | 8 |
| Very ugly or 'not right' | | Markedly unattractive | | Moderately unattractive | | Slightly unattractive | | Not at all unattractive |

3. To what extent does your feature(s) **currently** cause you a lot of distress?

| 0 | 1 | 2 | 3 | 4 | 5 | 6 | 7 | 8 |
| Not at all distressing | | Slightly distressing | | Moderately distressing | | Markedly distressing | | Extremely distressing |

ASSESSMENT FORMS AND PROGRESS CHARTS

4. How often does your feature(s) **currently** lead you to avoid situations or activities?

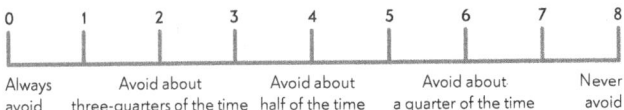

5. To what extent does your feature(s) **currently** preoccupy you? That is, you think about it a lot and it is hard to stop thinking about it.

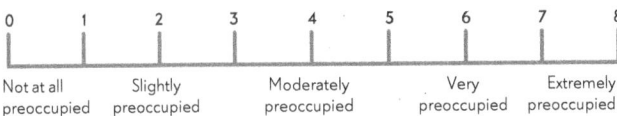

6. If you have a partner, to what extent does your feature(s) **currently** have an effect on your relationship with them (e.g. affectionate feelings, number of arguments, enjoying activities together)? If you do not have a partner, to what extent does your feature(s) **currently** have an effect on dating or developing a relationship?

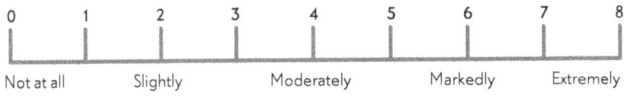

7. To what extent does your feature(s) **currently** interfere with your ability to work or study, or your role as a homemaker? (Please rate this even if you are not working or studying: we are interested in your ability to work or study.)

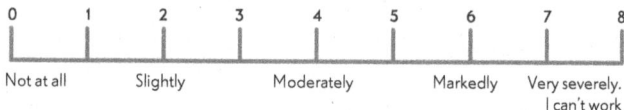

Not at all / Slightly / Moderately / Markedly / Very severely. I can't work

8. To what extent does your feature(s) **currently** interfere with your social life (with other people, e.g. parties, pubs, clubs, outings, visits, entertaining at home)?

Not at all / Slightly / Moderately / Markedly / Very severely

9. To what extent do you feel your appearance is the most important aspect of who you are?

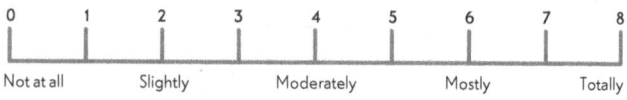

Not at all / Slightly / Moderately / Mostly / Totally

Source: Based on Veale et al. (2012).

Further details of the questionnaire are published in:

Veale, D., Ellison, N., Werner, T., Dodhia, R., Serfaty, M. and Clarke, A. (2012) Development of a cosmetic procedure screening questionnaire (COPS) for body dysmorphic disorder. *Journal of Plastic Reconstructive and Aesthetic Surgery*, 65(4), 530–532. http://dx.doi.org/10.1016/j.bjps.2011.09.007

ASSESSMENT FORMS AND PROGRESS CHARTS

Chapter 4

Body image questionnaire

This is the same questionnaire as that included for Chapter 2, above.

Please answer the following for how you have felt about your appearance over the past week.

1. How often do you **deliberately** check your feature(s) (not accidentally catch sight of it/them)? Please include looking at your feature(s) in a mirror or other reflective surfaces like a shop window, or looking at it directly or feeling it with your fingers.

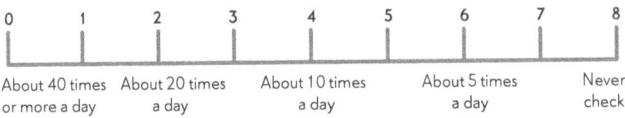

2. To what extent do you feel your feature(s) are **currently** ugly, unattractive or 'not right'?

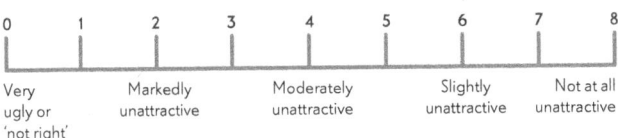

3. To what extent does your feature(s) **currently** cause you a lot of distress?

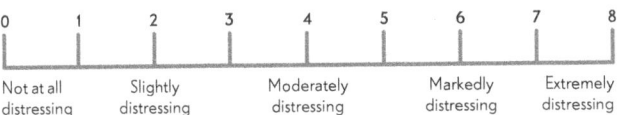

4. How often does your feature(s) **currently** lead you to avoid situations or activities?

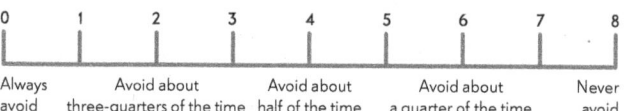

5. To what extent does your feature(s) **currently** preoccupy you? That is, you think about it a lot and it is hard to stop thinking about it.

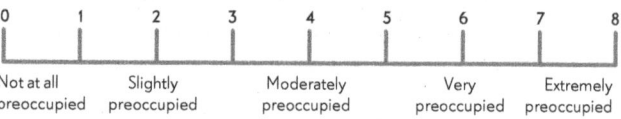

6. If you have a partner, to what extent does your feature(s) **currently** have an effect on your relationship with them (e.g. affectionate feelings, number of arguments, enjoying activities together)? If you do not have a partner, to what extent does your feature(s) **currently** have an effect on dating or developing a relationship?

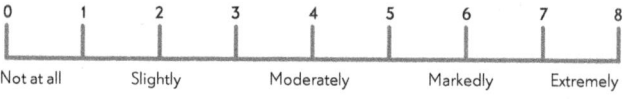

ASSESSMENT FORMS AND PROGRESS CHARTS

7. To what extent does your feature(s) **currently** interfere with your ability to work or study, or your role as a homemaker? (Please rate this even if you are not working or studying: we are interested in your ability to work or study.)

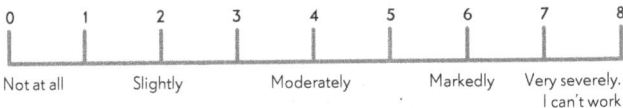

0	1	2	3	4	5	6	7	8
Not at all		Slightly		Moderately		Markedly		Very severely. I can't work

8. To what extent does your feature(s) **currently** interfere with your social life (with other people, e.g. parties, pubs, clubs, outings, visits, entertaining at home)?

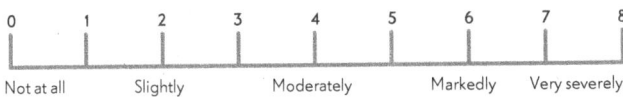

0	1	2	3	4	5	6	7	8
Not at all		Slightly		Moderately		Markedly		Very severely

9. To what extent do you feel your appearance is the most important aspect of who you are?

0	1	2	3	4	5	6	7	8
Not at all		Slightly		Moderately		Mostly		Totally

Source: Based on Veale et al. (2012).

Appearance anxiety questionnaire

Please tick the box that best describes the way you have felt about your appearance or a specific feature OVER THE PAST WEEK, INCLUDING TODAY.

Name _____ Date _____

	Not at all (0)	A little (1)	Often (2)	A lot (3)	All the time (4)
1. I worry about my appearance					
2. I check my appearance (e.g. in mirrors, by touching with my fingers or by taking photos of myself)					
3. I compare aspects of my appearance to others					
4. I think I look ugly or 'not right'					
5. I avoid situations or people because of my appearance					
6. I think about how to camouflage or alter my appearance					
7. I am fearful of being humiliated or rejected because of my appearance					

ASSESSMENT FORMS AND PROGRESS CHARTS

8. I avoid reflective surfaces, photos or videos of myself					
9. I try to camouflage or alter aspects of my appearance					
10. I brood about past events or reasons to explain why I look the way I do					
11. I am focused on how I feel I look rather than on my surroundings					
12. I discuss my appearance with others or question them about it					
13. I try to prevent people from seeing aspects of my appearance within particular situations (e.g. by changing my posture, avoiding bright lights)					
14. My life is restricted because of my appearance (e.g. my ability to work, study, have a social life)					
Total:					

Valued directions form

UNDERSTANDING YOUR VALUES	
Area	Valued direction
1. **Intimacy** What is important to you in how you act in an intimate relationship? What sort of partner do you want to be? If you are not involved in a relationship at present, how would you like to act in a relationship?	
2. **Family relationships** What is important to you in how you want to act as a brother/sister; son/daughter; father/mother or parent-in-law? If you are not in contact with some of your family members, would you like to be, and how would you act in such a relationship?	
3. **Social relationships** What is important to you in the way you act in the friendships you have? How would you like your friends to remember you? If you have no friends, would you like to have some and what role would you like in a friendship?	

ASSESSMENT FORMS AND PROGRESS CHARTS

4. **Work** What is important to you in your work? What sort of employee do you want to be? How important to you is what you achieve in your career? What sort of business do you want to run?

5. **Education and training** What is important to you in your education or training? What sort of student do you want to be? If you are not in education, would you like to be?

6. **Recreation** What is important to you in what you do to follow any interests, sports or hobbies? If you are not following any interests, what would you ideally like to be pursuing?

7. **Spirituality** If you are spiritual, what is important to you in the way you want to follow a spiritual path? If you are not, would you like to be and what do you ideally want?

8. **Voluntary work** What would you like to do for the wider community? For example, voluntary or charity work, or political activity?

9. **Health/physical well-being** What is important to you in how you act for your physical health?	
10. **Mental health** What is important to you generally in how you look after your mental health?	
11. **Any other values that are not listed above**	

> # Chapter 5

Vicious flower (see overleaf)

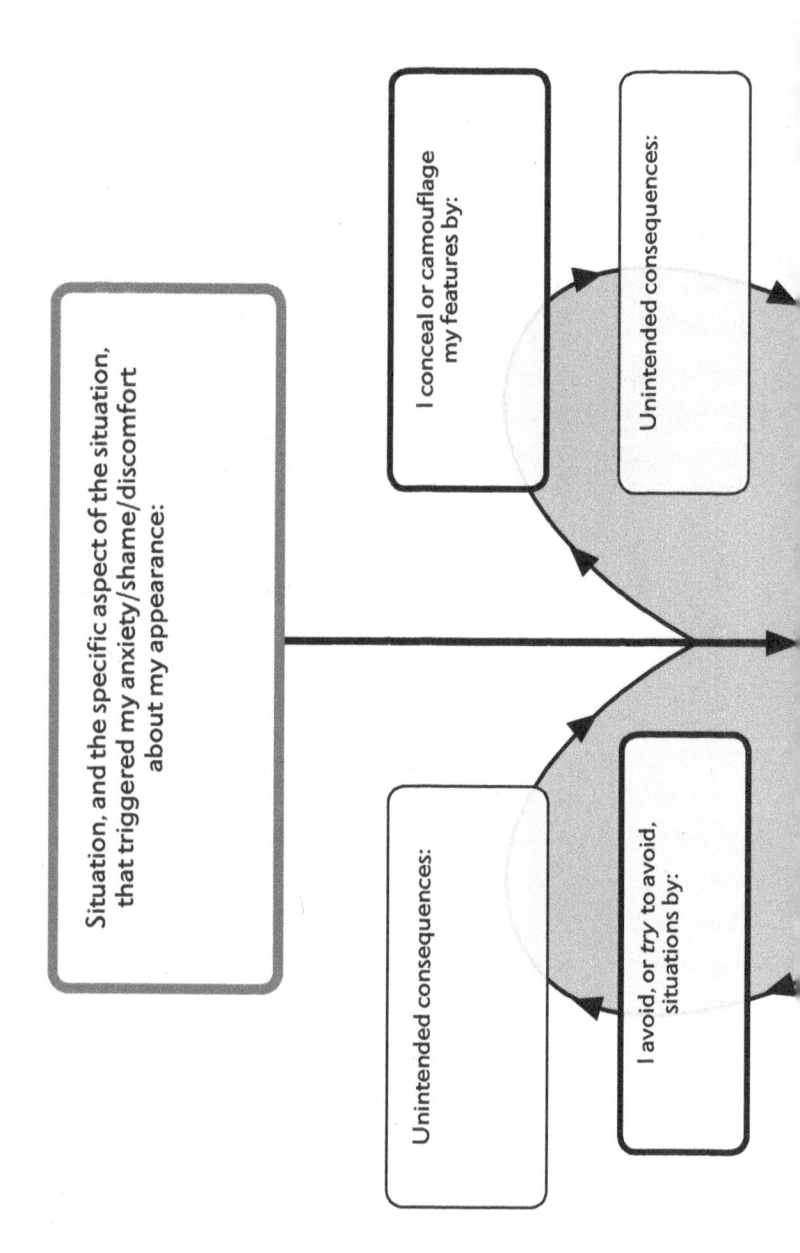

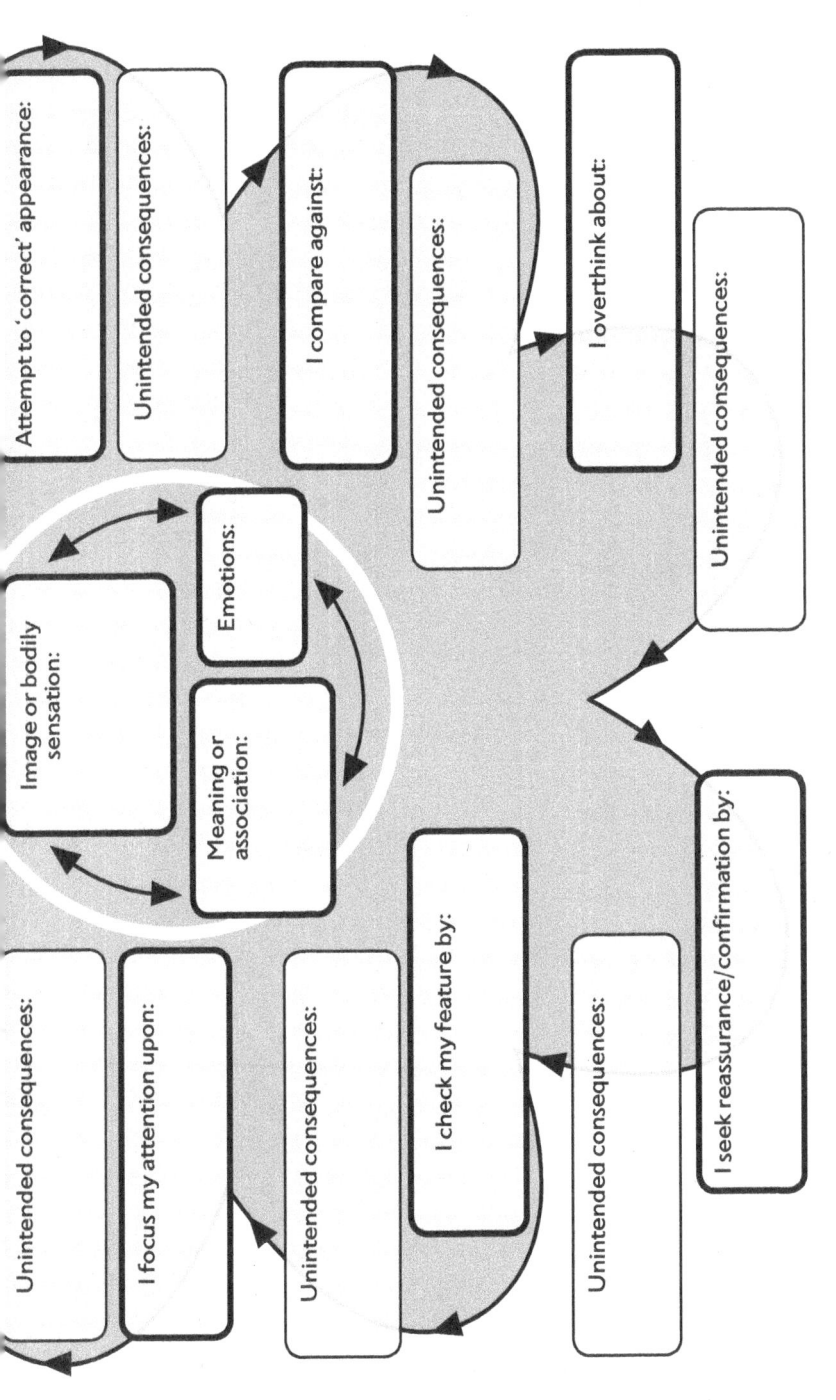

Chapter 6

Thought-monitoring chart

THOUGHT MONITORING CHART

WEEK BEGINNING

Write in your most common intrusive thoughts and images about your appearance, and tick the relevant column each time you have that thought, or add the total from your tally counter.

	Mon	Tues	Wed	Thurs	Fri	Sat	Sun
I have thoughts that:							
I have thoughts that:							
I have thoughts that:							
I have thoughts that:							
I have an intrusive image of:							
have an intrusive image of:							

ASSESSMENT FORMS AND PROGRESS CHARTS

Monitoring self-focused attention chart

MONITORING SELF-FOCUSED ATTENTION CHART						
Date	Situation	% attention on self	% attention on task	% attention on environment	Total (100%)	Distress (0–100%)

Record of attention training

RECORD OF ATTENTION TRAINING

Rating scale

−3: entirely focused on your own thoughts and feelings or the impression you have of yourself

0: attention divided equally between being self-focused and externally focused

+3: entirely externally focused on a task (e.g. listening to someone) or the environment (e.g. what you can see or hear)

Date	How self-focused I have been generally today (-3 to +3)	How long the training lasted	Number of sounds I used	Any other comments

ASSESSMENT FORMS AND PROGRESS CHARTS

Brooding and worrying self-monitoring chart

BROODING AND WORRYING SELF-MONITORING CHART

WEEK BEGINNING

Write in your most common brooding and worrying thoughts, and tick the relevant column each time you have that thought, or add the total from your tally counter.

	Mon	Tues	Wed	Thurs	Fri	Sat	Sun
I brood about:							
I brood about:							
I worry about:							
I worry about:							
I attack myself about:							
I attack myself about:							

Comparing self-monitoring chart

COMPARING SELF-MONITORING CHART							
WEEK BEGINNING							
Write in your most common comparing thoughts and tick the relevant column each time you have that thought, or add the total from your tally counter.							
	Mon	Tues	Wed	Thurs	Fri	Sat	Sun
I compared my:							
I compared my:							
I compared my:							

Chapter 7

Hierarchy of exposure to feared triggers

HIERARCHY OF EXPOSURE TO FEARED TRIGGERS	
Trigger (object, place, person, situation):	**Estimated distress (0–100)**

Exposure record sheet

EXPOSURE RECORD FORM

Exposure task	Level of discomfort	Duration of discomfort	Coping strategies	Testing your expectations	Next steps
Write out the date and what you actually did:	0–10 at the start and when it was at its maximum?	How long did the maximum level of anxiety last for?	What helpful things did you do to tolerate your anxiety? Did you use any unhelpful ways of coping (for example, any safety behaviours)?	What did you learn about how your body image works? Did your experience strengthen Theory B?	How might you progress from here – for example, repeating, extending or developing this exercise, or moving on to an alternative task?
	Start: Maximum:				
	Start: Maximum:				
	Start: Maximum:				

ASSESSMENT FORMS AND PROGRESS CHARTS

Frequency of checking

DATE _____

	Mon	Tues	Wed	Thurs	Fri	Sat	Sun
I check in a mirror for a long duration (e.g. applying make-up, grooming)							
I check briefly in a mirror or reflective surface (e.g. window)							
I check by looking at a feature directly without needing a mirror							
I check the 'picture in my mind' or memory of how I last looked							
I check by feeling my skin with my fingers							
I check my feature using a camera on my phone							

I check the feeling of elasticity or amount of fat by pinching my skin							
I check by measuring my feature							
I try to convince others about how unattractive my feature is							
I ask others to confirm the existence of my defect							
I seek reassurance about whether my feature has got worse							
I seek reassurance about whether my feature is camouflaged (for example, by make-up)							

ASSESSMENT FORMS AND PROGRESS CHARTS

The Hospital and Anxiety Depression (HAD) Scale

THE HOSPITAL AND ANXIETY DEPRESSION (HAD) SCALE

Please read each group of statements carefully, and then pick the one (by writing the number in the box) that comes closest to how you have been feeling in the past week and write that number in the box. Don't take too long over your replies: your immediate reaction to each item will probably be more accurate than a long-thought-out response.

		Anxiety	Depression

1. I feel tense or 'wound up':

   3 Most of the time
   2 A lot of the time
   1 From time to time, occasionally
   0 Not at all

2. I still enjoy the things I used to enjoy:

   0 Definitely as much
   1 Not quite so much
   2 Only a little
   3 Hardly at all

3. I get a sort of frightened feeling as if something awful is about to happen:

   3 Very definitely and quite badly
   2 Yes, but not too badly
   1 A little, but it doesn't worry me
   0 Not at all

	Anxiety	Depression
4. I can laugh and see the funny side of things: 0 As much as I always could 1 Not quite so much now 2 Definitely not so much now 3 Not at all		☐
5. Worrying thoughts go through my mind: 3 A great deal of the time 2 A lot of the time 1 From time to time but not too often 0 Only occasionally	☐	
6. I feel cheerful: 3 Not at all 2 Not often 1 Sometimes 0 Most of the time		☐
7. I can sit at ease and feel relaxed: 0 Definitely 1 Usually 2 Not often 3 Not at all	☐	
8. I feel as if I am slowed down: 3 Nearly all the time 2 Very often 1 Sometimes 0 Not at all		☐

ASSESSMENT FORMS AND PROGRESS CHARTS

	Anxiety	Depression

9. I get a sort of frightened feeling like 'butterflies' in the stomach:

    0 Not at all
    1 Occasionally
    2 Quite often
    3 Very often

10. I have lost interest in my appearance:

    3 Definitely
    2 I don't take so much care as I should
    1 I may not take quite as much care
    0 I take just as much care as ever

11. I feel restless as if I have to be on the move:

    3 Very much indeed
    2 Quite a lot
    1 Not very much
    0 Not at all

12. I look forward with enjoyment to things:

    0 As much as I ever did
    1 Rather less than I used to
    2 Definitely less than I used to
    3 Hardly at all

13. I get sudden feelings of panic:

    3 Very often indeed
    2 Quite often
    1 Not very often
    0 Not at all

	Anxiety	Depression
14. I can enjoy a good book or radio or TV programme: 0 Often 1 Sometimes 2 Not often 3 Very seldom		☐
TOTAL	Anxiety ☐	Depression ☐

Add up your scores for anxiety (in the left-hand column) and depression (in the right-hand column).

The scores can be summarised on a chart completed at regular intervals so that you can monitor progress.

If you score 9 or more on the depression sub-scale, you are probably experiencing depression. Similarly, if you score more than 9 or more on the anxiety subscale, you are probably experiencing an anxiety disorder. Higher scores (15 or more on the depression subscale) could mean that a self-help book might not be suitable for you, and you might need to seek additional professional help.

ASSESSMENT FORMS AND PROGRESS CHARTS

Chapter 9

Cost–benefit analysis form

COST-BENEFIT ANALYSIS OF _____	
Costs – for you and other people. Consider short- and long-term costs.	**Benefits** – for you and other people. Consider short- and long-term benefits.

Chapter 10

Skin-picking self-monitoring form

SKIN-PICKING SELF-MONITORING FORM									
Date/time	Duration: How long did you pick for?	Location: Where were you?	Activity: What were you doing before picking?	Strength of urge to pick on a scale of 0 to 10, where 0 is no urge	Degree of awareness of picking on a scale of 0 to 10, where 0 is no awareness	Notable feelings before you picked	Notable thoughts or images before you picked	Notable sensations before you picked (e.g. itching or burning)
1.								
2.								

ASSESSMENT FORMS AND PROGRESS CHARTS

Habit reversal form

HABIT REVERSAL FORM

Site: Where did you pick?	What effect did picking have on your feelings?	What effect did picking have on your thoughts?	What effect did picking have on your sensations?	How strong was your effort to resist picking on a scale of 0 to 10, where 0 is no effort at all?	What did you do to try to resist picking?
1.					
2.					

Chapter 11

Alternative explanations form

Date/time	What happened?	What did you think?	How could you challenge this?	How could you test it out?

Index

abdominoplasty, 345–7
Abilify, 391
abuse, 8, 37, 50, 52, 55, 56, 60, 66, 69, 94
acceptance and commitment therapy, 35, 75, 332
accidents, 3, 19, 60, 61, 65, 69
accommodation, 254–5
acne, 6–7, 19, 45, 65, 299
acting 'as if', 141–2, 182
ACTION, 246
activities, 239–46
actors, 60–61, 69
adolescence, 6–8, 19, 28, 56–7, 60, 66, 93–4, 256
aesthetic sensitivity, 59
ageing, 9, 121, 337
aggression, 42, 110, 259
alcohol, 45–7, 199, 211, 230, 252–3, 332
  medication and, 371–2
allies, 255
alprazolam, 199
alternative directions, 154, 177, 180, 208, 211, 218
Anafranil, 382
anorexia, 3
anti-depressant medication, 252, 365, 368–91, 397
anti-obsessional medication, 31, 45, 370, 381–2
anti-psychotic medication, 391–2
anxiety, 52, 53–5, 68, 97–8
  medication and, 371
  serotonin and, 64
  severity of, 74–5
  social anxiety disorder, 29, 41–2
appearance, 1–22
  adolescence and, 6–8, 19, 28, 56–7, 60, 66, 93–4

anxiety questionnaire, 74
  comparisons and, 10–12, 75, 110–12, 135, 172–80
  culture and, 4, 9–10, 60–62, 75
  media and, 5–6, 8, 10, 11-12, 60–61, 69, 75
  self and, 138–40, 144
  self-esteem and, 4, 8, 12, 19, 41, 67, 68, 170, 252, 302
  value of, 299–302
appetite, 18, 41, 63, 229, 253, 379–80
Arab cultures, 61
aripiprazole, 391
art and design, 59, 68
associations, 93–7, 136
attentional bias, 108–9, 151–4
attractiveness, 1–22, 60–61
  beauty myths, 15
  culture and, 4, 9–10, 60–62, 75
  halo effect, 14
  media and, 5–6, 8, 10, 60–61, 69, 75
  socioeconomic conditions and, 10
  symmetry and, 5, 28, 43
autism, 43
avoidance, 46, 74, 103–6, 112, 184
  family support and, 258, 259
  of mirrors, 97, 106, 195, 215, 216–17, 218
  of socialising, 14, 17, 18–19, 26, 74, 106, 115, 184, 230

baseball caps, 300, 307, 315
BEAT, 406
beauty myths, 15
beauty products, 121
Beck, Aaron, 30
behavioural activation, 238–46
behavioural experiments, 185, 186
benzodiazepines, 393

449

'Big I, little i', 140
bipolar disorder, 381
birthmarks, 303, 306–7
blame, 257
body dysmorphic disorder (BDD), 23–7
    causes, 52–72
    comorbidities, 38–49
    maintenance of, 56, 87–134, 135, 142, 170
    prevalence of, 27–9
    questionnaire, 24–7
    severity of, 73–5, 80–81
    treatments, 29–33, 365–95
    triggers, 56, 64–7, 69–70, 106, 169, 181, 185, 191–2, 222
    untreatable, 268–9
    visible difference and, *see* visible difference
    vulnerability to, 55, 58–64, 67–9
body hair, 13, 28
body image, 2–22
    adolescence and, 6–8, 19, 28, 56–7, 60, 66, 93–4
    comparisons and, 10–12, 75, 110–12, 135, 172–80
    culture and, 4, 9–10, 60–62, 75
    feedback and, 4, 7, 11, 57, 60, 67, 102, 137, 184
    media and, 5–6, 8, 10, 12–13, 60–61, 69, 75, 338–40
    neurology and, 3, 53–5, 59, 62–4
    'normal', 2, 12–14, 338–40
    self-esteem and, 4, 8, 12, 41, 67
body image questionnaire, 73
body integrity dysphoria (BID), 36
body language, 2, 4, 16, 318–19
body modification, 37
body odour, 47–8
body piercing, 13, 37
body shame, 98–100
body-focused repetitive behaviours (BFRBs), 271–98
    analysis of, 279–85
    disruption of, 293–4
    exposure therapy, 294–8
    habit reversal, 288–91
    monitoring of, 286–7
    reduction of, 292–3
    shame of, 278–9
    triggers, 279–82, 293
Bögels, Sandra, 157

borderline personality, 48–9
Botox, 121, 337
boundaries, 66–7, 256
brain, 3, 53–5, 59, 62–4, 71
brain surgery, 394
Brazil, 61
breastfeeding, 371, 390–91
breasts, 6, 7, 28, 37–8
    cosmetic surgery on, 335–6, 338–40, 355
British Association for Psychotherapies, 405
British Association of Plastic Surgeons, 356
brooding, 113–16, 135, 165–72
Buddhism, 65
bulimia, 401
bullying, 7–8, 13, 43, 56–7, 65, 94, 137, 251
Butler, Gillian, 42

camouflage, 111, 112, 118–19, 130, 174, 205, 216
    visible difference and, 300, 307, 315, 317
cancer, 10, 33, 227, 303, 335–6
catastrophising, 97, 261, 315–16
celebrities, 6, 49–50
Centre for Appearance Research, 15, 35, 332
Changing Faces, 308, 309, 319, 327
charisma, 16
charities, 406
checking behaviours, 14, 17–18, 74, 80, 81, 83, 106, 184, 199–218
    anxiety and, 97, 213
    as compulsive, 23, 42
    avoidance of, 106
    comparisons and, 111, 112
    family support and, 258
    frequency of, 203–12
    monitoring of, 199–218
    motivation for, 212–14
    unintended consequences, 120, 206, 207, 210
cheek biting, 271
cheerleading, 260
chemotherapy, 303
children; childhood, 5, 61–2, 66, 71
    abuse and, 8, 37, 50, 52, 55, 56, 66, 69
    boundaries and, 66–7
    cosmetic surgery and, 355

INDEX

medication and, 373–4
neglect and, 56, 60, 66, 69
visible difference and, 324
chlorpromazine, 391
Cialis, 379
citalopram, 370, 372, 374, 376
cleft palates, 303
clinical psychologists, 401
clomipramine, 372, 374, 382–5, 390, 391
clonazepam, 393
clothing visible difference and, 315, 317
clothing, 12, 13, 14, 16, 43, 47, 102, 106, 119, 197
coaching, 260
cognitive behavioural therapy (CBT), 29, 30–32, 35, 36, 45, 48, 56, 348, 358, 396–407
  family and, 255, 261, 265, 267–8
  medication and, 366, 368, 373
  visible difference and, 308–16, 332
Coming Off Antidepressants (Glenmullen), 389
communication, 263–5
comparisons, 10–12, 75, 110–12, 135, 172–80
compassion, 49, 66, 101, 136, 198–9
Compassionate Mind Workbook, The (Beaumont and Irons), 39
concealing visible difference and, 300, 307, 315, 317
concealing, 111, 112, 118–19, 130, 174, 184, 205, 216
confirmation, 45, 47, 102, 117–18, 205, 218–20
conversation, 319–21
coping strategies, 100–34, 158, 181, 184, 185
  avoidance behaviours, 46, 74, 103–6, 112, 184
  checking behaviours, *see* checking behaviours
  comparing, 110–12, 135, 172–80
  concealing, 111, 112, 118–19, 130, 174, 184, 205, 216
  correcting, 9, 13, 17, 23, 29, 37, 50, 84, 117, 121–2, 314, 330–31, 334–64
  overthinking, 74, 112, 113–16, 135, 165–72, 238–9, 247–51
  reassurance, 45, 47, 102, 117–18, 205, 218–20, 258

  self-focused attention, 74, 107–9, 112, 135, 154–72
  unintended consequences, 102–33, 174, 176, 197, 206, 271, 284, 292
correcting, 121–2
cosmetic surgery, 9, 13, 17, 23, 29, 37, 50, 84, 117, 121–2, 314, 334–64
  abroad, 357
  appropriateness of, 359–64
  brooding and, 110, 113, 205
  children and, 355
  cultural factors, 27, 61
  DIY, 38, 121
  family participation and, 122, 258
  finding a surgeon, 344, 356–8
  happiness and, 344–54
  media and, 338–40
  objective opinions, 340–44
  pressure from others, 355–6
  regulation of, 356–8
  risk factors, 358–9
  timing of, 354
  visible difference and, 330–31
counselling, 398
counselling psychologists, 402
counsellors, 402
counter-factual comparisons, 110
courage, 187
Covid-19 pandemic, 12
craniofacial conditions, 303–4, 331
cultural factors, 4, 9–10, 60–61, 75

dating, 26, 41, 60, 83, 106
decoupling, 289–90, 297–8
defusing, 142–3
dental procedures, 121
Department of Health and Social Care, 405
depression, 29, 39–41, 52, 66, 98, 229–53
  behavioural activation, 238–46, 251–2
  cosmetic surgery and, 354
  lifestyle changes and, 252–3
  medication for, 252, 370
  overthinking, 238–9, 247–51
  primary problem, 231
  severity of, 74–5, 231–5
  suicidal ideation, 237–8, 354, 372–3, 376, 380, 397, 399
dermabrasion, 337
dermatological conditions, 33, 65, 68, 273
dermatological procedures, 23, 29, 121

dialectical behaviour therapy, 49
diazepam, 393
diet, 63, 68, 211, 239, 252–3, 294
dimensional comparisons, 110
disfigurement, *see* visible difference
disgust, 55, 98–9
divorce, 24
dog bites, 303, 327–8, 347
dogs, 110, 174
dopamine-blocking medication, 392–3
drug misuse, 45–7, 199, 211, 230, 252–3, 332
dysmorphophobia, 23

ears, 150–51, 355
eating, 236, 252–3, 294, 315
  appetite, 18, 41, 63, 229, 253, 379–80
  disordered, 3, 359, 401, 406
  gut microbiota and, 63
  junk food, 63, 68, 239, 252
  overeating, 211, 239, 252
Eating Disorders Association, 406
eczema, 60, 68
education, 59, 68
Efexor, 374, 386
electroconvulsive therapy (ECT), 394
emotional disorders, 37, 63, 48–9
emotionally unstable personality disorder (EUPD), 37, 48–9
emotions, 1, 97–8, 261
employment, 8–9, 15, 24, 69, 106
epilepsy, 384
escitalopram, 370
exercise, 121, 183, 239, 252, 292
exposure and response prevention (ERP), 183–228
  challenge of exposure, 193–6
  courage and, 187
  examples of, 220–26
  frequency of exposure, 196
  graded exposure, 187–9
  length of exposure, 193
  monitoring, 199–220
  obstacles to, 226
  response prevention, 185, 196–7
  safeness and, 187
  task list, 189–90
eye contact, 4, 16, 102, 307, 315, 318–19

facial expressions, 1, 318
facial rejuvenation, 12

fairy tales, 5
family, 24
  cosmetic surgery and, 122, 258
  genetic inheritance, 52, 55, 58, 66, 68
  participation of, 104, 257–9
  support from, 31, 254–70
  therapy and, 255, 258, 261, 267–8
  withdrawal from, 106, 230
fashion industry, 11
FEAR, 189
Ferrari, Lolo, 37–8
fibrous foods, 63
fillers, 121
films, 5, 50, 177
first impressions, 1, 16
fluoxetine, 370–75, 378–80, 389, 390, 397
fluvoxamine, 376, 378
focusing out, 303
food, *see* eating

Garland, Judy, 50
gay men, 61
generalised anxiety disorder (GAD), 44
genetic factors, 52, 55, 58, 66, 68
genitalia, 28, 37
Geodon, 391
ghosts from the past, 8, 57, 91, 153, 196, 221, 337
Gilbert, Paul, 53
global processing, 59
goals, 76, 81–6
GPs (general practitioners), 344, 404
guided self-help, 396
gut microbiota, 63

habit reversal, 288–91
hair colour, 8, 13
hair pulling, 271, 272
haircuts, 4
Haldol, 391
halo effect, 14
haloperidol, 391
happiness, 6, 15
  cosmetic surgery and, 344–54
  positivity bias and, 59–60
  visible difference and, 14, 15, 35, 300, 310
health anxiety, 44–5
height, 60, 65
HIV/AIDS, 62

INDEX

homeostasis, 181
Hospital and Anxiety Depression Scale, 75, 231–5, 375
humour, 262–3, 324
hypnosis, 30
hypnotherapy, 30, 398

images, 90–92
internal mirror, 163
interpretation pie chart, 150
Islam, 61

Jackson, Michael, 50
Jane Eyre (Brontë), 5
jumping to conclusions, 150–51
junk food, 63, 68, 239, 252

laser treatment, 337
life experiences, 56–7, 58, 69, 93–7
  abuse, 8, 37, 50, 52, 55, 56, 60, 69, 94
  bullying, 7–8, 13, 43, 56–7, 69, 94, 137
  neglect, 56, 60, 69, 71
lifestyle changes, 252–3
lip biting, 271
listing problems, 80–81
literature, 5–6
Lizardman, 38
lofepramine, 378
lorazepam, 393

make-up, 12, 13, 14, 43, 48, 80, 119, 194, 205
Manage Your Mood (Veale and Willson), 39, 46, 238
manner, 16
marketing, 10
Martell, Christopher, 246
meanings, 93–7, 136
media, 5–6, 8, 10, 12–13, 60–61, 69, 75
  cosmetic surgery and, 338–40, 349
  social media, 11–12, 111, 177, 180
  television and film, 8, 10, 60–61, 50, 69, 177
medical conditions, 62
medication, 31–2, 66, 199, 252, 365–95, 398, 399
  alcohol and, 371–2
  anti-depressants, 252, 365, 368–91
  anti-obsessionals, 31, 45, 370, 381–2
  anti-psychotics, 391–3
  children/adolescents and, 373–4

dosages, 372, 373, 375, 382, 397
pregnancy and, 371, 390–91
psychedelics, 33, 393–4
serotonin and, 31, 63–4, 369–81
side effects, 374–81, 383–4
stopping/reducing, 385–90, 393
suicidal ideation and, 372–3, 376, 380
therapy and, 366, 368, 373, 398
tranquillisers, 393
meditation, 292
men, 28
  body image ideals, 6, 12, 28
  breast development, 6, 28
  muscle dysmorphia, 28
  penis size, 28
mentalisation-based therapy, 49
microbiome, 63
mirrors, 109
  avoidance of, 97, 106, 195, 215, 216–17, 218
  checking in, 3, 17, 23, 80, 81, 97, 106, 109, 120, 130, 149, 203–17
models, 11, 69
moon face, 62, 303
Moritz, Steffen, 289
Moss, Kate, 340
muscle dysmorphia, 28

nail biting, 271
National Health Service (NHS), 336–7, 344, 355, 356–7, 398, 404
National Institute for Health and Care Excellence (NICE), 29, 348, 404
neglect, 56, 60, 66, 69
neurology, 3, 53–5, 59, 62–4, 71
Neysa Jane BDD Fund, 406
nitrazepam, 393
noses, 17–18, 49, 81, 84, 93, 105, 138, 185, 220–26, 314
  cosmetic surgery on, 314, 341–4, 351–3
nurse therapists, 402

obesity, 10, 358
obsessive-compulsive disorder (OCD), 29, 42–3, 59, 370, 404
olanzapine, 391
olfactory reference disorder (ORD), 47–8
Orlan, 38
Overcoming Health Anxiety (Veale and Willson), 45

Overcoming Obsessive Compulsive Disorder (Veale and Willson), 42
Overcoming Social Anxiety and Shyness (Butler), 42
Overcoming Worry and Generalised Anxiety Disorder (Freeston and Meares), 44
overthinking, 74, 112, 113–16, 135, 165–72
   depression and, 238–9, 247–51

paroxetine, 371, 372, 374, 386, 389, 390
participation, 104, 257–9
Partridge, James, 308
Paxil, 374, 386, 389
penis size, 28
perfectionism, 43, 59, 68
personalisation, 312–14
personality, 13, 58, 59, 66
   disorders of, 37, 48–9
phantom limb pain, 3
photographs, 217
   avoidance of, 18, 83, 218
   checking behaviour use, 120, 217
   comparisons to, 17, 81, 177, 180, 217
   exposure therapy and, 217
   modification of, 11
   selfies, 91, 203, 215
   social media and, 11, 83
pimozide, 391
pinnaplasty, 355
polycystic ovary syndrome, 62
port wine stains, 303, 306–7
positivity bias, 59–60
post-traumatic stress disorder (PTSD), 59
posture, 16, 318
pregnancy, 108, 339, 371, 390–91
probiotics, 63
professional help, 396–407
Prozac, 370–75, 378–80, 389, 390, 397
psychedelic medications, 33, 393–4
psychiatrists, 401
psychoanalysis, 398
psychodynamic therapy, 30
psychological factors, 59–60, 65–7
psychotherapists, 402
psychotherapy, *see under* therapy
puberty, 6–8, 19, 93–4
Puerto Rico, 61

questionnaires
   acting 'as if', 141–2

alcohol problems, 47
appearance anxiety, 74
body image, 73–4
cosmetic surgery, 359–64
depression, 40, 75, 231–5
Have I got BDD?, 24–7
skin picking, 274–8
social anxiety, 42
valued living, 75–86
quetiapine, 391

reassurance, 45, 47, 102, 117–18, 205, 218–20, 258
reboxetine, 378
Reinventing Your Life (Klosko and Young), 252
relationships, 15, 18–19, 24, 57, 59–60, 69, 252
   dating, 26, 41, 60, 83, 106
   visible difference and, 310
response prevention, 185, 196–7
rhinoplasty, 314, 341–4, 351–3
Risperidal, 391
risperidone, 391
role models, 77, 82
rose-tinted glasses, 59–60
Rumsey, Nichola, 308

sadomasochism, 37
safeness, 187
safety behaviours, 102–5, 112, 120, 122–3, 130, 158, 181
   checking, *see* checking behaviours
   concealing, 111, 112, 118–19, 130, 174, 184, 205, 216
   exposure therapy and, 183–5, 189, 190, 194, 196–7, 199, 202
   family support and, 258, 259
   reassurance, 45, 47, 102, 117–18, 205, 218–20, 258
   visible difference and, 315
scars, 5, 8, 18, 60, 61, 65
schizophrenia, 48
selective serotonergic reuptake inhibitors (SSRIs), 369–81
   children/adolescents and, 373–4
   dosages, 372, 373, 375
   serotonin and, 31, 63–4, 369–81
   side effects, 374–81
   suicide and, 372–3, 376, 380
self-acceptance, 138–40

INDEX

self-attacking thoughts, 114–16, 165–72, 202
self-confidence, 16, 302
self-criticism, 67, 114, 169, 187, 229
self-esteem, 4, 8, 12, 19, 41, 67, 68, 170
  cosmetic surgery and, 345–7
  depression and, 170, 252
  visible difference and, 302, 303
self-focused attention, 74, 107–9, 112, 113–16, 135, 154–72, 184
  exposure therapy and, 197–8
  motivations, understanding of, 163–80
  task-concentration training, 157–63
self-mutilation, 37
selfies, 91, 203, 215
Seroquel, 391
serotonin, 31, 62–4, 369–81
Seroxat, 374, 386, 389
sertraline, 372, 373, 374, 378, 380, 386, 390
sex; sexuality, 6, 42, 46, 53, 63, 345–7
  medication and, 375, 378–9, 384
shame, 97, 98–100
shyness, 59, 137
single people, 9, 18, 24
skin, 6–10, 18–19, 65, 93, 185–6
  acne, 6–7, 19, 45, 65, 68, 299
  disorders of, 33, 65, 68, 273
  picking of, 121, 271–98
  procedures on, 23, 29, 121
  puberty and, 6–7, 19
  tanning/whitening, 10
sleep, 18, 41, 44, 68, 229, 230, 239, 252
smallpox, 9
SMART goals, 82
smiling, 318
smoke detectors, 251, 323
smoking, 358
social anxiety disorder, 29, 41–2
social factors, 60–62
social media, 11–12, 83, 111, 177, 180
social skills, 16, 35, 302, 304, 308, 316–21, 327
socialising, 1, 4, 14, 15, 17, 115
  avoidance of, 14, 17, 18–19, 26, 74, 106, 115, 184, 230
  comparisons and, 111, 112
  depression and, 39, 41
  exposure therapy, 185–6
  images and, 90
  phobia of, 29, 41–2
  safety behaviours and, 102

skills, development of, 16, 35, 302, 304, 308, 316–21 327, 333
  visible difference and, 34, 300, 302–4, 306, 308, 316–21, 327, 333
socioeconomic conditions, 10
South London and Maudsley Trust, 404
St John's wort, 371
staring, 304, 306, 307
steroids, 28, 62, 303
substance misuse, 45–7, 199, 211, 230, 252–3, 332
SUDs (standard units of distress), 191
suicidal ideation, 237–8, 354, 372–3, 376, 380, 397, 399
sulpiride, 391
sunlight, 253
support (family and friends), 31, 254–70
  anxiety and discomfort, 261–2
  blame and, 257
  coaching/cheerleading, 260
  communication, 263–5
  downplaying and, 266–7
  help seeking and, 257, 263–5, 267–8
  humour, 262–3
  own needs and, 260–61
  participation and, 104, 257–9
  setbacks, 262
  therapy and, 255, 258, 261, 267–8
support groups, 406
swimming; swimwear, 106, 191, 193, 217, 345
symmetry, 5, 28, 43

task-concentration training (TCT), 157–63
tattooing, 13, 37
teasing, 6, 19, 34, 43, 52, 56, 65–6, 91, 94, 251
television industry, 8, 10, 60–61, 69, 177
temporal comparisons, 110
theories A and B, 128–33, 183, 185, 197, 198, 213, 220–21
therapy, 29–32, 396–407
  acceptance and commitment, 35, 75, 332
  BFRBs and, 277, 285
  cognitive behaviour, *see* cognitive behavioural therapy
  compassion focused, 49, 66, 101, 136, 198–9
  counselling, 398
  dialectical behaviour, 49

exposure, 183–228
family and, 255, 258, 261, 267–8
hypnotherapy, 30, 398
medication and, 366, 368, 373, 398
mentalisation based, 49
psychedelic assisted, 33
psychoanalysis, 398
psychodynamic, 30, 398
substance misuse and, 45
transactional analysis, 398
visible difference and, 308–16, 332
thinking, 135–82
  acting 'as if', 141–2, 183
  attentional bias, 151–4
  defusing, 142–3
  distancing, 143–4, 146–9, 202
  jumping to conclusions, 150–51
  labelling, 143–5
  overthinking, 74, 112, 113–16, 135, 165–72, 238–9, 247–51
  records of, 145–6
  self-acceptance, 138–40
  self-attacking thoughts, 114–16, 165–72, 202
  self-focused attention, 74, 107–9, 112, 135, 154–72
  tolerance of uncertainty, 149–50
  triple column method, 136–7
  visible difference and, 309–14, 318
thought–event fusion, 142
threat-focused attention, 74, 107–9, 112, 135, 154–72
thyroid problems, 62, 303
Tigerman, 38
tolerance of uncertainty, 149–50
transactional analysis, 398
trauma, 55, 56, 60
trazodone, 378
tricyclics, 381–5
trifluoperazine, 391
triggers, 56, 64–7, 69–70, 106, 169, 181, 185, 191–2, 222
triple column method, 136–7
tummy tucks, 345–7

ultra-processed foods, 63, 68
uncertainty, 149–50
unintended consequences, 102–33, 176, 197
  avoidance behaviours, 105–6
  BFRBs and, 271, 284, 292
  checking behaviours, 120, 206, 207, 210
  comparing, 110–12, 174, 176
  concealing, 118–19
  correcting, 121–2
  overthinking, 113–16
  reassurance, 117–18
  safety behaviours, 102–5
  self-focused attention, 107–9
University of the West of England, 15

Valium, 393
valued directions, 75–86, 153, 167, 170, 176, 177, 179, 180, 208, 211
Veale, David, 404
venlafaxine, 374, 386
verbal skills, 319–21
Viagra, 379
vicious flower, 87–134, 135
  body shame, 98–100
  emotions, 97–8
  images, 90–92
  meaning, 93–7
  responses, 100–34
visible difference, 3, 5, 14, 15, 16, 19–20, 33–6, 56, 60, 65, 68, 299–333
  comments and, 304, 305, 306, 327
  interpretation and, 306–8
  questions and, 304–5, 306, 319, 321–6
  skin-picking and, 275, 276
  socialising and, 34, 300, 302–4, 306, 308, 316–21, 333
  staring and, 304, 306, 307, 319, 326–7
  surgical solutions, 330–31
  therapy and, 308–16, 332
  thinking styles and, 309–12, 318
vitiligo, 317
vulnerabilities, 56, 58–64, 67–9

waist-to-hip ratio, 9
walking, 236, 253
Warhol, Andy, 49–50
weight, 7, 10, 13, 14, 28, 60, 62, 65, 345–7
Withers, Carl, 50
women, 6, 9, 11, 12, 28
worry questions, 248
wrinkles, 18, 337

ziprasidone, 391
Zoloft, 386
Zyprexa, 391